Hanna

Politics, (

PHILOSOPHY AND SOCIETY
General Editor: Marshall Cohen

ALSO IN THIS SERIES:
RIGHTS
Theodore M. Benditt
ETHICS IN THE WORLD OF BUSINESS
David Braybrooke
MARX AND JUSTICE: *The Radical Critique of Liberalism*
Allen E. Buchanan
RONALD DWORKIN AND CONTEMPORARY JURISPRUDENCE
Marshall Cohen (ed.)
LUKÁCS, MARX AND THE SOURCES OF CRITICAL THEORY
Andrew Feenberg
THE REVERSE DISCRIMINATION CONTROVERSY
  A Moral and Legal Analysis
Robert Fullinwider
WORKERS' RIGHTS
Mary Gibson
THE MORAL FOUNDATIONS OF PROFESSIONAL ETHICS
Alan H. Goldman
FEMINIST POLITICS AND HUMAN NATURE
Alison M. Jaggar
HANNAH ARENDT: POLITICS, CONSCIENCE, EVIL
George Kateb
PATERNALISM
John Kleinig
ECOLOGICAL ETHICS AND POLITICS
H. J. McCloskey
A PHILOSOPHY OF FREE EXPRESSION: *And Its Constitutional Applications*
Robert F. Ladenson
THE LIBERTARIAN READER
Tibor R. Machan (ed.)
MORAL PROBLEMS IN NURSING: *A Philosophical Investigation*
James L. Muyskens
READING NOZICK
Jeffrey Paul (ed.)
AND JUSTICE FOR ALL: *New Introductory Essays in Ethics and Public Policy*
Tom Regan and Donald VanDeVeer (eds.)
SEX, DRUGS, DEATH, AND THE LAW
  An Essay on Human Rights and Overcriminalization
David A. J. Richards
KANT'S POLITICAL PHILOSOPHY
Patrick Riley
EVOLUTIONARY EXPLANATION IN THE SOCIAL SCIENCES
  An Emerging Paradigm
Philippe Van Parijs
WELFARE RIGHTS
Carl Wellman

Hannah Arendt
Politics, Conscience, Evil

GEORGE KATEB

Rowman & Allanheld
PUBLISHERS

320.530924
K15h
144607
May 1988

ROWMAN & ALLANHELD

Published in the United States of America in 1984
by Rowman & Allanheld
(A division of Littlefield, Adams & Company)
81 Adams Drive, Totowa, New Jersey 07512

Library of Congress Cataloging in Publication Data
Kateb, George.
    Hannah Arendt, politics, conscience, evil.

    Bibliography: p. 198
    Includes index.
    1. Arendt, Hannah. 2. Political science. I. Title.
JC251.A74K37   1983   320.5'3'0924   83-6213
ISBN 0-8476-6757-X
ISBN 0-8476-7558-0 (pbk.)

86 87 88 / 6 5 4 3 2

Printed in the United States of America

Contents

Acknowledgments   *ix*

Preface   *xi*

1   The Theory of Political Action   *1*

2   Totalitarian Evil   *52*

3   Politics and Absolute Morality   *85*

4   Modern Democracy   *115*

5   Modernity   *149*

Appendix   The Life of the Mind   *188*

List of Selected Writings on Hannah Arendt   *198*

Index   *201*

To Victor and Albert Mesnooh

Acknowledgments

I want to thank Marshall Cohen for suggesting that I try to develop my views on Hannah Arendt, and for showing patience while the work was being done. Benjamin Barber and Richard Poirier carefully read parts of the manuscript and made a number of helpful comments. Those who offered encouragement and critical response include Joseph Epstein, Reuben Garner, John Hollander, Thomas Kearns, Leo Marx, Anthony Parel, Melvin Richter, Austin Sarat, Peter Stern, Bruce Towner, Sheldon Wolin, and Elisabeth Young-Bruehl.

I would also like to thank Floyd Merritt, the Reference Librarian at Amherst College, for his help, Cherene Holland for her skillful editorial work, and Marjory Bowser, Dorothy Ives, and Dianne Kaplan for typing parts of the manuscript in various drafts. I am particularly grateful to Lurline Dowell for word-processing the whole last draft.

Last I would like to thank the Trustees of Amherst College for their generous sabbatical and leaves policy, which furthered my work.

Parts of Chapter 1 and of the Appendix appeared, respectively, in *Political Theory* 5 (May 1977), pp. 141-82, © Sage Publications, Inc., and *American Scholar* 48 (Winter 1978-79), 118-26.

Preface

Hannah Arendt (1906–1975) was one of the eminent political theorists of the last half century because she dealt strenuously and faithfully with many of the great recurrent questions of political theory. Yet her passion for an old subject accompanied the wish to identify and delineate the novel or unprecedented features of modern political life. This is not to say that she sought guidance or solace for modern troubles in premodern writers. Rather, because of the horrors perpetrated in the public realm during her lifetime, she came to have an all-absorbing interest in politics, whether ancient or modern, heroic or collegial, evil or constitutional. She began by reflecting on totalitarianism, but she did not stop there.

Arendt's work on both political modernity and the recurrent questions of political theory demonstrates considerable originality. I hope that I have not obscured her originality by my anxious commentary. Her work surely can induce anxiety: Her fame depends as much on the anxiety she aroused as on anything else. She always seemed to be saying painful things, or unpleasantly exotic ones. Yet though many of those made anxious had not read her but depended on gossip, there is ample reason to come away from her work feeling unsettled. In particular, her overt as well as implicit critique of leading aspects of the culture of democratic individuality and of its political system—constitutional representative democracy—is not only challenging but also threatening.

Much of my discussion is an effort to convert my anxiety into a profitable receptivity. The delight comes from the gift Arendt had of suggesting fresh ways for defending the objects of her critique. Although I am interested in her whole achievement and not just in her interrogation of modern democracy, I have tried to make her work yield assistance to the theory of modern democracy. My aim, however, is not an impossible synthesis, not reconciliation. The otherness of Arendt's thought is the source of its advantage to the theory of modern democracy, as well as to our general reflection.

Hannah Arendt

Politics, Conscience, Evil

Chapter One

The Theory of Political Action

Hannah Arendt closes *On Revolution* by quoting part of the choral poem in *Oedipus at Colonus*. In her translation, the lines are: "Not to be born prevails over all meaning uttered in words; by far the second-best for life, once it has appeared, is to go as swiftly as possible whence it came."[1] This is the desolate wisdom of drunken Silenus, tutor of Dionysus, otherwise expressed in the formulation that it is best not to have been born, and second-best, to die young.[2] Arendt writes as if she more than merely understood these words, as if she had come to believe them, or would believe them were it not for one thing, the polis and its life of action. Without the polis, who could "bear life's burden"?[3] At times she suggests that the worst burden is mere knowledge of our mortality. The life of the polis with its chance for immortal fame or because of its intensity could thus be accepted as a kind of eternity.[4] More characteristically, however, life's greatest burden is the pain and frustration we are all familiar with, as well as the demonstrated incapacity of most objects, activities, and human relationships to satisfy.[5] Exempted from this indictment, the life of action, of political action, is thus the one vindication of life. It is a vindication, not a sought-after consolation or compensation or pledge of something beyond and better than itself. Its "splendor" causes all other concerns to become weightless or forgotten.[6] It is good in itself. Such is the judgment Arendt attributes to Theseus, king of Athens and protector of Oedipus. We must see that she sincerely shares this judgment, even though her philosophical groundwork is not pessimism but wonder at and gratitude for Being. But this philosophical attitude can come under strains that it can barely survive. Her invocation of Sophocles is no mere rhetorical flourish. No higher claim for politics can be imagined than that which she makes. The claim is shocking and foreign to the prepossessions of most of us. Indeed, her work as a whole is usually found shocking and foreign whenever it is seriously attended to, certainly in America. The source of this response is precisely in Arendt's conception of politics, in what it is, what it excludes, why it is good. The last page of *On Revolution* is simply the most concentrated expression of that conception; and for that reason it is perhaps the most shocking and foreign moment in her writings.

The Deficiency of Most of Life's Activities

Freedom and *worldliness* can serve as the terms that stand for what Arendt prizes most. She regularly connects them; she sees them as dependent on each other. Freedom exists only when citizens engage in political action. Political action can take place only where there is worldliness—a common commitment to the reality, beauty, and sufficiency of the culture or way of life that sustains political action, as well as a commitment to political action itself. Political action looks in turn to the conservation or augmentation of the way of life that sustains it. Arendt thus uses *world* to mean both a culture (a polis, for example), which is the scene and inspiration and source of meaning for political action, and more narrowly, the course of political action in the public realm.

All the other activities of life, with the ambiguous exceptions of thinking (or understanding), scientific knowing, and contemplation, are not free but done in bondage to one or another kind of master or done in unredeemable futility or impotence. All these activities, including thinking and contemplation, but with the exception of fabrication (artisanship or craftsmanship), artistic creation, and organized science, are not worldly but private, either in the sense of being done in private or for private purposes, or in the sense of taking place inside oneself. Arendt regards unworldly activities with skepticism, distaste, or scorn;or she acknowledges their necessity grudgingly and sometimes with shame;or she praises them in a way that at times keeps one off balance, so strained or unusual are the terms of her praise. She makes these things seem either unreal or too real.

To say, therefore, that political action alone is equal to the task of challenging Silenian wisdom is to say that freedom and worldliness are the only values that make life worth living. Or, more precisely, that the Greeks before Plato understood life in this way and lived out of that understanding, as did the Romans of the Republic and a few others. In our age, for the most part, we can live that life only vicariously through philosophical understanding. Our condition is such that one of the highest tasks of philosophy is to make believable to those who love philosophy a view in which something other than philosophy—namely, political action—could present itself as worthy of perhaps an equal devotion. After all, the people who invented philosophy were the very ones who invented political action. Arendt's mission as a philosopher is to attempt the recovery of the idea of political action in a culture that she thinks has (except episodically) lost the practice of it and in which almost all philosophy is united, if in nothing else, in denying intrinsic value to it. At best, where there is not aversion, there is reluctance, condescension, or indifference. The mere right understanding of political action—the understanding that men of action in the past had of what they were doing—is now, for the most part, absent.

We can approach Arendt's defense of the primacy of political action by noticing her judgments of nonpolitical things. The power of her thought to shock and alienate is vividly shown in these judgments. It is not that political action is simply the sole pale survivor of her work of criticizing and depreciating nonpolitical things—as if, provoked to deny what everybody else affirms, she at last finds one thing no one else praises and chooses to praise it. It is, instead, that her praise of political action derives some of its energy from her radical revaluation of the nonpolitical. Which is to say that her commitment to the values of freedom and worldliness is basic; her double passion is to differentiate man from nature and save man from phantasm. Given this passion, her judgments about nonpolitical things and political action follow with equal necessity and equal force.

In making such a radical revaluation Arendt must strike anyone not reflexively sympathetic as at least initially shocking and foreign in the way that Nietzsche more famously does. And what finally matters for the reader of Arendt, as for the reader of Nietzsche, is not necessarily to be persuaded. I would take Arendt as, first, appealing for our suspension of disbelief (to use a phrase of Coleridge's that is used too much), so that the novelty of her judgments not automatically condemn them in our eyes; and second, as wanting to change subtly the manner by which we hold our own contrasting judgments in order to loosen the hold our judgments have on us. That there may be conversion to her views, not just a susceptibility to her influence, is not impossible. But it is hard to imagine that that would have pleased her very much. She did not want to be a prophet, just an educator. The aim must be to admit her disturbing thoughts into our usual circle of thoughts and allow them to do what they will.

The Human Condition is Arendt's most elaborate and complex revaluation of the nonpolitical; it also contains the fullest theoretical vindication of political action, even though *On Revolution* is amazingly rich in such vindication and shifts our attention from the polis to modern life. In these two books and a number of essays, a general consistency of attitude is found. The bodily or biological, the domestic, and the social, on the one hand, and the egotistically or romantically inward, intimate, or private, on the other, fail to measure up to the criteria of freedom and worldliness. Their failure is neither moral nor esthetic but existential; any of them taken as a sufficient life diminishes a person's experience and hence the person. Thus, whether Arendt's subject is ancient or modern political action, her revaluation of the nonpolitical is constant, even though that revaluation is originally undertaken and most concentrated when the subject is ancient political action.

The activities Arendt associates with the biological, the domestic, and the social are those "that should be hidden."[7] "[Bodily] functions and material concerns should be hidden."[8] In ancient times not only were these activities kept out of sight, but so were those who engaged in them even when not engaged in them, such as women, slaves, and laborers. Arendt writes as if the thought and practice of antiquity and indeed of Europe until the modern age in regard to the hidden is properly human. (She does praise in passing the modern liberation of women and workers from darkness.)[9] Insofar as the human being is tied to natural function, to its unending cycle of the distress and palliation of the body's desires or the induced desires of modern, consumerist society, the human being is human only in name. The distinction between private and public coincides ultimately with the opposition of shame and honor.[10] Public life is a rupture with a life lived merely as a series of pleasures and pains. From private life, love and friendship are spared her revaluation, of course. About them she says only a few words, but they are passionate ones.[11]

It would be wrong to see fastidiousness as operative here, as if Arendt were posing as an aristocrat shunning her peasants because they smelled bad and had too many babies. Some of her most ferocious pages are written in denunciation of the decadence of the *ancien regime*.[12] Furthermore, the seeming bourgeois remoteness from nature, represented by conspicuous consumption, is not more worldly than the life led close to the edge and without respite from scarcity and toil. Yet it cannot be denied that when Arendt speaks of what should be hidden, she characteristically has the laboring mass in mind, the *animal laborans* in enormous number. They, more clearly than any other group, never rise above life as a self-perpetuating but fundamentally unchanging process. The process is imperishable, but every part of it is perishable. The laborer lives only to die;[13] he turns everything, including what is meant to last, into the stuff of consumption. He devours the world; time devours him. The laboring mass fails to arrest nature's course. The worst horror is that "within the life process itself....it is idle to ask questions that presuppose the category of means and end, such as whether men live and consume in order to have strength to labor or whether they labor in order to have the means of consumption."[14] The horror comes from the inability of the human agent to stand apart from his environment and achieve a human identity. By his dependency on nature and his reduction of artificial goods to the uses of nature, he is submerged in nature. Where nature is ascendant, there is no freedom or worldliness. The capacity for political life implies an ability to be alienated from the processes of natural life.[15] And nature is in the ascendant as much in the daily life of "jobholders" in our economy of waste,[16] superfluity, and advanced technology as it was in the "hidden" life lived in premodern times.

For Arendt *animal laborans* triumphs over the craftsman, whom she calls *homo faber*, and the man of action for the first time in modern times. One of the several ways in which she differentiates modern times from all preceding history is precisely by signaling that triumph. She sees advanced society in the West as organized in submission to the principle that life is the highest value.[17] In an unusually threatening section of *The Human Condition* (no. 44), she traces the modern preoccupation with preserving and prolonging life to the Christian doctrine of the immortal soul. This doctrine makes human individuals precious by differentiating them from all the other (expendable) creatures that lack immortal souls. She suggests that the secularized residue of that doctrine is the sense of preciousness of the individual's life on earth. Derivative from that is what the religious doctrine could never have countenanced: an emphasis on "happiness," a debased hedonism devoid of courage and devoted to no purpose other than the satisfaction, or attempted satisfaction, of the body's need or the body's vanity. She applauds the potency of modern technology to relieve misery,[18] even though in some of her most risky passages she wonders whether the relief from the experience of necessity might not so further dilute life as to lead to a "lifeless life."[19] In any case, a hard life and a miserable life are not the same.[20] Arendt goes so far as to deride *animal laborans* for thinking "that mortal men could be happy."[21] She claims that "only children are capable of intense happiness."[22] Despite this austerity (not asceticism), she never trifles with the suffering of the poor. What she means when she says that modern society elevates life to the position of primacy is that it elevates a kind of cowardice—a "self-indulgent egotism with its infinite variety of futile miseries."[23] The triumph of this outlook must mean the ruin of the political realm. There can be no economic self-absorption if there is to be political action. She disagrees with Aristotle on a number of things, but she is at one with him when he says that human life is action and not production.[24]

There is another kind of self-absorption equally fatal to the political realm. It is at the opposite end of the spectrum from bodily self-absorption. That is the concern of the self with the self, with its own inwardness. In attacking this concern—it is not hyperbole to say that she *attacks* this concern—Arendt is at her most iconoclastic. In one of her earliest American writings, she quite simply says, "Man....is more than thought, because more real and more free."[25] Her treatment of the inner life is one aspect of her theorizing on the various activities of mental life altogether. She also makes connections between these activities and political action. Among those she takes up are introspection and empathy, on the one hand, and thinking, intelligence (skill in reasoning), knowing, judging, and contemplation, on the other.[26] Thinking and judging have a (problematic) place in political life; intelligence and knowing and having a thirst for knowledge are properly at home in science and whatever resembles science; contemplation is the end-state of speechless wonder at Being, or the inactive contemplation of truth or forms or models. The object of her unequivocal indictment is none of these latter mental activities, even though a life dedicated to any of them is a life withdrawn from political action.

Arendt never says with finality what the existential status is of spending a life in mental life, even though at one point she calls thinking the "freest and purest" of all human activities.[27] Her ambiguity on this subject is a teasing one. The easy thing to say is that she spent her own life in mental life.[28] Yet that life resulted in worldly products, in books and essays, and what is more, these writings deal almost entirely with the nature of political action or with particular political actions. (For a further discussion of her view on the existential status of life as thinking, see the Appendix.)

There is no equivocation, however, in Arendt's attitude toward mental life when it takes the form—the formless form—of introspection or of empathy. She typically uses the word "subjectivity" as a pejorative term. She frequently refers to the heart and the mind as dark, as dark places, as a "chartless darkness."[29] To spend a life watching oneself, refining one's self-perception, trying to catch the feeling or the impulse as it leads its evanescent existence, trying to be fulfilled in one's own inner process is to misspend one's life. There is no freedom or worldliness here. Presumption is added to waste when a person thinks that he can exploit his self-understanding, such as it is, in order to understand others, or to put himself in their place and thus have their feelings and thoughts, indeed to become those others, now this one, now that one.

Arendt goes far in this essentially antiromantic enterprise. One of her earliest works, *Rahel Varnhagen*, is her most extended meditation on the existential inadequacy of the inner life. From the start she has been at war with one of modernity's proudest pursuits. The reason for her hostility is starkly simple: No one can know himself. Consequently, no one can pretend that on the basis of his self-knowledge he can absorb the whole world or that the climax of self-knowledge is the realization that the whole world is already inside himself. Her skepticism is radical, even though she calls on the imagination to help us penetrate into the inner cave.[30] The imagination can never do as much as the cultivators of the inner life want done, but at least it can do something. At the same time, the technicians of the inner life, especially the psychoanalysts, are dismissed as pseudoscientists and curiosity-seekers.[31] Arendt also takes aim at Dilthey and his followers, who claimed that the understanding of history consisted in the effort to "re-live" the experiences of the dead through some deepened self-acquaintance. She charges such practitioners or would-be practitioners with leading a "parasitic" life, of disingenuously converting their failure to have a political life of their own into an opportunity to live the lives of others, to have many lives vicariously, as if a vicarious life had the same reality as a real one.

The cultivation of the inner life is thus a symptom of a general "world alienation,"[32] a flight from reality and toward dreaming or unheroic illusion. No one can know himself; no one can know others. Humanity cannot know what humanity is: "This would be like jumping over our own shadows."[33] The desire to substitute the inner life for a worldly life is understandable, but for Arendt not forgivable.

In sum, man abdicates from the world and fails to be free when he contents himself with the activities of consumption (which are natural and under necessity, no matter how artificial or refined) or with the activities of consciousness (which are arbitrary and alien, no matter how intense and intimate). In the modern age, the many consume or aspire to consumption, and the few withdraw into themselves. Both are prisoners.

The Existential Supremacy of Political Action

We must now look somewhat more directly at political action itself and understand what Arendt sees in it. We must try to apprehend how it is that freedom and worldliness may rebut, if not refute, the wisdom of Silenus.

At the outset, Arendt's conception of political action is hard to comprehend. And there is no doubt that she would have us feel the difficulty of the subject, if for no other reason than to disabuse us of the belief that we already understand it without the intervention of philosophy. But for all the difficulty, one can make out a general sense. That sense is by no means familiar or common in our culture: Arendt's remoteness from received ideas is as definite in her philosophy of political action as we have seen it to be in the judgments she passes on the nonpolitical activities of life. Although she avoids making any explicit claim for herself, she knows her philosophy is original, or substantially original. She maintains that if not Jesus, then St. Augustine was "the first to formulate the philosophical implications of the ancient political idea of freedom."[34]

The articulation of the very meaning of political action, on the other hand, can be found in "the body of non-philosophical literature....poetic, dramatic, historical, and political writings" of Greece and Rome.[35] That articulation, however, is not systematic. The hostility of Greek philosophers after the death of Socrates and the philosophical incapacity of the Romans make it extremely arduous to rescue the original meaning of political action. The Christian centuries were not hospitable to an understanding of this subject, except in the Italian Renaissance, thanks mostly to Machiavelli. Arendt's project, then, is to do what has never been done: to supply a philosophical account of the meaning of political action. The basic stuff that Arendt the philosopher will work over is the nonphilosophical literature of Greece and Rome. Arendt will recover its "treasure."[36] Her ambition is enormous.

We must notice that as time went on Arendt worked to theorize the peculiarly modern examples of genuine political action: founding constitutions; participation in revolutionary council governments; and civil disobedience.[37] It would be wrong, however, to think that she abandoned her passion for the world of the Greek polis. She simply added another passion. Direct citizen participation is the element common to her ancient and modern commitments. Yet it cannot be denied that her tone and emphasis changed somewhat in her later writings. Politics as the will to heroic greatness, to glory, politics as agon, remains with her when she speaks of modern revolutions, but she makes room for the more modest, almost nameless politics of the councils or civil disobedience. The important point is that "the existential supremacy of political action," as I have called it, shows itself equally in ancient and modern action whether or not the agon is present.

The questions raised by her analysis of action in the polis are also raised by her analysis of modern political action. It is true, however, that sometimes her modern analysis makes it a little easier to try to answer these questions. Much of the following analysis, however, is based on the theory Arendt originally presented with the polis in mind.

She says, "The *raison d'être* of politics is freedom, and its field of experience is action."[38] The *reason* for which people ought to organize a common political life and the reason they have organized it when they have been a truly political people is to have the daily actuality of freedom. Freedom becomes a direct *aim* only when a people make a revolution and thereafter deliberately create the frame for the daily actuality of freedom.[39] The organization or frame or form for freedom, for the action that expresses or manifests or embodies freedom, is the constitution or public space or public realm. Only where there is such a realm and citizens use it to be free can we say that human beings rival nature: They "can establish a reality of their own."[40] (The new methods that scientists have developed for "acting into nature" may equal political action in the quality of rivaling nature's creativity. Such works, however, lack the ability to illuminate human existence, the "existentially most important aspect" of action.)[41]

There are many deeds and acts to which we give the name "political." Not many of them show forth freedom in Arendt's sense of that term. At least she does not think they do. Her standards are strict; she applies them narrowly. She is willing to grant in passing that freedom is not confined to the public realm, that it is "the hidden source of production of all great and beautiful things."[42] More than that, "we can find traces and signs in almost all his [man's] activities."[43] But freedom develops fully only when it is not hidden but appears in political action in a visible space. The prevailing idea in Arendt's work is that the only vehicle of freedom is political action.

A number of questions emerge from Arendt's account. First, what is the existential achievement of political action? Second, what are and are not the modes of political action? Third, what damages or denatures political action?

To Arendt, the illumination of human existence is the most important existential aspect of action. The ability of political action to illuminate human existence marks it as the rebuttal to the wisdom of Silenus. What is the illumination? How can political action achieve such existential salience? I think that Arendt's answer can be put as follows. Life's burden can be better borne—indeed, one can become reconciled to one's existence—not if one knows who one is (no one can know himself), but if one is known by others as he knows them, and known not as the cultivators of the inner life define knowing, but, as the great poets and dramatists exemplify knowing, through creative or mimetic power.[44] Each knows that he is known, and knows others. This is knowing others in a special sense—knowing as recognition, not as propositional knowledge. For this knowing and being known to be possible, there must be a public realm in which men are expected to act, and do act, by word and deed.

Arendt emphasizes the *revelatory* quality of political action. In political action alone is a person revealed. There alone is light. All other places are dark, and in them the person remains obscure. In his nonpolitical life, he is reduced to his biological species-being, or to the typicalities of social conduct, or to a losing struggle to preserve an amorphous personality against social pressure,[45] or to dependence on the unreachable, inexpressible substratum of his mental life.[46] The political self, publicly presented, is thus the real self or what must pass for the real self. The real self can be only a defined self; it cannot be the infinite possibilities of inner process and outward response. Political action is the great definer and concentrator of the self, the great stimulus to the formation of a self out of its own welter. Political action introduces coherence into the self and its experience. Such coherence is redemptive. Narrative, dramatic, or poetic art perfects the coherence.

The very nature of the human self combined with the discipline of political action imposes restrictions on the extent of the revelation concerning individuals. "Innermost motives" can never become known either to one's inner eye or to the watchful observation of public eyes. Hence, they are not revealed. It is hopeless (and politically ruinous) to expect such a revelation.[47] If true self-knowledge or knowledge of others is defined as knowledge of innermost motives, then the knowledge is unattainable by any method. Yet the self-knowledge that comes to us from the observation of others is superior to the self-knowledge we gain by introspection.[48] Our "sense of unequivocal reality is so bound up with the presence of others that we can never be sure of anything that only we ourselves know and no one else."[49] Arendt thus drives her thesis of the real self as the worldly self very hard. Her contrast between the inner chaos and the shining world is never more acute than when she writes of the revelatory powers of political action. It is almost as if she welcomed the discipline of political action (when rightly done) as an excluder of most of the content of the human heart and mind. Not only is that which goes on in the house best kept there and not allowed to spill outside, so too is that which goes on in the person.

There is a second restriction on the revelation, which is probably an intensification of the first. The self that is revealed, as a whole and not just facets and particulars—the person as "who" rather than as "what"[50]—is hidden from the person but appears clearly to others.[51] Not only are there certain things no one, not even I, can know about myself, there are certain things that others can know about me better than I can, and there are certain things that I can learn about myself only from others. It is thus the case that the most important thing of all—who I am—I cannot know, only others can. I cannot enter political action in order to know myself; I can only get to know myself somewhat better, and then thanks only to the political copresence of others. Furthermore, so fluid or mutable or subject to fortune is even the real or worldly self that one can be said to have attained an *identity* only after one's involvement is finished, with death. One's life becomes a story, a biography; the intangible becomes tangible.[52]

In this context, without mentioning Solon's contention that we should count no man happy until he dies,[53] Arendt seems to be repeating the formulation but suggesting a new interpretation for it: That to have an identity is, and is alone, to be happy, but only the dead have identities. The misfortune is that not many of them do, since so few have ever had the chance for political action. In a remarkable passage on Achilles, Arendt says that among these lucky few, fewer still, perhaps only one—Achilles—gained his identity by a great deed and then died before later events could confuse that identity. Achilles is the hero *par excellence* because he delivered the full significance of his deed to his narrator. We can say of him that he not only suffered his experience and enacted his story, but that he "made" his story.[54] The most extreme hero "must not only risk his life but expressly choose, as Achilles did, a short life and premature death."[55] This sentence is an ironic affirmation of Silenian wisdom: The best life is a short life. Usually, no single act or event can "deliver and save a man, or a nation, or mankind."[56]

With these two restrictions established, the revelatory capacity of political action may be more positively described. The political actor, in Arendt's portrait of him, is part deliberate and part self-surprising, part personal and part impersonal. Her emphasis shifts from one text to another. Thus the nature of the "who" revealed is somewhat variously rendered. I find three main depictions of the political actor, and of the spirit in which he acts. The qualities projected by the actor in each case overlap, but the net sense is different from depiction to depiction. Nevertheless, in all depictions Arendt tries to show that in revealing persons, political action also illuminates the general human condition.

The First Analysis. The political actor reveals that he has latent strengths that are awaiting the opportunity to manifest themselves, transformed by stylization as they are in the passage from natural propensity to public display. When the political actor shows these strengths—courage, judgment, self-control, eloquence—in a publicly remarkable style, he has revealed himself as virtuosic. He possesses *virtù* (in Machiavelli's usage),[57] or he manifests the human ability to engage in activities that "leave no work behind....but exhaust their full meaning in the performance itself," an ability conceptualized by Aristotle as *energeia*.[58] (Arendt seems to prefer *energeia* to *praxis*, perhaps because of Aristotle's equivocations, as the result of which *praxis*, political action, is sometimes described as instrumental in part.)[59] He has revealed himself as a distinctive *performer*.[60] Because the performance relies heavily on natural propensities, the political actor as performer is less deliberate, more self-surprising, and more personal than the actor in Arendt's two other depictions. We should stress, however, that Arendt has no patience with the idea of self-expression,[61] either in the realm of action or in that of craft or art. Action, like anything creative, is not an emanation or an unconditional unfolding, but an uncertain initiative in a preexistent and largely unpredictable world.[62] The actor changes himself and the world as he acts. He shows himself and others that he is more than he knew.

The Second Analysis. Arendt presents the political actor as one who hides much in order to reveal more. He wears a mask. But the mask in the ancient theater hid the face yet allowed the actor's true voice to come through. She reverts to the Roman conception of persona, a political and legal personality (carrying rights and duties) that the public realm ascribes to each citizen, and without which there would be only the natural, naked, unformed ego. The analysis is not wholly clear,[63] but it deserves some attention because Arendt is suggesting that for a man to keep his mask on is not to make himself a hypocrite. To the contrary, without worldly conventions there can be no honesty. The unmasked face is the unprotected self, which must dissolve into a self-consuming, self-destroying, single-minded passion like rage or hate. A hypocrite, on the other hand, is one who when unmasked reveals that there was nothing behind the mask: He is a compulsive role-player, changing from one role to another, able to feign even naturalness, and finally succumbing perhaps to self-deception, to being an actor without knowing it, paradoxically filling himself with emptiness.[64]

To wear a mask is to sustain a persona, a role, a position, an identifiable character. It is not a distortion of Arendt's meaning to say that she believes that it is the highest responsibility of the citizen to protect his mask so that in the artificial composure of his appearance the truth of his words may sound. Of course there are many masks, but their differences are much less important than the differences between persons, which their common wish to speak truthfully establishes.[65] The distractions of personal idiosyncrasy, the hopeless struggle to keep on remembering who one truly is, and the impossibility of having an identity without having a public identity and of having a public identity without having a publicly defined identification all conduce to the view that the public action of a persona, a person masked, is one of the great sources of a certain kind of truthfulness in the world.

The political actor in this analysis is more deliberate, less self-surprising, and more impersonal than in the preceding analysis.[66] The revelation is not so much of the actor as of the truth that the particular occasion requires. This truth is not the truth of great thought, nor is it the truth of mere information and communication. The point is "finding the right words at the right moment."[67] The aim is rational persuasion, not lying or sophistry. In a society committed to political life, there will necessarily be a commitment to talk; and the talk through the masks of many united but various individuals will be a continuous generator of truth, truth about the common world, yet truth that may have more than local significance. Such is the revelation promised.

We should notice, however, an apparently contrary moment where the notion of masks and roles is not abandoned but circumscribed. In an unpublished speech given when she won a prize, in the last year of her life, Arendt refers to the ability of a person to change the masks that cover the inner self. Uncharacteristically, she speaks as if the inner self had a determinate reality and was not instead comprised of latencies awaiting their occasions. She refers to "my naked 'thereness,' identifiable, I hope, but not definable and not seduced by the great tempation of recognition *as* such and such, that is, as something which we fundamentally are *not*."[68] With these words she takes off the mask of her theory and allows her public self to speak in behalf of the inner self. Yet her preponderant sense is that the inner self has no "thereness." Masks alone create the object of attention.

Much earlier, almost at the beginning of her career in America, Arendt projected a notion of roles that also seems at variance with her preponderant sense. She sympathetically expounds the French existentialist idea that only by constantly changing roles, or alternatively, by choosing "to play at being what one really is,"[69] can one escape the bad faith that consists in thinking that one is identical with one's function, one's job, one's position in society, as an animal is identical with itself. Later, she explicitly repudiates a life of constantly changing roles. Although she loathes the bad-faith loss of self in any *function*, she sees such loss as equivalent to the loss of consciousness of oneself as not natural, as forgetfulness of the difference between nature and convention. Wearing a mask or playing a role in political life, however, is a deliberate adoption of a commitment to consistency in the face of unforeseeable events. It is not life lived in imitation of natural process. At the same time, Arendt ultimately believes that "what one really is" cannot be played at: It does not preexist the role. The point is to choose a role knowingly and accept its discipline freely. The best role is that of citizen. And to play a role in public life is to do more than play.

The Third Analysis. Arendt says that political action (when rightly done) permits the actor to escape the self. He reveals the peculiar human capacity to be free—to be free of self. This analysis is an extreme version of the second.

Whereas in the second analysis, the actor was understood as sustaining a role that had typical or representative aspects[70] but which also depended in part on his individual character, the actor in the third analysis is even more deliberate and impersonal. He *creates* a role and enacts it in accordance with his conception of what the role requires. He thus illuminates existence by redeeming some bit of life from the determinisms of the psyche. The revelation of this generic human capacity is, I think Arendt thought, the most profound existential achievement of political action.

Arendt's discussion, brief, dense, and somewhat obscure, is found in "What Is Freedom?" She introduces the concept of *acting from a principle*, as distinguished from acting for a purpose or goal or acting from a motive. She says, "Action, to be free, must be free from motive on one side, from its intended goal as a predictable effect on the other."[71] Motives and aims or goals are always present as "determining factors," but action is free "to the extent that it is able to transcend them."[72] In a slightly changed formulation, she says that, "Action insofar as it is free is neither under the guidance of the intellect nor under the dictate of the will—although it needs both for the execution of any particular goal."[73] Arendt is trying to purge the definition of right political action from inner determination, whether it be that of the assertive will, the calculating intelligence, the impassioned heart, or the urges of the body or spirit. She is also trying to indicate that there may be action that is impersonal, but not in the sense of dispassionate or impartial (much as she admires these latter qualities). Perhaps a clumsy, indeed inhuman, word is more accurate than "impersonal"—namely, "depersonalized." To act from a principle is to act in a depersonalized way.

What is a principle? It is not a moral principle in the usual sense. It is an idea or value, general in nature and universal in validity; it comes to one from outside and inspires "from without." It appears in life, however, only when a given political actor acts from it: "The appearance of freedom, like the manifestation of principles, coincides with the performing act."[74] It is not an inner event, nor does it die with the act's completion. Arendt gives these examples: honor, glory, love of equality, distinction, and excellence, but also "fear or distrust or hatred."[75] (There are echoes perhaps of Montesquieu on the informing and sustaining principle of each form of government.)[76]

It is hard to distinguish between principles on the one hand and motives, intentions, purposes, and goals on the other. Motives (and the rest) can be general in nature and universal in validity. The exhaustion or satisfaction of motive in one person does not preclude exhaustion or satisfaction for someone else. Furthermore, a purpose or goal may be a policy and hence something outside the actors' selves, and the strategy in pursuit of the policy may be as free from the peculiarities of the psyche and as implicated in the discipline of the world as acting from a principle. Still, despite the obscurity of the notion, Arendt seems to be struggling with an idea that others have developed or that could be developed. It may be that what she puts forward resembles formally (and only formally) the existentialist concept of *project*. The project is a task without boundaries; one can never say that it is done, yet the whole meaning of it is found in every action done for its sake. ("For the sake of" does not mean "in order to.")[77] It is never realized.

That one adopts a principle does not prevent another from adopting it; it is inexhaustible. To act from a principle is not only to be inspired by it, but to manifest it. A political actor does not *pursue* honor, for example; he does all that he does honorably, or he does honorable deeds.[78] A principle is not a consideration external to the act and satisfiable by a neutral method. One acts from a principle when one spends one's political life, one's worldly career, dominated by the effort to live up to the objective requirements of a single loyalty, and to do so at whatever cost to one's interests. What is involved is not altruism, but self-forgetting—self-forgetting as death-forgetting.[79] Or the political actor must try to lead a double life, in the sense of giving an inferior place to his interests and needs. Or he must let his principle color or tinge his every act no matter what his motive or goal. (I do not know how to put her thought exactly.)

Additionally, one will certainly have to interpret the requirements of one's loyalty: What to do is not automatically dictated by the principle. For the same reason, some room for play will be given to one's temperament. The least concern, however, will be for one's authenticity. Unstylized natural promptings must be kept out of sight. (She prizes honesty, even sincerity, but authenticity is impossible. To want it is not to know the first thing about oneself or about selves.) To live for a single loyalty is to lose the self and gain the world. To live outside oneself and for the sake of acting from a principle is to live freely, free of the necessities of body, heart, and mind. To live with others loyal to the same or to a different principle is to live in a free world. Living in this manner is to be human, at last.

In this third analysis, political action reveals the greatest of all human capacities: to be born a second time. Completing the blasphemy is Arendt's sympathetic commentary on Machiavelli's self-description, "I love my native city more than my own soul." She says, "Most of Machiavelli's arguments against religion are directed against those who love themselves, namely their own salvation, more than the world; they are not directed against those who really love God more than they love either the world or themselves."[80] Thus there is radical discontinuity between political action and everything else on earth and in heaven. And this doctrine, she says, Machiavelli held as a Christian believer; she holds it as one who thinks that only a fool could be an atheist. We are witness to her blasphemy as well as to Machiavelli's: She means to be understood in that way. She means us to understand Lincoln in the same way, when he defined his aim as preserving the Union, not abolishing slavery.[81] (She ignores the fact that Lincoln thought the Union worth preserving because it rested on the principle of equal human dignity.) To push the matter to the limit, it is as if Arendt were saying that only the earthly immortality of glorious political action withstands Silenus's wisdom; heavenly immortality would not suffice. The reversal of Plato on where the place of darkness is is now joined by the reversal of Christianity on what salvation is. Thus, the highest existential advantage to the person as political actor is coincident with the greatest service he can do for his world. One becomes individuated through self-loss.

One might add that the revelations of action are perfected only in art, the great poems, plays, epics, histories. The story about the virtuoso or persona or principled actor is the last word about who he was. Stories thus contribute as nothing else can to the illumination of human existence.[82] The best stories are about public words and deeds that shine, that compel further attention by their beauty. Arendt comes close to saying that we exist in order to be turned into stories, and that we are justified by the stories we provoke or inspire writers to tell. And the stories provoke and inspire others to act. There would be no stories without us: We are their matter. But we would not have a human life, a life worth living, without stories. We spoil life and obstruct art, however, if we try to shape our actions or lives into a story or deliberately set meaningfulness as an aim or end.[83] In any case, whatever the actor's intention may be, the storyteller, thanks to the "backward glance" that is his privilege, "always knows better what it was all about than the participants."

The actor's own account may be useful, but it cannot attain the "significance and truthfulness" of the later story. The reason:

> What the storyteller narrates must necessarily be hidden from the actor himself, at least as long as he is in the act or caught in its consequences, because to him the meaningfulness of his act is not in the story that follows.[84]

Achilles, as the greatest hero, is alone exempt from this anticipated dependence.[85] Furthermore, the story should reveal the meaning of action "without committing the error of defining it."[86] Art thus shares the burden of withstanding the wisdom of Silenus, so long as the art is worldly.[87] This is not to justify life as an esthetic phenomenon, but to define human life as intelligible meaning.[88]

WHAT ARE THE MODES OF POLITICAL ACTION?

Although the emphasis in the preceding discussion has been on the existential importance of political action for the actor, taken singly as one who both experiences the joy of action and furnishes a revelation by his performance, Arendt is intent on showing how political action must be done in company with others and for the sake of all. There is no meaning otherwise. A line from Tennyson's "Ulysses," slightly changed, captures the gist: To drink delight of action with my peers. The whole poem, never cited by Arendt, conveys her sense of political action. Action is a common enterprise. Human plurality is the basic condition of action. I would interpolate the inference that only a diseased subjectivity could possibly say, with a character from Sartre's *No Exit*, that hell is other people. If that is hell, the reason is that the life lived with them is solely private.

Arendt says that plurality has a twofold character—equality and distinction. If political actors were not equal, they could not understand each other and work together. If they were not distinct from each other, they would not need words or deeds to make themselves understood; they would not have the inestimable opportunity for communicating *themselves* rather than merely messages.[89] There could be no political world if individuals were all of the same mind and saw things from the same perspective. Reality is guaranteed by variety, whereas when there is "prolongation or multiplication" of any one identity or perspective, as in the household, reality is shadowy.[90] In the public realm a person's identity is established by the play of different opinions about him; just as his own "truth" is enhanced in contention with the truths of others. He is real to himself only because he is publicly real to others. Public life is a condition of both relation and separation;[91] it can be destroyed by too much closeness (unanimity or brotherhood, for example) as well as by solitude, loneliness, or isolation,[92] or by factional hostility or "pull and pressure and the tricks of cliques."[93] The worldly scene of political action, in Arendt's description, is the place of sanity and the very paradigm of sanity.

As for the egalitarian element of human plurality, Arendt invokes the Greek term *isonomy* and reads it to mean not equality of condition, but a condition that makes men equal. It is a condition of "no-rule."[94] Only in political life are the talents that are needed potentially in all men. In all other spheres of life the differences between people engender inequalities, and usually rightly so.[95] Politics can exist only in the public realm; and, therefore, equality can exist only there.

Political action, then, takes place in the company of diverse equals. What is political action? Arendt frequently distinguishes between words and deeds, or between talking and doing, as the basic modes of action. But given all that she excludes as not properly political, the distinction cannot stand.[96] It must collapse, with the result that there is only one true mode of political action, and that is speech, in the form of talking or occasionally writing, as with the Declaration of Independence[97] and other manifestoes or addresses to the world, writing that should be read aloud.

Arendt's work is often concerned with war and revolution, but when she praises any war or revolution, she does not praise what she accepts as necessary and justifiable deeds of violence—with the exception of Rome's "great notion of a war," in which the warring parties become partners "by virtue of the new relationship established in the fight itself."[98] Yet she may mean to include feats of bodily strength and valor that may result in death, provided that such strength does not turn into violence, which, by her definition, always needs equipment or "implements,"[99] and may be divorced from courage. In any case, physical feats cannot be "brutal,"[100] and they merit praise only in the form of resistance to violence.[101] The deeds of young revolutionaries would fit, though uneasily, into an extended version of her theory, at least as well as the deeds of Achilles and other warriors. Also, there are physical actions, examples of "symbolic speech" and gestures that count primarily as communication because of their luminosity or exemplariness, or their instantaneous intelligibility.

On occasion, Arendt *defines* political action as political speech,[102] she also says that "most acts....are performed in the manner of speech,"[103] and she insists that speech must always be joined to action, if action is to possess its revelatory quality.[104] But what action does her theory allow us to name as political except for talking or writing? My point is probably obvious. What else but speech could political action essentially be, once violence is excluded as non-political, and such physical activities as labor and craft (and play, too)[105] are conceptually opposed to political action?

One theoretical consequence of insisting on action as speech is to call into question Arendt's location of action in the same category—the *vita activa*—as labor and craft (or work). Action, like the processes of thinking and knowing, is constituted by words and is free of materiality and its necessities, as labor and craft cannot be. The freedom is in the immateriality, which includes of course, the symbolic and notational (mathematics and music) as well as the verbal. If the freedom is there, so is the dignity. Which is to say that Arendt's analysis may lead us to claim kinship between what she sometimes sets starkly at odds: the life of action and the life of the mind.

If action is speech, it is clear that a political actor cannot be represented in political action. One must have words to say and say them oneself. Political action is therefore direct participation in the conversation of diverse equals, or more rarely, in written composition for the occasion. The typical result is a conclusion: a decision, a choice, a judgment, a rule. The master intellectual virtue displayed in action is *phronesis*, insight, refined common sense.[106] Arendt refers without elaboration to a second stage—achieving or carrying through.[107]

What are the modes of speech as action? Arendt refers to "speech-making and decision-taking, the oratory and the business, the thinking and the persuading;"[108] "predicative or argumentative speech;"[109] the processes of "persuasion," "negotiation," and "compromise;"[110] "the discussions," "the deliberations, and the making of decisions;"[111] and "the joys of discourse, of legislation, of transacting business, of persuading and being persuaded."[112]

THE CONTENT OF POLITICS.

What is the subject matter of such speech? That is, what is the content of political action? This is a vexed question to which Arendt herself sometimes gives a perplexed answer. Quoting Jefferson on how the ward system of government he had sketched, once begun "only for a single purpose" would "soon show for what others they [were] the best instruments," she concedes that the notion of wards shows a "vagueness of purpose."[113] Undeniably, a certain vagueness marks Arendt's own thought on the question of the content of political action. The vagueness is not really dispelled when in a revision of this passage she abruptly converts the wards into "instruments" for "breaking up" mass society or permeating it with a self-constituted "grass roots" elite.[114] Yet as she grew ever more occupied with American political life, she evolved a compelling answer, even if it still falls short of being a full one.

For Arendt to say that political action is not a means to some end beyond itself, that it is valuable in itself, still does not indicate what the content of the action is. Turning to games, perhaps the closest analogy to Arendt's notion of action, we see that a game may be played for its own sake—that is, for the exhilaration of the play itself—though we are ordinarily obliged to try to win and not just feel good playing. Analysis nevertheless pays attention to the nature of the game itself, to the rules that constitute and regulate the play, as well as to any particular contest played by and within the rules. We can go on to say that the content of any kind of game is itself. A game is not "about" anything outside itself; it is its own sufficient world. It is often confined to its own spatial field. Can we say, similarly, that the content of political action is itself? Yes, while remembering that unlike politics many games are without speech. We can say that the content of political action is politics in the sense that political action is talk about politics.

Ideally, politics is its own content in the sense that it is its own subject. To act politically is to talk about politics. What does that mean? Where does Arendt's emphasis lie? Either she is saying that the only great or fine revelatory public talk turns out to be talk about politics, or she is possessed of the formalist wish, present without defense, that politics should have nothing internal to itself but itself. Both elements appear or are implied but without being either distinguished or comparatively assessed. The first element is probably closer to her intention. That means that the only talk that can be counted on to achieve the existential worth promised by political participation deals with matters that are political. Other matters are important, but important matters are often boring.

Such talk takes the form of discussion that aims at having a vote or making a decision. Thus the talk is not idle, academic, or gratuitous. It has a practical conclusion and issues in responsibilities and unpredictable patterns, in sacrifices and dangers. For that fact, political action is only partly analogous to a game. It is too serious, too bound up with the deepest existential questions, as well as with the most mortal stakes to be literally a game. At the same time, the occasions for political talk arise from the need to respond to events that may impinge from the outside or erupt unexpectedly. Here, too, the analogy with a game lapses: All the events of a game (to leave aside what is accidental) are the events of the game's play. Also, politics tames and refines conflicts that would exist in a fiercer state unless politics existed, while a competitive game creates its own kind of conflict that would not otherwise exist. And because these things are true, a game can be completely intelligible—as political action can never be—and totally free of human nature, free of motives, hidden or obvious, while political action must fight free of human nature.

Still, what is talk about politics actually about? It deals with the creation of the conditions that make itself possible or with the preservation of those conditions. Put less glibly, discussion that is properly political pertains either to the creation (or founding) of a constitution or form of government, or to the defense of a constitution or form against internal erosion or external attack. Arendt's premises are that a set of political arrangements, rules, procedures, and conventions is a supremely important human artifice,[115] and that the discussion it engenders may be free of such unpolitical impurities as economic self-interest and group interest. In a political (politicized) culture, these impurities will be much less important than people living in an economistic culture like our own can easily imagine.

Whenever the Greek polis occupies the center of Arendt's reflection, the question of the content of political action does not seem to be acceptably answerable. We are true to Arendt's understanding if we use as illustrations of properly political talk the speeches in Thucydides. They deal with war and peace; with particular moments when judgment must be made concerning guilt and innocence, punishment or reprieve; and with the rhetorical need to speak even with guile or hyperbole, about the nature of the city itself, its way of life, its *telos*, its distinctiveness. The almost formal antagonism of units helps to define the content of public discussion: how to win, how to play. All citizens are in it together, act as one, are affected equally, actually or potentially. The content here is grim because it is so closely attached to war, often aggressive war or desperately defensive, and thus attached to violence, which Arendt usually refuses to situate at the conceptual center of political action. There seems to be little in normal politics that is also ideal, or normal politics seems minor in comparison to grand politics, the politics of adventure and emergency.

From the perspective I propose, the content of politics in the Greek world concentrated itself too insistently on the defense or pretended defense of a constitution against external attack—"constitution" understood here, of course, in the extended sense of defining a whole way of life. Politics as the lethal antagonism of units—as distinguished from the moderated and rule-governed antagonism inherent in the domestic politics of republics and constitutional democracies—crowds the scene. The gamelike quality of politics turns into a bloody caricature. The difference between proper politics and power politics becomes too faint. At one point Arendt almost accepts foreign policy as the only true *modern* politics because it is full of "hostilities and sympathies" that are not economic in nature.[116] Usually, however, she expresses aversion to power politics: the ruthless struggle for mastery or position or jurisdiction, or "power as the only content of politics, and....expansion as its only aim."[117] But that is what the politics of the polis was at its most intense and memorable. Or when not that, it often was class war. Politics was not, unfortunately, the mere pacification of neighbors so that the bloodless and lovely war of daily politics could go on undisturbed. If anything, daily politics, even when not class war, was a wargame, a conditioning for war.[118] Arendt, however, tries to attribute power politics solely to the modern imperialist bourgeoisie sponsored by Hobbes. But Hobbes learned about power from Thucydides.

Once out of the Greek world, the properly political content of politics becomes less frightful. The heroic and the agonistic do not vanish, but they lose their cruelty. Glory is earned without imposition and self-imposition. Politics remains, however, genuinely political to an equal degree. The two main kinds of content of political deliberation (besides that which emerges from the lethal antagonism of political units) that dominate Arendt's analysis are (1) the creation (or founding) of a constitution or form of government and (2) its defense against internal erosion. When writing about those modern revolutions that culminate in the creation of new constitutions, and about the practice of civil disobedience in America, she finds the appropriate center of her conception of the content of political action. Beyond the need of her theory for a satisfactory resolution, her conception catches a fair part of the usually unspoken sense of those who want politics seen as an activity sharply distinct from all others, even if they do not seek the purely political as intensely as she does.

Deliberation about a new constitution is creation in the highest political sense, and it shows more than any other kind of political action, the capacity to begin, to start something new, to interrupt the automatisms of man's life and save something from nature's downward tendency. Arendt says that no other capacity "except language, neither reason nor consciousness, distinguishes us so radically from all animal species."[119]

Arendt does not want political creation in this sense to be understood as a kind of instrumental activity. She always tries to exclude the means-end relationship from the proper conception of political action. She will not see constitution-making as making at all. I suppose her implication is that a constitution is not a program or policy. Nor is it a blueprint or design for a utopia or a whole society. A founding is not lawgiving in the Platonic or Rousseauist sense. It has no goal; it does not make an object. Rather, it is the creation of a frame of institutions for indefinite future possibilities of political action, and the frame itself is changed by what it contains—by the experience it shapes and accommodates. It therefore has no fixed shape itself. It has only a career inspired by certain principles.

Arendt devotes *On Revolution* to the experience of the American and French revolutionaries in trying to establish new political institutions. Arendt's great interest is not in all founding, but in the efforts made to found a form that would provide a way of having the revolutionary spirit survive the end of the revolution.[120] Despite the enduring greatness of the American Constitution, it failed to do this no less than the French effort.[121] The creation of representative institutions is the death of unprofessionalized, unpartisan grass-roots participation in discussions of the highest importance. The amazing fact is that in revolutionary circumstances the newly liberated common people spontaneously created small face-to-face councils for public business. These councils then were superseded, or crushed. They contained, in Arendt's judgment, a political situation as genuine as that of the city-state. The tragedy of revolution is the failure of the council form to endure, since the greatness of revolution is the miraculous efflorescence of political talk by people hitherto private and silent. It is important to notice that when Arendt discusses the quality of participation in councils she does not make anything of virtuosity or persona or principle, all of them connected with the wish to shine and excel and stand out before one's equals. She refers, in the case of the councils during the Hungarian Revolution, to the traits of "personal integrity, courage and judgment."[122] Yet these latter qualities are certainly compatible with the wish to shine or excel, even though the council form may tend to temper its various expressions, especially pride in virtuosity.

Arendt realizes that the preservation of the revolutionary spirit in America by means of recurrent constitutional conventions would have been too disruptive or "more likely have debased the act of foundation to a mere routine performance."[123] A form of government that institutionalizes the creative practice of founding is thus not imaginable. But to institutionalize direct participation, while extremely difficult in the modern age, is at least a coherent ideal. She therefore takes seriously Jefferson's ward system of government for America and is sympathetic to any European attempt to project institutional arrangements for council government.[124] Only with such forms can freedom as direct participation be given an institutionalized place in the modern age. By this analysis, the best that people have now is decent government and civil liberty—not freedom, not political action, not the direct participation of diverse equals in the public business. As we shall soon see, Arendt advances beyond this analysis.

Grand politics in the modern age, then, is exemplified by the deliberate effort to specify a set of political arrangements, rules, procedures, and conventions, get them accepted, and get them started. Although Arendt does not dwell on the drafting and the process of ratification of the American Constitution, it is clear that the intelligence, dignity, and passion that went into the countless discussions concerning the document satisfy the highest standards of political action. The question remains, however: If Jefferson's ward system had found a place in the Constitution, if the Constitution were not so single-mindedly dedicated to the avoidance of direct popular participation in federal politics, what would political activists do? What would they talk about? What would be the content of their political action? The theoretical need is to say what the properly political content of normal politics is. And away from America, what is the content of the politics of council government? Perhaps in this latter case we could say that the precariousness of all these European experiments led to defensive concerns of a genuinely political nature, and that the newness necessitated a daily effort to work out the meaning, the logic, the implications, of council government itself. But suppose they had survived? We would be left with that vagueness she acknowledged. In general, up to this point, Arendt's theory leaves us only service on juries and perhaps town meetings as an unproblematic example of modern political action.[125].

When she came to reflect on civil disobedience in America, Arendt found the key to the properly political content of normal politics. It is odd, of course, to associate civil disobedience with normality, but one of the unexpected elements of Arendt's analysis is that she advocates a regular constitutional niche for irregular action. Whether or not this proposal is a plausible one, the fact remains that civil disobedience is a principal mode of defense of any constitution that embodies representative democracy. But it is not the only mode. The general point is that the properly political content of normal politics is defense of a democratic constitution against internal erosion. At the same time, such defense allows participatory citizenship to find a home in representative government.

Erosion is an unending threat to anything so full of impediments to government as a democratic constitution committed to individual rights. Therefore, unending attentiveness to the vicissitudes of such a constitution is one good way of being a citizen. The attentiveness of truly political citizens is directed at office-holders, because so many of the pressures on office-holders are pressures on the constitution, while so many of their temptations are temptations against the constitution, especially in the executive.[126] Despite the assertion made in *The Origins of Totalitarianism* that "Lawfulness sets limitations to actions, but does not inspire them,"[127] the gist of Arendt's later thought is precisely that a concern to protect or perfect lawfulness is a great modern mode of political action. Her conceptualization of civil disobedience in America is primarily as action designed to protect or perfect the Constitution. By extension, any political action undertaken for that cause—all public deliberation that pertains to any feature of a democratic constitution and that issues in decisions, inquiry, further debates, protest, symbolic speech, and luminous or exemplary action—is the properly political content of normal political action. The idea can and must be extended to office-holders.

In accordance with Arendt's standards, then, the civil rights and antiwar movements in the United States are prime examples of citizenly action, and the hearings on the impeachment of President Nixon were the supreme political involvement for the members of the House Committee on the Judiciary. In general, office-holders engage in genuine political action when their deliberations and decisions touch directly or lightly on constitutional matters.

I do not suggest, however, that citizenship as constitutional action, (in regard to citizens not in office) could hold a place in Arendt's estimation as high as participation in council government. Constitutional action—beyond mere attentiveness—is episodic, while participation in councils is supposed to be full-time. For being full-time, it is central in a person's attainment of identity; episodic action is likely to contribute only a fragment to identity.

By the lights of this conception in which politics is the content of politics much of what conventionally counts as political action in the modern age is ruled out. On the one hand, governmental management of the economy is ruled out as properly political (though, of course, Arendt never denies that economic matters will and must occupy office-holders). On the other hand, the state's endeavors in behalf of socioeconomic reform or revolutionary reconstruction are also ruled out. The formalist wish, the wish for a "pure politics" may underlie these exclusions. But the arguments Arendt uses throughout her work refer to other considerations. Gathered together, these reasons are that the pursuit of economic policy and the exertions of reform and reconstruction meet few if any of the several criteria she sets for truly political action: It must involve the relations of equals; it must proceed by persuasion, not coercion; it cannot be instrumental; it cannot deal with interests or life processes; it must deal with matters that are uncertain and do not permit of one and only one right answer or solution; it must receive its discipline from serious or even urgent questions; and it must be comprised of great or fine revelatory talk, free of jargon or technical vocabulary. The more purposive public activity is, the more elitist it must be and the less citizenly it can be. Actually, only the criterion of seriousness is met by governmental management of the economy or reformist or radical activity.

It would be easier on Arendt's readers if instead of suggesting that the content of political action is itself she had said that no matter what political speech and deliberation deals with—no matter what its subject matter—it could be genuinely political, provided it were carried on in the right spirit. To accept any content as compatible with political action is, in effect, to downgrade all content while preserving it. The right spirit would be to debate and discuss with the hope of winning, certainly, but also for the love of the involvement, for the sake of playing or watching, and to regard the integrity of the constitution that inspires, guides, and limits the debate and discussion as more important than any particular result or set of results. Every public issue could be seen as having a political *aspect*, with the emphasis on such agonistic elements as competition, rivalry, and maneuver, as well as on the complementary elements of fellowship and common loyalty of rivals. Indeed, much of *nonpublic* life could also be seen to have a political aspect. The right spirit can find politics in any relation, or make politics out of it. But such a reading unfortunately fails to grant Arendt some of her major criteria for political action—especially those that require the presence of high seriousness and the complete absence of interests and life processes. If we nevertheless adopt this perspective, although we do not follow Arendt, we also do not follow the conventional position concerning the content of political action.

MODES OF ACTION THAT ARE NOT POLITICAL

From this account of political action as the speech of diverse equals concerning the public business, whether in the Greek or modern fashion, there naturally arises an initial answer to the question, What are *not* the modes of political action? That answer is that all relations that we conventionally call political are not genuinely so if they are relations of inequality. Of the several criteria for true political action, the criterion of equality is centrally important in separating it from everything else that may go under its name. The one unequal relation that may possibly involve true political action is that which is done in compliance with authority or within limits set by authority. Arendt says that authority, foreign to Greek experience,[128] relies on neither coercion nor persuasion[129] and is typified by the Roman Senate and by the United States Supreme Court as interpreter of the Constitution.[130] The problem is not to show that freedom and equality are compatible (they are inextricably joined), but to show "how to reconcile equality and authority."[131] It turns out that authority is above everything else reverence for the past act of founding the polity and for the words and intentions of the founders.[132] It is not a daily relationship between political office-holders and the rest of the people.[133] Such reverence, such willingness to be guided or even bound, is not incompatible with freedom,[134] in Arendt's preponderant judgment, provided the revered polity allows dissent. The toleration of dissent implies consent to a constitution, and thus the object of reverence is the object of rational acceptance as well.[135]

For us, the major point is that, in general, relations of inequality disallow truly political action. Either these relations lack speech or the speech they contain is indirect or devoid of mutuality and give and take. The relations where speech is lacking include violence and force. The relations where speech is indirect include voting and being represented. The relations where speech is devoid of mutuality include ruling, commanding, administering, and coercing. Arendt insists that not only the objects of violence and force, and those who are ruled, commanded, administered, or coerced, are deprived of a real political relation, but also those who use violence or force, or who rule, command, administer, or coerce. The beauty of equality is in knowing and being known by others. Where there is inequality, this human knowledge is destroyed by muteness or distorted by the illusions that the relations of superiors and inferiors breed. Those who use violence or force do not talk and hence do not reveal themselves; their victims are not revealed. Those who rule (and the rest) do what they do instrumentally, exploitatively, or manipulatively.[136] They do not engage the world in a way by which they come to be known or come to know others; and thus the speech embedded in these relations is not revelatory. Arendt's point is not affected by whether those who rule (and the rest) do so beneficently or oppressively. But, in fact, the "only power that does corrupt is the power to rule."[137]

It would be foolish to deny the necessity for all these essentially nonpolitical activities; people could not get along without them. The point is to see them for what they are and not confuse them with each other or confuse any of them with political action. It would be just as bad to blur the distinction in practice; for example, to try to substitute political action for administration, as in the place of work or in economic relations in general. Correspondingly, the human qualities enlisted and favored by political action are not likely to be found in those who aspire to rule or administer and who do it well.[138] The right attitude is that of the Greeks: For the sake of preserving the conditions of political action, "each was more or less willing to share in the burden of jurisdiction, defense, and administration of public affairs."[139] Obviously, here Arendt is departing from Aristotle, who saw in ruling, in the executive and administrative offices, the greatest field for the action of citizens. She thus rejects the possibility of drawing the distinction he tried to draw between despotic rule over slaves and constitutional rule over equals. The latter consists in both ruling and being ruled in turn (rotation in office) and ruling those who will one day be rulers (older citizens ruling younger ones). Arendt reverts instead to the democratic idea that Aristotle mentions: that citizens *as citizens* neither rule nor are ruled.[140]

The underlying theoretical point here is that political action is a relation of equals. Almost as important is the point that political action is not a means to some end or ends lying outside itself, like protecting good men, saving souls, ensuring progress. Arendt not only dismisses as senseless the question of what the end of government is,[141] she says that only in the world of work (fabrication) is the means-end duality appropriate. Action is its own end: Its greatness as revelation needs no further validation, only philosophical elaboration. For Arendt, to press beyond the revelatory qualities of action is absurd because it is to demand an answer to the question, Why be human? Action has consequences, usually unforeseen, but its innermost meaning is untouched by them.[142]

As for the relation between the represented and representative, there is one difference from the essentially unpolitical activities just mentioned. The representative is free: He alone among those who occupy the superior position in these relations is in a company of equals, his fellow representatives, at least when they are not bound by their constituents.[143] Much more important, however, is Arendt's rejection of being represented as a form of freedom, of political action. That she prefers modern representative government to any other existent system may go without saying. The basis of this preference is negative: the absence of oppression and injustice, the presence of personal security and liberty. But that is not enough for the claim to be made that representative government works because of the participation, the action, the citizenship, of the vast majority. In a healthy representative government, the people *rule* their representatives; but they do not act, and hence they are not free. [144] We are not free.

We are not free, by definition, because we do not participate. Arendt says that actions and opinions, the very being of freedom, cannot be represented; only interest and welfare can.[145] Interests adhere to groups, opinions to individuals.[146] Freedom can be experienced only by individuals, and only directly. She goes so far as to say that there is "danger" in giving power only in the form of the vote: used as a device for the promotion of self-interest or the satisfaction of a mood, or of massed, undeliberated public opinion,[147] the vote is power "given to the people in their private capacity."[148] The clash of interest groups is not seen by Arendt as a kind of agonistic contest, but as the use of power as "blackmail," the introduction into public life of the unenhanced relation of winners and losers.[149]

Furthermore, participation does not matter in Arendt's theory because of its connection to individual consent or, even more, to individual will. She is fierce in her rejection of Rousseau—in part for his self-absorption; in part for the feelings he made fashionable; in largest part for the centrality he gave to the concept of will in political theory, and the way in which he tied human dignity to living by one's own will in all areas of life, not only the private.[150] She sees no dignity in doing what one thinks one ought to do, apart from what one's equals think, when all must do the same thing. What matters is not that others agree or disagree with oneself, but that one collaborates with others in the common task of deciding what all will do after all have directly expressed divergent opinions. There is no existential injury to a person who abides by a result he disagrees with. The collaboration dissolves the significance of will. Wills cannot be mediated or compromised without injury to their dignity; that is why will is not a political category.[151]

Opinions, on the other hand, can be mediated; that is, minds can instruct and affect each other and thereby gain in dignity. Her implication is that a law or policy is a common judgment, not an article of belief to which all must subscribe. The process of its enactment contains reasons of every sort on both sides. No one mind could accept or author all of them; nor could any side. A law or policy therefore cannot be seen as the victory of one preference over another, or as the victory of rule-makers over rule-followers. Collaboration creates something beyond personal preference, something impersonal or transpersonal. To succeed, collaboration requires division. It is almost as if there could be no law or policy unless doubt and dispute existed.

Arendt's aversion to will as a political category also shows itself in the refusal to understand law as command;[152] or to see a constitution as deriving its legitimacy from popular will rather than from political right;[153] or to see the strict *moral* necessity to have continuous popular consent to the content of all laws and policies[154] (provided those laws and policies do not violate the basic law, the constitution); [155] or to see in consent a phenomenon of the will rather than a general disposition to give support; or to define consent of the governed as anything but consent to be governed on certain terms; [156] or to find anything in the idea of sovereignty but a euphemism for tyranny.[157] This overall attitude is distilled in her discussion of kinds of social contracts in which she insists that the proper contract is between equals engaged in a common enterprise without any possession or claim of sovereignty over citizens and not the contract between a people and its rulers (a "vertical" contract).[158]

She thus wages war not only against Hobbes but also against the "Rousseauan-Kantian solution to the problem of obligation."[159] Autonomy and self-determination are either delusions or metaphors and are no standards for the organization of political life. Once again, Arendt gladly shows herself as shocking and foreign to our prepossessions.

In sum, there is only one mode of political action, only one form of freedom in the world—the direct participation of diverse equals in the conversation pertaining to the public business, which is the creation or preservation of a constitution. This is the only mode for ancients and moderns.

WHAT DAMAGES OR DENATURES POLITICAL ACTION?

The short answer is, all those emotions that damage or denature public speech—emotions that impede, circumvent, or distort it. (This answer is parallel to that given to the question concerning what modes of action are not political. We now look at this question not formally but experientially, by looking at some of the main emotions that provide part of the energy for essentially unpolitical modes of action.) When certain emotions find their way into a public realm that has contained a genuine political life, that life will be hurt or ended. Even where the public realm is not the place of political action (rightly understood), these emotions are not desirable for that realm, such as it is. They should rarely or never appear outside private life; even in private life they may sometimes be suspect.

Once again, Arendt's ability—positive desire—to shock our sensibilities is fully displayed. She finds that the following emotions (or feelings, passions, and sentiments) threaten the existence of the frame of action or a process of action once begun. They include love, goodness, conscience, compassion, pity, and ambition. Anyone could join in denouncing ambition, but the others are the energy of liberal or radical politics. As we have seen, liberal and radical politics is not politics by Arendt's understanding. This is not to say that she thought conservative politics any closer to the real thing; the contrary is the case.[160]

Ambition. Concerning ambition or the will to power, I would mention that, following John Adams, Arendt distinguishes it from emulation or the wish to gain the good opinion or admiration of others by excelling in action, even competitively. Ambition is the wish to come to power and acquire distinction from the mere occupancy of position, apart from what people think. The tyrant wants "to rise above the company of all men," while emulation makes men love the world and the company of others and drives them into public business. Arendt says that emulation and ambition are the "chief virtues and vices" of political man.[161] In order to discredit ambition and similar drives, she denies Nietzsche's assertion that the will to power impels all creatures and is the animating source of political life.[162]

Ostensibly Praiseworthy Emotions. To say that Arendt wants the ostensibly praiseworthy emotions and passions of love, goodness, conscience, compassion, and pity kept out of political life is not to say that she wants hatred, evil, ruthlessness, coldness, or cruelty kept in. There are specific political virtues, some of which are also conventional moral virtues, while some are morally ambiguous or indifferent. None is a vice, except in the light of either Socratic absolutism or Christian absolutism, from which, precisely, come the greatest threats to the ideal of political action. The best in private life is not the measure for what is best in political life.

At the risk of too much scheme, it can be said that love, goodness, conscience, compassion, and pity all hurt or abolish political action under all circumstances, and that in the midst of revolutionary circumstances compassion and pity have actually destroyed the chance to establish a lasting constitution for freedom. These interrelated emotions are to a peculiarly great degree separable from speech in their expression, and they may even despise speech or be driven to substitute direct, inarticulate action for it.

Love abolishes distance between people, the "in-between." But action not only connects people, it connects people in a way that also keeps them distinct, separate. This is not Nietzsche's pathos of distance that Arendt preaches: There is nothing hierarchical in the distance she insists on. Love is great; it is rare; it is too easily mistaken for romance; but whatever it is, it is antipolitical.[163] It leads to calamity when directly politicized, but its proper political transmutations are forgiveness and respect.

By *goodness*, Arendt means absolute goodness, Christ-like goodness. She presents two versions of it: one in the person of Jesus, the other in the person of Billy Budd. In an amazing meditation on Jesus she tries to read his life as the story of one who knew that goodness could never show itself in public without destroying both itself and the public realm.[164] One great cost in trying to have the best in private life be the measure for what is best in political life is that the private best is corrupted. Jesus taught that the one who did goodness must do it in secret, not talk about it even with himself, and must not know that he does it or must forget that he did it. His activity is "not even at home in the realm of privacy."[165] It is with profound insight into both private and public life that Jesus removed himself from political action. The climax of Arendt's presentation is an audacious gloss on Machiavelli's admonition that a prince must know "how not to be good." She says, "he did not say and did not mean that men must be taught how to be bad....[His] criterion for political action was glory ... and badness can no more shine in glory than goodness."[166] (She ignores Machiavelli's saying that the prince "should know how to do evil, if that is necessary.")[167] He meant that absolute goodness was antipolitical in its nature, and that it damaged and denatured itself if it felt itself driven to enter politics.

Arendt sees Herman Melville's *Billy Budd* as one of the deepest examinations of the inner meanings of the French Revolution[168] for the reason that it is about Jesus, or a Jesus figure. Billy is good in the sense that he is beyond virtue and vice. He is innocent, unworldly. Confronted with motiveless evil, innocence (already reticent) becomes speechless and in its—his—rage murders the evil one. She reads the story as a vindication of Captain Vere, the man who has the kind of virtue fit for the world. Unable to prevent the crime of absolute evil, he must, in his virtue, punish innocence, absolute goodness, when it acts.[169] Virtue, not goodness, can be embodied in lasting institutions: "Absolute goodness is hardly any less dangerous than absolute evil."[170]

Arendt's main discussion of *conscience* comes in the course of her defense of the practice of civil disobedience during the Vietnam War.[171] Until her essay on civil disobedience was published in 1970, she had preliminarily defined civil disobedience as the politics of conscience.[172] (I consider this change in her position in Chapter 3.) Thereafter, her interest is caught by what she calls "the greatest fallacy in the present debate," which is the assumption that the civil disobedients should understand themselves or be understood as "individuals, who pit themselves subjectively and conscientiously against the laws and customs of the community."[173] But the disobedient, she says, is not a conscientious actor, at least not after he joins others in public acts.

Conscience "is unpolitical;"[174] it shows an ultimate commitment to being able to live with oneself, to one's own spiritual welfare. To be political, one cannot love one's soul as much as one's country. At most, conscience has a place when resistance to atrocity is needed. It never escapes subjectivity, and when expressed publicly it turns into one opinion among many; it is debased.[175] It is essentially anarchic. It cannot be a principle of action, although it may be present at the start of action. What then is the right view? "It is my contention that civil disobedients are nothing but the latest form of voluntary associations, and that they are thus quite in tune with the oldest traditions of the country."[176] They revive the traditional American idea of free contractual fellowship for the sake of common action. Their principle is to get the government to abide by its constitution. The principle is political, and it inspires one of the few kinds of political action still possible for citizens in a mass representative democracy.

The treatment of *compassion* (feeling for the suffering of the person one can see) and *pity* (a general emotion of sorrow at the suffering of the many) is one of the most intricate and yet one of the most disturbing segments in Arendt's work.[177] In analyzing the inability of the French revolutionaries, and all later revolutionaries influenced by the French, to found a long-lasting constitution for freedom, to perpetuate the spirit of action that the turbulence of revolution had miraculously thrown up, she asserts that the revolutionaries, moved by particular compassion, and then by pity at the misery of the mass (who were suddenly released from darkness and found a voice in which to proclaim their need), tried to end suffering by political means. Such an effort must fail; and, in failing, it will also, by a process that is both inwardly determined by the progression of feelings and outwardly determined by the rush of action and reaction, lead inexorably to the end of the brief life of freedom, of the councils, or soviets, or Raete, all of which are the beginnings of a constitution for freedom.

Arendt's writing is about the Terror, and creates a terror of its own. The impact of mass suffering on sensitive and prepared souls, like those of Robespierre, Saint-Just, and Lenin, is overwhelming. Their sentiments become boundless. An initial commitment to worldliness, to maintaining the conversation of diverse equals, is brushed aside as trivial or, worse, as an obstacle to the solution of enormous problems. Power reverts to the center. Meeting opposition from other revolutionaries or from the counterrevolution, the center becomes despotic and rigid. "Pity, taken as the spring of virtue, has proved to possess a greater capacity for cruelty than cruelty itself."[178] And all this in a hopeless cause: Only administration and future technology can ever solve "the social question." Arendt does not put her point in quite this way, but I would hazard to do so: It is better to preserve freedom (for those few wanting to be free) by not trying to abolish misery than to lose freedom for all in trying and failing (when the conditions of life do not permit a technical remedy for misery). I am uncertain as to whether her sympathy might not lie with even those who would defend freedom against others whose misery led them to invade the public realm in order to destroy it.[179]

In case after case, Arendt has converted a moral virtue into a political vice and sometimes into the political source of a moral vice.[180] There is no cleverness or perversity at work in her revaluation; rather a single-minded adherence to the unique and supreme existential achievement of political action as revelatory speech.

The Moral Nature of Arendt's Theory

It is apparent that Arendt's conception of the political, both Greek and modern, is purged of a fair amount of what common opinion would situate in politics. She purges it of many practical functions and moral virtues. She also finds scant evidence of the genuinely political in the ostensibly political life of modern times. She is not friendly toward representative government. To say it yet again, she is not an ingratiating writer. At the same time, she is one of the most valuable students of political evil. One would expect that a thinker so intimately and philosophically aware of totalitarianism would let her horror pass into her feelings about politics in general,[181] or at least lead her to celebrate the decencies of liberal politics as the best possible or as the ideally best. Instead, the theorist of politics as the deliberate systemization of unspeakable evil (*The Origins of Totalitarianism*) or as the unthinking routinization of unspeakable evil (*Eichmann in Jerusalem*) reluctantly tolerates liberal politics *faute de mieux* while denying that it is the real thing. And she goes on to construct an image of true politics that often taunts us in its unavailability.

One's discomfort is intensified when it turns out that political evil bears a resemblance to ideal politics, that the worst is, at least in a number of respects, the perversion of the best, rather than being wholly unlike it. If Arendt manages to find the potentiality of immorality in morality, she also, if unwittingly, praises as the highest secular good a relation to the world that in its parodic form is the worst relation to the world.[182] Surely there must be something seriously mistaken in her approach if this is its upshot. Specifically, to purge true politics of love, goodness, conscience, compassion, and pity is to purge it of the largest part of moral inhibition. Some critics might therefore wish to conclude that it should not be surprising to find that Arendt's idealization runs the risk of making too close a connection to the abhorrent. If the actual cruelties, excesses, and depredations of Greek and Roman politics did not deter her in the first place from using this politics as the foundation of her philosophy, then what could we expect? Her distaste for bodily nature and for privacy, intimacy, and domesticity is also symptomatic. What should be surprising is that she bothered to study totalitarianism at all; or that, in studying it, she did not produce some elaborate way of coming to terms with it. Is she not an immoralist? Of course Arendt is not, but her ideal conception is morally troublesome.

None of the political virtues Arendt praises is a vice, except by some absolutist standard, and some of them are also conventional moral virtues. But that is not to say enough. She cannot guarantee that her ideal conception will be free of great immorality if realized; she does run the risk of some connection to the abhorrent. The reason is that she purges politics of too much: She is too pure in her moral and practical exclusions. She may also ignore things that should be included. Furthermore, doubts about the moral complexion of her theory remain even if totalitarianism and true political action do not bear some likeness to each other, or if they did and it rightly was said that the worst is invariably the perversion of the best.

THE RESEMBLANCE TO TOTALITARIANISM

Arendt's analysis of Nazism and Stalinism is, in its vastness and subtlety, unified by the thought that the totalitarian leadership was neither ruthless in its pragmatism nor driven by power lust. They were not despots or tyrants. They did not act out of crass motives; they did not see their action as a means to some delimited goals. To the contrary, they had no interests, no goals, no love of power for its own sake. They were profoundly antiutilitarian.[183] Also, the Nazis, although a conspiracy in power, had their own code of honor, and made mutual pledges, even if those of conspiracy.[184] All this establishes some little connection to ideal political action. In addition, the Nazis sought release from the bondage of nature, of reality; they sought to interrupt the automatism of all processes. They sought to have reality conform to their wish; they believed that everything is possible and acted to verify that belief. Which is to say that their activity, as conceptualized by Arendt, was an assertion of the unnatural or artificial against the natural or the everyday. But so in her view is political action when rightly done. I would add that her description of the ability of modern scientists to "act into nature" so as to work their will on it and change it as they please is a link between totalitarianism and political action. She explicitly likens the work of modern scientists to political action;[185] and she all but explicitly assimilates the totalitarian mentality and the scientific mentality.

Could it be said that if political action is speech the connection to totalitarianism vanishes? Hitler's speeches to the German masses had the kind of intoxicating rhetoric Arendt attributed to Robespierre's speeches before the French, and she does not look upon these speeches of Robespierre as his political action, but as a departure from it.[186] Hitler's activity was continuously violent or coercive and thus by definition not political. Is that not enough for us to be able to say that there is no connection between totalitarianism and ideal political action? Perhaps. Yet what about the relations among the top Nazis? Between the Roehm purges and the last years did they use violence against each other? Did they not use speech and make an audience for each other—if not public, then not private or social either? Did they not try to shine before each other and excel each other and live beyond their everyday selves, live as performers, or wearers of masks, or as men inspired by a principle like glory? They were a gang; but so may a body of citizens be a gang in relation to the outside. It may be that a general point is shown here in its most vivid light; namely, that although action is not undertaken because of its consequences, it still has consequences; and almost always those consequences are bad or mixed for those outside the company of actors. A theory of action must give that fact weight.

How much should be made of these formal similarities? It may be that unless Arendt's theory of political action contains within it other resources to break the connection with totalitarianism, action's hideous ape, then that theory may be more shocking and more foreign than is tolerable. It may be that this is the severest test that could be made of Arendt's theory of political action. On the other hand, perhaps I have made too much of too little, or of nothing. I do not know what to think. Let the matter be suspended.

DISALLOWING MORAL JUDGMENT

If we suspended the matter, there would still be cause for concern. The worry must be made explicit. Insofar as Arendt confines her thought to the action of the polis, she severs the whole point of political action—its revelatory existential achievement, its creation of human identity—from moral motivation or intention. Performing, wearing a mask, and acting from a principle are not *conceptually* tied to wanting to do the morally right thing, although of course each could be contingently tied. Only when political action is understood in relation to the creation or preservation of a modern constitution is the conceptual tie made, and only then does a political motivation coincide with some sort of moral one.

Obviously not every sphere of life must show the presence of moral motivation. Consider a social institution like a college. Ordinarily we do not expect a college to have any purpose but the pursuit of right understanding. We are not likely to think that this pursuit is essentially animated by a moral motive or that its results are typically amenable to moral judgment. Right understanding is valuable for its own sake, valuable existentially but not necessarily morally. All we ask is that the pursuit take place within moral limits—that deceit or torture, for example, not be used for the sake of an increase of knowledge. We also may ask that a college in its institutional dealings with itself or the world not do injustice, that it not, for example, discriminate against women or minorities in its hiring practices. Yet the college does not exist to do justice. Analogously, Arendt in her Greek thinking suggests that political action does not exist to do justice or fulfill other moral purposes. The supreme achievement of political action is existential, and the stakes are seemingly higher than moral ones. This is the gist of Arendt's radicalism. But we must persist with at least one question: Does Arendt's Greek theory at least provide moral *limitations* on political action, even though it rejects moral *motivation*? Because her Greek conception is her first and most famous contribution—and one that she never abandoned or even examined again in the light of her modern conception—its moral meaning should be explored. Arendt fought any tendency to moralize her modern conception even minimally. Thus what I say about morality and the Greek conception sometimes applies to the modern conception as well.

On a few occasions Arendt clearly disallows moral judgments to be made on true political action. They are unguarded moments, shall we say; but perhaps they should at least be noticed because they expose the temptations to which lovers of politics are liable. For example, she says that the "Greek agonal spirit" knows no morality, only the wish to excel.[187] With this remark she certainly distances herself from the Aristotelian notion of action. Although the agonistic aspect of action is sublimated in Aristotle, his is surely a Greek perspective on action. When he says that action is valuable for its own sake and is not merely a means, the force of his judgment is that action matters because of the moral and morally intellectual virtues it ideally requires the display of. He sometimes suggests either that the ends of action may not matter or that the ends matter only if they result from the exercise of the relevant virtues. (At other times the value of action as means is affirmed.) But since action matters because it needs and uses virtues that are themselves indissolubly connected to morality, genuine action itself must necessarily be indissolubly connected to morality. It is no sin to revise Aristotle, but Arendt's flat assertion makes her sound more Homeric or Nietzschean than she centrally means to be.

In another example, Arendt talks about particular acts in a way that seems to strengthen one's alarmed sense that her general theory of action can too easily accommodate great substantive evils, even the system of evil known as totalitarianism. She says, "Every good action for the sake of a bad end actually adds to the world a portion of goodness; every bad action for the sake of a good end actually adds to the world a portion of badness."[188]

She adds that in action, but not in production, "the means are always the decisive factor." Notice that her use of the word *means* to explain the paradox is not in accord with her usual rejection of the categories of means and ends. What she is saying is that where a response to a situation displays a political virtue (say, courage) the response is humanly admirable, no matter how morally bad the purpose, whereas a response that demonstrates a political vice (say, faithlessness to one's word) depresses life, no matter how morally good the purpose. Indeed, the political virtue excuses the bad purpose; the vice condemns the good purpose.

Arendt is thus setting down a neat reversal when she should instead be allowing for an asymmetry. We can say that faithlessness is always blameworthy, but that courage in a good cause is different from and better than courage in a bad one, because in the former case its beauty and hence its memorability are enhanced by its association with something good other than itself; for example, a sense of morality. But take her solely on her own terms: Is courage in a bad cause better for the world than faithlessness in a good one? I do not know how to answer without sounding like a utilitarian. However, I would like to avoid the inappropriate estheticism (of politics as gesture) to which Arendt's passage tends,[189] for in this context she is not adopting the position that it is better to fail by good actions to achieve a good purpose than succeed by bad actions. This is the excellent moral position of proceduralism, which is not foreign to her but unfortunately is not evident here.

On another occasion, Arendt distinguishes political action from human behavior, and says that only human behavior, the locus of motives and consequences, is to be judged by moral standards. Action, contrarily, is judged only by its greatness because its nature is "to break through the commonly accepted and reach into the extraordinary, where whatever is true in common and everyday life no longer applies because everything that exists is unique and *sui generis*."[190] She thus uses a quasi-Kantian distinction with an anti-Kantian intent. The morality ruled out is not absolutism in its Socratic and Christian forms, but ordinary morality. She seems to be not only against Socrates but also against Polemarchus; she seems to side with Alcibiades. Greatness is its own morality. It is as if the wrongs about to be done are known to be wrongs but excluded altogether from the deliberations preceding a decision, and as if the judgments made afterward took no account of the wrongs actually done. Political speech is made submissive to violent activity. Arendt is playing with fire.

Now there are familiar phenomena about which it is morally acceptable to believe that it would be inappropriate to expect general moral limits on activity. These phenomena include games and contests of many sorts; the agonistic spirit is intrinsic to them. But they are games: They are restricted and self-enclosed activities and do not reach to the integrity of the person. They have no moral point. Politics may. This is one more difference between games and political action that we must add to those mentioned earlier. To be sure, we expect players not to cheat. But not cheating means only playing by or within the rules of the game, rules internal to the game. Immoral political action seems more than a broken rule in a game, no matter how hard we try to use a player's cheating as pointing beyond the game to some truth about his character or about the moral life in general. How then could it be morally acceptable to treat political action exactly as if it were only a competitive game? (We shall see below that Arendt tries to devise an "internal" morality for politics.)

There are also two related sorts of phenomena, not games, where some schools of moral judgment permit systems of impure or immoral conduct for the sake of a morally desirable *result*. There is no doubt that in both cases judgment, driven by a moral motive, facilitates its acceptance of facts it does not like by hinting that if the results are good the selfish conduct is gamelike. Not only is the moral motive absent in both cases, but there is no voluntary acceptance of moral limits or inhibitions.

The first case works by a benign invisible hand. A morally desirable result automatically ensues from the self-interested but not mutually injurious activity of the participants. "Private vices, public benefits." The second is the stability that is reached when all the participants aspire to injure each other, but each has only enough power to preserve himself but not injure another. The outward semblance of morality is achieved without anyone being moral, and this situation is held to be morally acceptable. This is a caricature of the Madisonian vision of the tenth *Federalist* paper.

Arendt's positions in the several comments I have referred to ignore moral limitations altogether while foregoing any concern with morally desirable results. Common judgment concerning market behavior and the balance of factions at least invokes results. If amorality is one kind of immorality, then in a few moments of recklessness Arendt celebrates immorality. What could transmute immoral greatness into moral acceptability? How can a great speech in favor of a wicked policy be exempted from moral judgment? How can morally unlimited action be anything but gravely immoral? We are now directly faced with the Greek and Roman experience from which Arendt began her theory, not with the pervertedly political world in which the Nazi leaders lived. Let us not, however, make anything more of these reckless moments. In fact, Arendt has a way of dealing with the terrible consequences of greatness. She relies on the human capacity for forgiveness.

ARENDT'S VIEW OF POLITICAL MORALITY

We have so far been dealing with the margins of Arendt's thought on morality. Throughout her work she is aware of the moral dangers of her theory, and she works to reduce them. In her reflections on *The Pentagon Papers* (where she attributes a kind of totalitarian mentality to the war strategists and problem-solvers without calling it by that name), she says that "the deliberate denial of factual truth—the ability to lie—and the capacity to change facts—the ability to act—are interconnected; they owe their existence to the same source: imagination."[191] Action and lying both want to change the world.[192] At another point, she says that every genuine political action is a beginning and as such carries with itself "a measure of complete arbitrariness"; that is, a break in time and causation.[193] It approaches the miracle: It seems to come out of nowhere, and not to be reducible to explanation. Yet when beginning is seen as founding a new polity, making a break in a continuity of human life, the arbitrariness may show its ugly possibility by treating human beings like "material" that awaits its proper forming, if the founders mistakenly confuse acting with doing as making.[194] She also declares that there is an "inner affinity between the arbitrariness inherent in all beginnings, and human potentialities for crime."[195] She is conscious on these occasions of the closeness of her ideal to the bad, if not of the closeness of her ideal to the worst. But consider some of the arguments she makes in order to reduce the moral dangers of her theory, dangers that are especially serious when her theory's center is the polis.

For Arendt, the morality of political action is *a selective version of ordinary morality*. Despite the passing remarks quoted, it would be wrong to believe that Arendt thinks that ideal political action is altogether exempt from moral judgment, or that it has a morality that is neither absolute nor ordinary, but its own peculiar and self-sufficient morality—as if *morality* were a word so vague or elastic as to cover all complete codes of conduct whatever their content.

One may say that no difference exists between political morality and ordinary morality in everyday life; that the only difference is between ordinary morality and absolute morality. There is one possible way to sustain this argument. The standard of ordinary morality is that no self-sacrifice is required; no conduct is ruled out, provided that it is necessary for the preservation of life, rights, and gravely important interests. By that standard, we can live our everyday lives without too much moral strain. (Ideally, the motive in treating others right is regard for them and what is due them, rather than enlightened self-interest or fear of punishment.) A settled society keeps us far from desperation and its necessity. At the same time, ordinary morality does not tell us to spend our lives positively promoting the well-being of others. However, political action is often taken in crisis or danger or under necessity. Office-holders have to do what ordinary morality allows, but allows reluctantly. Everyday life is not the realm of the lesser evil; theoretically, political life is. (Of course, in actuality, political life is often the realm of surplus evil that is rationalized as necessary.) Both are covered by the same morality, but everyday life is luckier in its circumstances.

Arendt would not accept this complete absorption of political morality into the ordinary morality of everyday life. To Arendt, political morality is a *selective* version of ordinary morality, meaning that it assumes the heightened presence of certain desirable qualities of character in the actor and expects that those qualities will preclude moral atrocity, even though their display is not morally motivated. There will after all be limits.[196] The qualities are sometimes morally praiseworthy and sometimes not easily assigned their moral designation. Further, Arendt would always resist diminishing political action (or even government) by thinking of either as merely a necessary evil.[197] Political action is valuable in itself: It is that which withstands the wisdom of Silenus. Thus, Arendt tries hard to demonstrate that political morality can be strictly deduced from the very nature of political action.

Arendt is suggesting that the most important quality of character needed by the ideal political actor is the will to act. This presupposes courage: the guarantor of the will to act and of other qualities as well;[198] "the political virtue *par excellence*, the one virtue without which political freedom is wholly impossible."[199] It takes courage, she says, merely to leave the sheltering darkness of privacy;[200] it also takes courage to forget or minimize the value of life and its interests.[201] The will to act is the will to see and be seen, speak and listen, decide and be bound by decision, take chances and court failure, shine and be outshone. (The will to act is far removed from the selective version of ordinary morality produced by the public practice of due process, with its emphasis on forbearance, scruples, and remorse.) The will to act, for these reasons, implies a respect for those one considers one's equals. It does not, of course, command universal respect because it does not consider men as men, only as citizens.[202] The passional richness comes from fellow-feeling, solidarity, loyalty. The will to act can exist in a person only when he acknowledges a reality outside himself, some reality besides his body's needs and his heart's waywardness; when he acknowledges the reality of others, especially in their worldly being as fellow citizens. His truest need is others.[203]

From the will to act politically follow a number of dispositions that are also praised in everyday life. Some others would not be praised, but they would not be condemned. For Arendt, two dispositions that flow from the will to act are more important than any others.[204] The first is the readiness to keep one's word or promise and to honor the commitments that one has freely made to others so that all may act in concert. This disposition keeps one in action; it lets others know that one's presence can be counted on. Arendt says that its power is so great that it transforms sinners into a community that "need not reflect this 'sinful' side of human nature."[205] The second is forgiveness, the basis for which is "they know not what they do."[206] Forgiving is like undoing; promise-keeping is like controlling what we will do. She goes so far as to say these are the only moral precepts "that are not applied to action from the outside....They arise....directly out of the will to live together with others in the mode of acting and speaking, and thus they are like control mechanisms built into the very faculty to start new and unending processes."[207] They comprise the "internal" morality of political action.

The easy response to Arendt's enormous claims for *promise-keeping* is that there is honor among thieves. Not many groups can hold together no matter what, but some of the worst, in their eros or fanaticism, may. Such groups make commitments that should never be made, or, if made, kept. These commitments are void from the outset. In ignoring the content and context of commitments, she takes us too close to the mystique of oath.

On *forgiveness*, the easy response is that no one is entitled to forgive me for the wrong I have done except the person to whom I have done wrong. A group may be united in a readiness to forgive each other, but still no general spirit can take the place of strict accuracy in moral accounts. Beyond that, the person I may have injured could very well not be in the group. Without his presence, his voice, who can say for him that I am forgiven? To use Arendt's own formulation: An opinion cannot be represented. The consequences of action, the deeds that have followed from speech, reach to those outside the circle of speakers.

The easy responses cannot be overcome. Promise-keeping cannot form a barrier to atrocity. Eichmann kept faith with his leader. Who can forgive what he and his superiors did? Arendt herself cannot, and she says so powerfully at the end of *Eichmann in Jerusalem*.[208] Even in the midst of her discussion of forgiveness in *The Human Condition*, she speaks of the unforgivable: radical evil that can be neither forgiven nor punished.[209] If Eichmann was not a political actor, by her conception, he was at least the agent of those who were, or those who resembled actors, although pervertedly. Furthermore, the other dispositions that flow from the will to act, together with the fundamental virtue of courage, are not closed to bad men or even evil men. It is difficult to find any "internal" consideration adduced by Arendt that can assure us that action as speech will not in some circumstances—and *perhaps* in *most*—transgress moral limits. Additional moral traits from private life, indeed from the best in private life, must be mixed with the political virtues for the sake of drawing some of the poison out of action. (Arendt herself must reintroduce "animal pity" as an indispensable trait for persons in all circumstances, despite her fear of it in politics.)[210]

Most important, an acceptance of limits is not enough. Moral motivation must be reintroduced, and eventually she does reintroduce it. That action may often be revelatory and therefore existentially supreme for those who engage in it, and that it may be beautiful for the outsider to witness, read about, or contemplate, is not sufficient. The phenomenon of totalitarianism, which she did so much to conceptualize, must haunt us as we attend to her thought on the ideal. It is not really possible to overlook the conceptual resemblance.

One further element in Arendt's philosophy bears on the relation between political action (in her Greek sense) and morality. That is her view of *thinking* and its political implications. Fittingly, her initial discussion of thinking was provoked by the public response to her book on Eichmann, who was not able to think (in Arendt's special sense) and was therefore able to administer a policy of atrocity.[211] The ability to think has something to do with telling right from wrong.[212]

Arendt's discussion is oblique,[213] and it is somewhat guarded, because thinking is essentially private and removes the person from life in the world, at least inwardly. To praise thinking too highly would jeopardize her entire enterprise of restoring the luster of freedom and worldiness, and she knows it. Yet she goes on to explore the relevance of thinking for political action. Her reflections are part of the larger effort she makes to determine whether political action, from its own nature, generates enough morality of limitations to keep it free of serious wrongdoing and atrocity. It is as if just by reflecting further on totalitarianism she was forced to reflect further on the moral implications of political action in general.

What is thinking? It is a "relentless and repetitive"[214] activity that in its purest form is a quest for meaning, and it gets its energy from an erotic need to have meaning.[215] The activity never achieves its aim; it is *aporetic*. It regularly interrupts doing.[216] "There are no dangerous thoughts; thinking itself is dangerous....Thinking is equally dangerous to all creeds and, by itself, does not bring forth any new creed."[217] Its exemplar is Socrates. He is that kind of person in whom "the thinking activity....regardless of whatever qualities a man's nature, his soul, may possess—conditions him in such a way that he is incapable of evil."[218] The stuff of Socratic thinking is the conduct of life. The primary mode of thinking is the internal dialogue carried on in solitude between me and myself. To be conscious of oneself is to divide oneself, to become inevitably two-in-one.[219] Arendt says that from the very activity of thinking Socrates made two propositions follow. The first is, "It is better to be wronged than to do wrong." The second is (in paraphrase) that it is better that multitudes should disagree with me than that I, being one, should be out of harmony with myself and contradict myself.[220] Actually, the second is the source of the first. Arendt says that Socrates teaches that it is much easier to live with oneself if one does not have to endure the self-reproach, the self reproaching itself in internal dialogue, when one has done wrong.[221] Consciousness thus breeds conscience, "secular conscience,"[222] the capacity to have afterthoughts when one is alone. To avoid wrongdoing (the force of conscience is prohibitive and speaks only in negatives; it does not initiate or inspire action)[223] is a way of avoiding torment. To avoid torment one must govern one's life by the precept that "it is better to be wronged than to do wrong." This is the basis for Socratic moral absolutism.

Arendt insists that only a few could ever have Socrates' dedication to thinking. In any case, if everybody could imitate Socrates, there would be no political action, no commitment to the world, no will to act. A political actor is "never alone and always much too busy to be able to think."[224] Socrates is one kind of absolutely good man. The morality of the citizen cannot be that of any kind of absolutely good man, any more than the activity of a citizen can be that of the philosopher.[225] The world of action needs the (Socratic) good man only in emergencies, in bad times.[226] He will then do some teacherly deed, the one way a philosopher can act without distorting philosophy and without "violating the rules of the political realm."[227] But his acts are either refusals, like deciding not to escape from prison when he has a chance to; or not joining everybody else in some mindless rush to criminality;[228] or merely telling the truth when "everybody lies about everything of importance."[229]

We have already seen that in "Civil Disobedience" Arendt does not think conscience is a political virtue. But at least in three essays—"Personal Responsibility Under Dictatorship," "Truth and Politics" (published before "Civil Disobedience"), and "Thinking and Moral Considerations" (published after)—she is willing to see the political value of an antipolitical activity like thinking, the source of prohibitive conscience, and the political relevance of the antipolitical person, the thinker, whether he be the philosopher, or the historian possessed of impartiality as between his people and their enemy or as between winners and losers.[230] Perhaps she was revising her own theory in order to avoid unacceptable implications of an immoral sort. She admits the value of prohibitive conscience, although not that of activist conscience. Still, the Socratic man is outside politics; he is a rarity; his appearance cannot be counted on; he may fail. Only a few Germans refused to collaborate with the Nazis, even at the risk of death, "not because the world would then be changed for the better, but because only on this condition could they go on living with themselves."[231] Their habit of thinking not only empowered them to see honestly what was going on but also to feel that they would rather be dead than unable to live peacefully with themselves. But this habit is all too rare.

Is there something that can be counted on more regularly and that is part of the political world? Her answer is not completely clear. She speaks of "thinking in its non-cognitive, non-specialized sense as a natural need of human life."[232] In this sense, thinking "is not a prerogative of the few but an everpresent faculty of everybody."[233] She does not develop this notion. She also does not explicitly distinguish between self-sacrificing absolute morality rooted in a continuous absorption in thinking and ordinary morality sustained by thinking as "an everpresent faculty of everybody." Within a generally decent political system that respects opposition but aberrantly commits atrocities or even undertakes an atrocious policy, all that is needed to resist atrocity is an ordinary sense of moral limits, continuously active. The trouble is that she does not make even everyman's thinking anything more than "a marginal affair in political matters."[234]

Arendt seems to provide a way out of these perplexities by identifying a kind of thinking that, if not peculiarly political, is perfectly at home in the world of political action as speech. She calls it judging and adapts Kant's notion of it as presented in *The Critique of Judgment*. It takes on a special urgency in the present context as, for Arendt, it took on a special urgency in the paper she wrote during the controversy raised by her book on Eichmann. She says that the thinker, rare in himself, may trigger in others the politically usable version of thinking, namely, the faculty of judging. Encouraged by the thinker, a disposition to question one's ideas and examine one's life may loosen deference to any given body of rules and thus enable one to judge a particular case on its own terms. Judging is not the ability to remain in harmony with oneself, but the related ability "to think in the place of everybody else," and even when alone to think "in anticipated communication with others with whom I know I must finally come to some agreement."[235]

One must be able to make present to mind the standpoints of the absent or to show respect for the divergent perspectives of others present. This activity is not empathy, the arrogant annexation of the personalities of others, but imagination, the effort to understand how others look at the world.[236] It can manifest itself only in the presence of others.[237] The great political virtue of judging is, finally, that one can "judge *particulars* without subsuming them under those general rules which can be taught and learned until they grow into habits."[238] Judging, like action, is a mode by which automatism is broken. It is "the most political of man's mental abilities."[239] Where it exists, atrocity and serious wrongdoing (and here I am making an inference) will be resisted, if not prevented. (She does not cite the decision of the Athenians to reverse themselves and decide not to massacre the Mitylenians, but she could have.) Eichmann wholly lacked the ability to judge, because he was unable, to begin with, to engage in even the rudiments of thinking.

My fear is that judging is too frail a support for the hope of keeping an only slightly altered Greek conception of political action while reducing the dangers of its countenancing immorality. Judging may extend only to the company of actors. The others may remain unimagined, unrepresented, in the inner dialogue of the individual and in the process of public speech in which judging makes its appearance in the world. All that the faculty of judging can guarantee is that those one recognizes as one's equals will be taken into account. The demand that all be recognized as one's equals, that one not equate humanity with one's group, does not necessarily follow from the activity of judging. Unless citizens think—that is, engage in the very activity that is the source of judging, engage in some amount of abstract, universal thought—they are certain to do great wrong. Yet Arendt characteristically purges political action of thinking and shoves thinking to the sidelines. Therefore, even when all the other political virtues are added to judging, the result is not morally acceptable because of all that is left out and that is needed to avoid gross immorality. Arendt's selective version of ordinary morality is *too* selective.

But Arendt is not teaching immorality. If she could have been persuaded that the likely tendency of her Greek conception is the commission of great evil (not totalitarianism, but the evils of Athens and Rome), she would have altered that conception. Her books on totalitarianism give warrant for that. They presuppose a passionate and unshakeable loyalty to the elements of basic morality at whatever cost to the glory of action and the grandeur of culture. The trouble is that this loyalty when transferred to her analysis of political action would have to take the form of improvised moral judgments that would not come from the conception itself. Our quarrel is not with the Greeks, but with Arendt for accepting them too completely, out of season.

A substantial revision would have to be made of Arendt's Greek conception if it is not to be charged with immoralism. Another reason to revise is that we may wish to retain it as a source of guidance for political imagination and, maybe, for action that we want partly or loosely or artfully to resemble the action of the polis. The revision might have the effect of reducing the existential achievement of political action. The definition of action as speech would remain. Speech, however, should not be so strictly tied to the circle of peers. It would be stressed that if action is speech, speech is action. All the moral virtues Arendt excludes must be reintroduced, but with some account of the situations in which they would likely have a proper place and of the modifications they would have to endure. The most important moral virtue reintroduced would be caring about consequences. Explicitly rejected must be Arendt's claim that the innermost meaning of action is untouched by consequence.[240] Ideally, one must be able to act for the sake of action and yet respect moral limits. Citizens must think, even if without Socratic relentlessness. More of the inner life, to its own cost, would have to attain public expression for the sake of curbing the excesses of decisions made. The public realm, too pure, is corrupt. The lines between activities as well as between states of being cannot be drawn as sharply as she would like them. The aim, in sum, would be to revise Arendt's Greek conception to create a view of the citizen as public actor whose will to act is accompanied by a moral sense that is not absolutist, yet although ordinary, may be more tested and complex than the ordinary morality of daily life, precisely because it is public. The emphasis remains negative: to respect moral limits, even while acting for the sake of action.

Above all, however, we must insist on remembering that so long as action is understood in Arendt's Greek sense, it is necessarily cojoined to coercion and violence, even though to act is not the same as to administer or execute. The completion of action is often violent activity: Decision aims at enforcement.

Such public action is experientially indissoluble from doing harm. Even if Arendt's conception found room for some other content—say, public policy in a broad sense—the moral concern remains. Assume the consequences of decision and enforcement were confined to the deciders: the possibility of harm would not vanish. The harm (comprised of penalties, sacrifices, overridden claims and interests) would vary greatly in scope, frequency, and intensity, but its potentiality would always be there. The conversion of people into mere means or noxious things adheres to the deliberation of citizens. Practically every step costs. That does not mean that it must be unallowably wrong to engage full-time in political action or to be part of government. It does mean that the lesser evil must be, in fact, the dominant ethic of any public realm. It also means that a full-time engagement in politics is inseparable from grave moral dangers. That action is also revelatory is one great existential advantage that may be plucked from necessity. But this advantage cannot blind us to its inevitable cost.

Before turning to the way in which Arendt's modern conception of political action allays the moral dangers present in her Greek conception, I would like to make a drastic suggestion about the Greek conception. I propose that if the place of action were not located in the world (except now and then), but rather in any place else, the moral dangers would recede or become manageable. The point is to break the connection between freedom and worldliness—at least if the world means by definition the public political realm. This break would also be a break with implication in government as coercion or violence, as necessary harm. Is it possible more or less within the confines of Arendt's Greek conception to relocate political action? (Arendt's modern conception of political action is at least equally eligible for such relocation.) She probably would have instantly recoiled from the notion. Yet, is there enough support in her writings for this notion so that it could plausibly be said that her theory was not being saved by being betrayed?

One must try to show that despite its content much activity when looked at as relations between persons is political in nature and often is enjoyed for that reason. As Huizinga has shown in *Homo Ludens*, there is an agonistic aspect to countless activities. Although Arendt scorns play, she prizes agonistic exertion: There is no use in making anything of the verbal difference. Just to consider American society, a number of kinds of nonpublic citizenship already exist. There is what one may call the *lesser* citizenship that comes from direct participation in the internal life of voluntary associations. (We have also seen the intermittent effort to convert hierarchical organizations into political ones, whether they be factories, armies, or prisons, and thus to spread lesser citizenship.) There is the continuing effort to give domestic and even intimate relations a modified citizenly quality (even if the emphasis is not agonistic) and so produce a *private citizenship*. There is the *pervasive citizenship* intrinsic to the life of business association and competition, in all that "job-holding" Arendt mocks.

American society now has or is trying to develop these kinds of citizenship. All involve action as speech. All are pervaded by the reality of equality or by the wish to achieve it. All may be inspired by the wish to perform or to sustain a persona or to act from a principle. All permit some of the revelation Arendt expects of political action. All provide the chance to start something new, and they show more than "traces and signs" of freedom. All are serious. All lend themselves to being made into stories. Thus in American society there is a great deal of participation and the thirst for more. Its social life is political. Indeed, Arendt's Greek conception of action helps us to look again at our daily life. By becoming more aware of its political actuality, we may have reason to think better of it. Her thought may even encourage us further to reimagine our daily life and work to make it more political, and therefore more satisfying and more dignified.

Is there anything in Arendt's writings that could excuse us for relocating political action? Only a little. She remarks that something like political action existed in monasteries,[241] but that the prohibition against trying to excel hurt it. Arendt says about the Royal Society that it was an organization, and that an organization is always a political institution: Where men organize, they intend to act and acquire power.[242] She says without elaboration that action is possible in "small, well-defined sectors in the mass societies of the large powers."[243] She praises the courage of students even when their action was confined to campus politics and as such consisted in "small and relatively harmless enterprises."[244] All these observations are incidental.

After all the similarities between the various kinds of nonpublic citizenship and Arendt's Greek conception of political action are pointed out, too much has still been left out. Specifically, greatness has been left out: risking all for the sake of the city or country, putting one's life behind one's speech, saying the words that change or save the world, saying the words that help to shape the common fate. It is participating directly in decisions of the highest importance, of the greatest indefiniteness, that matters; not because one's autonomy is injured without such participation, but because one does not achieve full humanity except as an equal partner in the group whose decisions shape the common life. If one participates directly, it makes little difference whether one is in the majority or minority. The greatest opportunity is to know others and be known by them; and the best knowledge comes under the greatest pressure when the stakes are the highest. Ten people around a table are a political group, provided their talk is about public business and they are part of a public network of councils.[245] Although the kinds of non-public citizenship occasionally approach the seriousness Arendt finds only in sustained participation in the public realm—and have much else besides of a political nature to which she gives no attention—they do not lead to the existential achievement she seeks from political action. The world is what is most important. The place of citizenship cannot be transferred from the public realm, if we are to stay true to Arendt's ideal Greek conception. I propose that we not stay true; that instead we betray this conception in order to "save" our experience.

If we want to follow Arendt in confining political action to the public realm, her ideal Greek conception must be revised to avoid moral opprobrium: the consequences of action must become central. Yet, if so revised, what would happen to the wisdom of Silenus? It would seem that morality dims glory and glory wounds morality. There is no morally acceptable way by which the life of action, understood by reference to the Greeks, can rebut the wisdom of Silenus. Who now would accept the rebuttal on any other terms? The irony is that she invokes Theseus' rebuttal at the close of a book not on the Greek, but on the modern experience of politics.

At most, one could strain to find kinds of political action that are comparatively free of moral danger. None is, however, a full-time engagement. One thinks of the *local citizenship* present in towns and villages; the *caucus citizenship* of organized political parties; involvement in *jury service*; and involvement in some *referendums*. The *episodic citizenship* of those who enter the public realm only in response to intolerable situations and who struggle without violence to diminish or end these situations is morally problematic when lawbreaking is part of it. But it is otherwise free of moral danger. All these modes not only are or tend to be remote from association with coercion and violence, but they also are insulated from the harsh need to calculate consequences. Despite their genuinely political nature, however, they are not best thought about from the Greek perspective. If the rebuttal to Silenus requires the heroic and the agonistic, these morally safe activities would not suffice. However, one of them, episodic citizenship, is an integral part of another conception of political action found in Arendt's work—the modern conception. Let us also notice that one's voting in elections, so seemingly perfunctory, unheroic, and insignificant, is hardly safe morally, situated as it is in the entire field of public policy, of its deliberation and enforcement.

If we move away from the heroic and the agonistic, do we abandon Silenus altogether? At a number of points in her writings, Arendt speaks of trying "to reconcile ourselves to reality....to be at home in the world."[246] She assigns this task in one place to the activity of understanding (defined as she elsewhere defines thinking),[247] and in another to the poets and storytellers.[248] (This reconciliation is the furthest development of the power of writers to save political action from futility by making it memorable.) In speaking of this kind of reconciliation, Arendt seems to make the beginnings of an acknowledgment that not political action but only the activities of the mind, could possibly withstand the wisdom of Silenus. Even more significant, the only transference of action outside the public realm she emphatically makes is to locate the most intense and extensive activity in thinking, the dialogue of me with myself. She does this in the last words of *The Human Condition*[249] and ends a book in which she has done everything possible to avoid such words by surrendering to them. It is as if only a philosopher and poet as generous as herself could have been self-denying enough to imagine that political action could achieve what people had usually said only philosophy and poetry could achieve—to justify life. But political action, as she theorizes it with the help of the Greeks, cannot—at least not at a morally acceptable cost. Now and then Arendt says so. Only philosophy and poetry, the best fruits of thinking, can help us to withstand rightly the wisdom of Silenus. Or if they cannot, nothing can. And if they can, their content can never be confined to political action. The stuff of redemptive writing is as unconfinable as life itself.

The Moral Nature of Arendt's Modern Conception of Political Action

The conception of political action that Arendt is primarily known for contains intractable difficulties. Nevertheless, it is powerful enough to move us to look again at both our public life and our private and social life. She helps us see new richness; she helps us find further cause for dissatisfaction. Perhaps what I have been calling her Greek conception, her heroic and agonistic conception, is a great contribution, provocative, instructive, and fertile, whatever the variety of response it may elicit and whatever the uses that may be found for it. Therefore, in turning to her modern conception, I do not mean to imply that we can find in it an idea that alone would spare all the rest of Arendt's political theory from condemnation, that alone should make the difference between acceptance and rejection. It is not a *deus ex machina*.

Arendt never suggests even in the slightest way that another conception could supersede the Greek conception (or perhaps even equal it in beauty and nobility). Even when pressed by critics at a roundtable to defend her apparently contentless notion of political action she talks mostly about juries and town meetings.[250] Yet the fact is that the modern conception of political action as public speech and speechlike action for the sake of creating a constitution or defending it especially against internal erosion resolves at least some of the main perplexities that we have been examining, and still keeps political action fully in the public realm. Arendt does finally succeed in suggesting another conception of political action that solves its own moral problems and that exists not only as normal politics but also as grand. Just as the modern conception may help to make the question of the content of political action less obscure, so it may quiet moral qualms.

As we have seen, Arendt expounds her modern conception by reference to the incipient constitution present in council democracy in revolutionary periods; debate and discussion that issue in a new form of government (a democratic constitution with a bill of individual rights); and protest against the attempted circumvention of the American Constitution by executive agencies. These three examples of action share the trait of inherent or internal moral limits that go beyond the limits set by promise-keeping, forgiveness, rudimentary thinking, and judging. They all show political action enclosed within the limits of the principles of justice. In all cases a constitution or form of government that is putatively just frames the action. Even more, all three kinds of action can be seen as inspired by the moral motive, by a will to achieve or preserve justice, not merely to honor moral limits on action.

That citizens act for the sake of justice may initially preclude acting for the sake of acting, for the sake of reaping the existential and experiential rewards of action. They achieve an identity, and they experience the exhilaration of public action while and because they seek somthing else—justice. In fact, are they not more likely to reap the rewards if they do not seek them? The rewards, in turn sustain the effort. After a while the moral cause and the extraordinary advantages become inseparably one. If citizens enjoy the struggle in behalf of a moral cause—if they are inclined to do their political duty—they do not sully their involvement. Arendt insists, after all, on the possibility of public *happiness.*[251] Quite casually, she acknowledges that justice[252] or "moral motives"[253] may inspire political action. The acknowledgment is too casual for the very conception of political action that she develops from *On Revolution* to the end of her life. Revolutionary citizens; participants in constitutional deliberation at every level and on all sides of every dispute; and protesters defending a democratic constitution act with a moral intent and, at the same time, manage to act within moral limits. They seek justice justly. Only when revolutionaries or protesters turn violent do they forsake moral limits. They forsake moral limits because their moral intent itself forsakes limits—in ways that Arendt so powerfully renders.

What, after all, is a democratic council but a new form in which ordinary people claim their entitlements and proceed to work out the implications of this new form and defend it against attack (and against their own disinclination to face the rigors and ardors of participation)? What was the deliberation concerning state constitutions and the federal Constitution in America except deliberation concerning the nature of justice? What is the burden carried by protesters but the burden of defending while enlarging the meanings of a constitution of justice? Arendt's modern conception of political action still excludes the handling of economic issues and reformist or radically reconstructionist socioeconomic endeavors. Her sense is that the only kind of justice implicated in political action pertains to political rights and civil liberties. That may be too narrow, but at least her modern conception is free of amoral formalism. To be sure, Arendt's theory may leave office-holding in a philosophical limbo. Those who engage full-time in politics in a modern representative democracy have their genuinely political moments—moments that involve them with the constitution. Otherwise they are immersed in public policy and hence lost to Arendt's transfigurative powers. But her thought gives much more than it withholds.

Notes

1. Hannah Arendt, *On Revolution* (New York: Viking, 1962), 285. Hereafter cited as OR.
2. This sentiment is also expressed in a poem by Theognis. For Nietzsche's meditation on Silenus, see *The Birth of Tragedy*, trans. Francis Golffing (New York: Anchor, 1956), 29-30, 33. The entire book is central to understanding Arendt's work. Nietzsche's *On the Use and Disadvantage of History* is also especially relevant. Indeed, Nietzsche's influence on Arendt is pervasive. The Hegel of *The Phenomenology of Mind* is also crucial. Arendt often discusses Kant, yet his influence is shown for the most part in her tendency to make strict categorial distinctions, with some rigidity as the result. He is not a life-giving influence, as Hegel and Nietzsche are.
3. OR, 285.
4. Arendt, *On Violence* in *Crises of the Republic* (New York: Harcourt Brace Jovanovich, 1972), 165. Hereafter cited as OV.
5. In her last intended book, *The Life of the Mind*, Arendt once again takes up the choral poem in *Oedipus at Colonus*. She now translates the words as "Not to be born surpasses every *logos*; second-best by far is to go as swiftly as possible whence we came." (*Life of the Mind*, 2 vols., New York: Harcourt Brace Jovanovich, 1978, vol. 1, *Thinking*, 162. Hereafter cited as *Thinking*. Furthermore, in referring to lines from "The Garden of Proserpine," she speaks of Swinburne's "rejection of life as something that no man would wish to have twice." This formulation, a variant of Silenian wisdom, appears in "Bertolt Brecht: 1898–1956" in *Men in Dark Times* (New York: Harcourt, Brace & World, 1968), 233. She discusses Kant's versions

of it in Arendt, *Lectures on Kant's Political Philosophy*, ed. Ronald Beiner (Chicago: University of Chicago Press, 1982), 24-25. Hereafter cited as *Lectures*.

Arendt also refers to the discussion in Aristotle's *Eudemian Ethics*, I, IV-V, of Anaxagoras's answer to the question of why one should rather choose to have been born than not. He says, in her translation, "For the sake of viewing the heavens and the things there, stars and moon and sun." (*Thinking*, 133-34) She claims that this question preoccupied the Greek people, not only philosophers and poets. Yet, "The remarkable fact is that, so far as I know, this mood is nowhere mentioned as a source of Greek thought; perhaps even more remarkable, it has nowhere produced any great philosophy—unless one wants to count Schopenhauer among the great thinkers." (162) Whether or not Arendt is a great thinker, "this mood" is more than a mood in her work. She claims that this "feeling about life disappeared with the Greeks." (*Lectures*, 23) She reinstates it. It is as if her own return to the Greeks is a way both of sublimating the pessimism that totalitarianism induced in her and finding a worldly rebuttal to it.

6. OR, 285. She suggests that the search for a theodicy, or for a justification of life by reference to something outside it, derives from a pessimistic "suspicion of life," which "implies a degradation of the whole realm of human affairs." *Lectures*, 23-24. Alternatively, "Theodicies rely on the argument that, if you look at *the whole*, you will see that the particular, about which you complain, is part and parcel of it and, as such, is justified in its existence." (*Lectures*, 30). She prefers the Greek attitude, which takes "the particular event in its own terms, without relating it to any larger process in which it may or may not play a part." (*Lectures*, 56). Such an attitude is free of the need for a theodicy.

7. Arendt, *The Human Condition* (Chicago: University of Chicago Press, 1958), 72. Hereafter cited as HC.

8. Ibid., 73.

9. Arendt, "The Crisis in Education" in *Between Past and Future* (2nd ed., New York: Viking, 1968), 188.

10. HC, 73.

11. On love, see HC, 51-52, 242. An extended summary of her doctoral dissertation on the concept of love in St. Augustine is given by Elisabeth Young-Bruehl in *Hannah Arendt: For Love of the World* (New Haven: Yale, 1982), 490-500. Hereafter cited as Young-Bruehl. On friendship, see "On Humanity in Dark Times: Thoughts About Lessing," and "Waldemar Gurian: 1903–1954" in *Men in Dark Times*.

12. OR, 101–2.

13. HC, 246.

14. Ibid., 145.

15. Ibid., 120-21.

16. Ibid., 134.

17. Ibid., 313-20; OR, 58.

18. OR, 15, 60; Arendt, "The Cold War and the West," *Partisan Review* 29 (Winter 1962), 10–20.

19. HC, 120; also 71, 134.

20. OR, 63.

21. Ibid., 134.

22. Arendt, "The Too Ambitious Reporter," review of Arthur Koestler, *Twilight Bar* and *The Yogi and the Commissar*, *Commentary* 1 (January 1946), 94-95.

23. HC, 311.

24. Aristotle, *Politics*, I, 1254a.

25. Arendt, "What is Existenz Philosophy?" *Partisan Review* 13 (Winter 1946), 34–56.

26. For these distinctions, see HC, 171, 291; see also Arendt, "Understanding and Politics," *Partisan Review* 20 (July-August 1953), 377-92, at 377, 380; "Thinking and Moral Considerations," *Social Research* 38 (Autumn 1971), 417-46; and *The Life of the Mind, passim*.

27. Arendt, *The Origins of Totalitarianism* (rev. ed., Cleveland: Meridian, 1958), 473. Hereafter cited as OT.

28. On her personal disinclination to take part in politics, see the remarks she made at a conference on her work in Arendt, "On Hannah Arendt" in Melvyn A. Hill, ed., *Hannah Arendt: The Recovery of the Public World* (New York: St. Martin's, 1979), 303, 306. Hereafter cited as Hill.

29. OR, 195.

30. "Understanding and Politics," 392. See also her discussion of imagination's powers in *Lectures*, 79-85.
31. Arendt, *Rahel Varnhagen*, trans. R. and C. Winston (New York: Harcourt Brace Jovanovich, 1974), xviii. For the criticism of empathy, see Arendt, "Dilthey as Philosopher and Historian," review of H. A. Hodges, *Wilhelm Dilthey: An Introduction*, in *Partisan Review* 12 (Summer 1945), 404-6.
32. HC, 247-58; also "The Concept of History: Ancient and Modern" in Arendt, *Between Past and Future*, 53.
33. HC, 10.
34. "What is Freedom?" in Arendt, *Between Past and Future*, 167.
35. Ibid., 165.
36. Preface, Arendt's *Between Past and Future*, 3-15; OR, 284-85.
37. Compare Peter Fuss, "Hannah Arendt's Conception of Political Community" in Hill, 171-75.
38. "What is Freedom?" 146.
39. Ibid.
40. Ibid., 171.
41. HC, 230, 324.
42. "What is Freedom?" 169.
43. Ibid.
44. HC, 187-88.
45. OR, 137.
46. Arendt, "Heidegger at Eighty," *The New York Review of Books*, October 21, 1971, 50-54,
47. OR, 92-93.
48. Compare the remark of Aristotle:"[We] are better able to observe our neighbors than ourselves, and their actions better than our own." *Nicomachean Ethics* (1169b), trans. Martin Ostwald (Indianapolis: Bobbs-Merrill, 1962), 264.
49. OR, 92.
50. HC, 10.
51. Ibid., 179.
52. Ibid., 192.
53. Arendt says she follows Heidegger in seeing the real meaning of Solon's maxim as "no man can be called happy while he is still alive." It actually means: "No man is happy; all mortals on whom the sun gazes are wretches!" *Thinking*, 165, 249. The latter is her translation of *Anthologia Lyrica Graeca*. E. Diehl, ed., frag. 16. (The reference is incomplete.)
54. HC, 194.
55. Ibid., 192.
56. "What is Freedom?" 168.
57. Arendt, "What is Authority?" in *Between Past and Future*, 137; also "What is Freedom?" 153-54.
58. HC, 206.
59. Ibid., 195-96.
60. "What is Freedom?" 153-54; also HC, 207-11.
61. HC, 323.
62. Ibid., 168.
63. OR, 103-4.
64. OR, 98-99; also Arendt, "Truth and Politics" in *Between Past and Future*, 257-58.
65. HC, 175-76.
66. Compare what Yeats says: "There is a relation between discipline and the theatrical sense. If we cannot imagine ourselves as different from what we are and assume that second self, we cannot impose a discipline upon ourselves, though we may accept one from others. Active virtue as distinguished from the passive acceptance of a current code is therefore theatrical, consciously dramatic, the wearing of a mask. It is the condition of arduous full life. One constantly notices in very active natures a tendency to pose, or if the pose has become a second self a preoccupation with the effect they are producing. One notices this in Plutarch's *Lives*." *The Autobiography of William Butler Yeats* (New York: Collier, 1965), 317-18.
67. HC, 26.
68. Quoted in Young-Bruehl, 462.

69. Arendt, "French Existentialism," *The Nation* (February 23, 1946), 226-28,
70. *Rahel Varnhagen*, 57 ff.
71. "What is Freedom?" 151.
72. Ibid.
73. Ibid., 152.
74. Ibid., 152-53.
75. Ibid., 152.
76. See *The Life of the Mind*, vol. 2, *Willing*, 201-2. Hereafter cited as *Willing*.
77. HC, 154, 156-57; also "The Concept of History," 78-79.
78. "Truth and Politics," 241.
79. OR, 285.
80. Ibid., 290.
81. Arendt, "Civil Disobedience" in *Crises of the Republic*, 61. Hereafter cited as CD.
82. HC, 324, 184.
83. "The Concept of History," 77; Arendt, "Isak Dinesen: 1885–1963" in *Men in Dark Times*, 105-6.
84. HC, 192.
85. Ibid., 194.
86. "Isak Dinesen", 105.
87. HC, 168-69.
88. Ibid., 154-59; also OR, n. 4, 318.
89. HC, 175-76.
90. Ibid., 57.
91. Ibid., 52; also Arendt, "On Humanity in Dark Times: Thoughts about Lessing," 30-31.
92. OT, 474-79.
93. HC, 180, 203.
94. OR, 22-23.
95. Ibid., 283; also OT, 301; Arendt, "Reflections on Little Rock," *Dissent*, 6 (Winter, 1959), 45-56,
96. See the dialogue between Socrates and Gorgias on the degree to which speech comprises various activities. *Gorgias*, 450 ff.
97. OR, 127.
98. Ibid., 211.
99. HC, 200-204; also OV, 106, 143-45.
100. HC, 200.
101. Ibid., 203.
102. Ibid., 3, 27, 31; also OR, 81.
103. HC, 178.
104. Ibid., 178-79.
105. "The Crisis in Education," 183.
106. Arendt, "The Crisis in Culture: Its Social and Its Political Significance" in *Between Past and Future*, 221.
107. HC, 189, 222; also "What is Freedom?" 166.
108. OR, 26.
109. Ibid., 81.
110. Ibid.
111. Ibid., 115.
112. Ibid., 127.
113. Ibid., 258.
114. Arendt, *On Revolution* (2nd ed., 1965, Penguin, 1977), 279.
115. OR, 50; and n. 43, 315.
116. "What is Freedom?" 155. She seems to take a contrary position in OR, 71.
117. OT, 138.
118. See W. H. Auden, "Thinking What We Are Doing," review of HC, *Encounter* 12 (June 1959), 72-76.
119. OV, 179.
120. OR, 122. Compare Tom Paine: "The construction of government ought to be such as to bring forward by a quiet and regular operation all that extent of capacity which never fails to

appear in revolutions." *The Rights of Man*, 2nd pt. chap 3. He thought that representative institutions realized that aim.

121. OR, 242.
122. OT, 499.
123. OR, 237.
124. Ibid., 254-85; also Arendt, "Thoughts on Politics and Revolution" in *Crises of the Republic*, 231-32.
125. Hill, 317.
126. For an elaboration, see Edmond Cahn, *The Predicament of Democratic Man* (New York: Macmillan, 1961).
127. OT, 467.
128. "What is Authority?" 105.
129. Ibid., 93.
130. OR, 201.
131. Ibid., 283.
132. Ibid., 199 ff.
133. "The Crisis in Education," 191, 195.
134. "What is Authority?" 106.
135. CD, 88-89.
136. HC, 31, 57-58, 222.
137. Arendt (and others), "The Impotence of Power" in Alexander Klein, ed., *Dissent, Power, and Confrontation* (New York: McGraw-Hill, 1971), 222. Hereafter cited as Klein.
138. OR, 278.
139. HC, 41.
140. Aristotle, *Politics*, 1317a. In Chapter 4, I discuss the fact that she distinguishes between ruling and governing; the latter is what elective office-holders do in a representative democracy. There is some resemblance between Aristotle's constitutional rule and democratic governing.
141. OV, 150; HC, 229.
142. HC, 205.
143. OR, 239.
144. OV, 140.
145. OR, 272.
146. OR, 229.
147. Ibid., 227.
148. Ibid., 256.
149. HC, 205.
150. "What is Freedom?" 163-64. But she allows that Rousseau had roused Kant "in his manhood from moral slumber." (*Lectures*, 17.)
151. OR, 228.
152. OV, 193-94.
153. OR, 155-56.
154. CD, 84.
155. Ibid., 93.
156. OV, 139-40; also OR, 182, 281.
157. OR, 152; CD, 100.
158. Ibid., 167-73; also CD, 85-87.
159. CD, 84.
160. For her rejection of all such labels in regard to herself, see Hill, 333-34.
161. OR, 115-16.
162. Ibid., 280; also OV, 170-72.
163. HC, 242.
164. Ibid., 73-78.
165. Ibid., 78.
166. Ibid., 77.
167. Niccolo Machiavelli, *The Prince*, trans. George Ball (Baltimore: Penguin, 1961), 101.
168. OR, 77-80.
169. Arendt also speaks of a passive innocence: to suffer "more than anybody could have possibly

deserved." This was the fate of victims in death camps. Even the worst criminal among them "was as innocent as the new-born babe." The suffering was so inconceivable that the Socratic adage "better to suffer ill than do ill" loses its power to fortify. "The attempt of the Nazis to fabricate a wickedness beyond vice did nothing more than establish an innocence beyond virtue. Such innocence and such wickedness have no bearing on the reality where politics exists." Correspondingly, for Goering, "the death penalty is almost a joke." "The Image of Hell," a review of *The Black Book: The Nazi Crime Against the Jewish People*, and Max Weinreich, *Hitler's Professors*, in *Commentary* 2 (September 1946), 291-95,

170. OR, 77.
171. CD, 55-68.
172. Arendt (and others), "The First Amendment and the Politics of Confrontation" in Klein, 25-26, 28-29.
173. CD, 98.
174. Ibid., 60.
175. Ibid., 64, 68.
176. Ibid., 96.
177. OR, 61-94.
178. Ibid., 85.
179. Ibid., 280.
180. Compare Machiavelli's execution of a similar project in *The Prince*, chaps. 15-19.
181. "What is Freedom?" 149.
182. Compare N. K. O'Sullivan, "Politics, Totalitarianism and Freedom: The Political Thought of Hannah Arendt," *Political Studies* 21 (June 1973), 183-98. For Arendt's own discussion of the similarities between apparent opposites (but equally bad); in this case, the similarities of ex-Communists and Communists, see "The Ex-Communists," *Commonweal* 57 (March 20, 1953), 595-99.
183. OT, 417-19 and Chap. 11-12, *passim*.
184. OR, 182.
185. HC, 323-24.
186. OR, 115.
187. "The Concept of History," 67.
188. Arendt, "Hermann Broch: 1886–1951" in *Men in Dark Times*, 148.
189. In an article published earlier than the essay on Broch, "The Ex-Communists," 597, she speaks of good "deeds" for bad "causes," and the reverse. This usage is more in character. Unfortunately, she illustrates doing a good deed for a bad cause by the hypothetical case of a Communist behaving decently in order to make Communism more respectable. The "net effect would not be propaganda for Communism but a little decency." The illustration is strained and petty, and robs her formulation of its resonance. The oddity is that she does not praise those S.S. guards who capriciously performed occasional acts of mercy. She does express admiration, however, for a German doctor at Auschwitz who used his position *systematically* to alleviate camp conditions, even while contributing to the camp's functioning. But he is closer to subversion than to unexpected gesture. See Arendt, "Introduction to Bernd Naumann," *Auschwitz*, trans. Jean Steinberg (New York: Praeger, 1966), xxv.
190. HC, 205.
191. Arendt, "Lying in Politics" in *Crises of the Republic*, 5.
192. "Truth and Politics," 250.
193. OR, 207.
194. Ibid., 209-10.
195. Ibid., 210.
196. "Truth and Politics," 263.
197. OR, 134.
198. "What is Freedom?" 156.
199. Arendt, "Europe and the Atom Bomb," *Commonweal* 60 (September 17, 1954), 578-80. Here she discusses the terrible way in which living in a nuclear age affects the exercise of courage by changing the nature of war. See also her discussion of Kant's view that courage is "the sublime side of war." (Lectures), 53. Such a view suits only the prenuclear world.
200. HC, 36, 186.

201. "What is Freedom?" 156.
202. OR, 38-39, 147.
203. HC, 238, 244.
204. Ibid., 236-47.
205. OR, 174.
206. HC, 239-40. Luke, 23:34.
207. Ibid., 246.
208. Arendt, *Eichmann in Jerusalem* (2nd ed., New York: Viking, 1964), 277-79. Hereafter cited as *Eichmann*.
209. HC, 241. Concerning the limits of forgiveness,she also says that it cannot extend to "the extremity of crime and willed evil," which are fortunately "rare, even rarer perhaps than good deeds" (239-40).
210. *Eichmann*, 106.
211. "Thinking and Moral Considerations," 417-18.
212. Ibid., 422.
213. *The Life of the Mind* does not add much to the specific question of the relation between thinking and the avoidance of atrocity. See *Thinking*, 188-93. But, of course, it is her protracted effort to define the nature of *philosophical* thinking. See the Appendix.
214. HC, 171.
215. "Thinking and Moral Considerations," 437.
216. Ibid., 423.
217. Ibid., 435.
218. Ibid., 436.
219. Ibid., 442.
220. Ibid., 439.
221. Ibid., 442.
222. CD, 63, 68.
223. Ibid., 63.
224. "Thinking and Moral Considerations," 446.
225. "Truth and Politics," 245.
226. HC, 180.
227. "Truth and Politics," 247-48.
228. "Thinking and Moral Considerations," 445-46.
229. "Truth and Politics," 251.
230. Ibid., 262-63; also "Concept of History," 51-52.
231. Arendt, "Personal Responsibility under Dictatorship," *The Listener* 72 (August 6, 1964), 185-87, 205.
232. "Thinking and Moral Considerations," 445.
233. Ibid. See also *Thinking*, 4, 12, 53, 177, 188-93.
234. "Thinking and Moral Considerations," 445.
235. "Crisis in Culture," 220; also Appendix to *Willing*, 257-60.
236. "Truth and Politics," 241.
237. "Crisis in Culture," 220.
238. "Thinking and Moral Considerations," 446.
239. Ibid.
240. HC, 205.
241. HC, 54.
242. Ibid., 271.
243. OV, 181.
244. Ibid., 118.
245. "Thoughts on Politics and Revolution" in *Crises of the Republic*, 232-33.
246. "Understanding and Politics," 377.
247. Ibid.
248. "Truth and Politics," 262. See also *Thinking*: "who becomes immortal, the doer or the teller? Or: who depends on whom?" (133).
249. HC, 325.
250. Hill, 315-19
251. OR, 123-24; "Thoughts on Politics and Revolution," 203.

252. Hill, 311.
253. "Thoughts on Politics and Revolution," 203.

Chapter Two

Totalitarian Evil

In turning from true political action to totalitarianism we turn from the redemptive to that which immeasurably intensifies despair, from the rare best to the rare worst. Arendt's thought gives entrance to the realm of human deeds at their most criminal.

The Origins of Totalitarianism is about the pathologies of modern European history: the pathologies of racism and imperialism; and the actuality of totalitarianism, for which the word *pathology* is scarcely adequate. Arendt's book grows out of shock and horror and out of an even deeper grief. Although not victimized herself (except for a period of detention in France), Arendt writes in behalf of the victims: Jews as the main group, but also all the other victims of Europe's pathologies, Europeans, Africans, and Asians alike. She is persuaded that in regard to totalitarianism itself, "Human history has known no story more difficult to tell." But she warns: "Told as propaganda, the whole story not only fails to become a political argument—it does not even sound true."[1] She does not hide her feelings. She says, indeed, that to write about vast sufferings, *sine ira*, is to fail in objectivity and actually to condone them. She says that "a description of the camps as hell on earth is more 'objective,' that is, more adequate to their essence than statements of a purely sociological or psychological nature."[2] In a self-descriptive passage that is nevertheless free of vanity or posing, she sets down the nature of the ideal analyst of the worst horrors:

> If it is true that the concentration camps are the most consequential institution of totalitarian rule, "dwelling on horrors" would seem to be indispensable for the understanding of totalitarianism. But recollection can no more do this than can the uncommunicative eyewitness report. In both these genres there is an inherent tendency to run away from the experience....Only the fearful imagination of those who have been aroused by such reports but have not actually been smitten in their own flesh....can afford to keep thinking about horrors.[3]

Yet one remarkable feature of the book is generosity of understanding. As she explains in an autobiographical passage in her essay on Lessing, one way that émigrés like herself had of holding on both to some humanity in an inhuman world and to some reality in their "worldlessness" was "by seeking to the limits of their ability to understand even inhumanity and the intellectual and political monstrosities of a time out of joint."[4] In her case, this ability is indissociable from generosity. Recurrently, she expends great energy in the effort to make her readers see the world as some of the initiators or instruments of pretotalitarian pathology saw it. Her generosity does not extend to those responsible for the extermination of millions, to the upper ranks of Nazism and Stalinism; or to the masses who provided totalitarianism with its opportunity, its manpower, and its objects of organizational control. Nor does it extend to those toward whom some generosity might have been expected—for example, the typical European bourgeois. That the book is full of unexpected generosity does not, however, necessarily make its uneven distribution seem capricious. Rather, one can easily conclude that even Hannah Arendt's generosity has its limits. The long book has almost no heroes: Clemenceau and Bernard Lazare come closest to getting unequivocal praise. But some of the practitioners or abettors of pathology emerge from the book with a heightened humanity.

The aim of this chapter is to see what Arendt contributes to our understanding of phenomena that are repellent but that she means to approach. These phenomena comprise the necessary historical preconditions of totalitarianism and totalitarianism itself. The main text is *The Origins of Totalitarianism*.

The Place of Psychological Analysis

It must be stressed that the recipients of her generosity are practitioners and abettors of pathology: They are racists and imperialists, engaged in wicked endeavors and precursors of totalitarian evil. Thus they are not even initially likeable morally, as are the French and Russian revolutionaries whom Arendt subjects to her powers of understanding and who also emerge (in *On Revolution*) with a heightened humanity. Remember that Arendt pictures Robespierre, Saint-Just, and Lenin as overpowered by their sense of human suffering and led by that uncircumscribed sense into excesses. The racists and the imperialists, however, showed no sympathy for others: When they victimized others, they had not first been victimized by their own goodness. Still, Arendt works on them and tries to make some of them accessible to our fellow-feeling, if not liking.

The oddity is that Arendt deplored empathy. She attributed the wish to know others from the inside to a romantic predilection to shun action and substitute for it an obsessive and futile concern with the inner life. The cultivation of empathy was a form of spiritual arrogance. She also thought that the human heart, in its darkness, was unknowable, that inner motivation was hidden from both the person himself and from others trying to understand him. However, there is no word better than "empathy" to name what Arendt manifests in *The Origins of Totalitarianism* (and *On Revolution* and elsewhere). A passing remark she makes in her reply to Eric Voegelin's critique of *The Origins of Totalitarianism* is doctrinally uncharacteristic of her, but it is entirely accurate as an account of what she regularly does:

I am convinced that understanding is closely related to that faculty of imagination which Kant called *Einbildungskraft* and which has nothing in common with fictional ability. *The Spiritual Exercises* are exercises of imagination and they may be more relevant to method in the historical sciences than academic training realizes.[5]

This kind of imagination is not the same as the "enlarged mentality," which Arendt conceptualizes as either the ability to put oneself in the place of another or the ability "to think from the standpoint of somebody else."[6] Her gifts go well beyond these capacities, even at their most sensitive, and are related, no matter what she says, to fictional ability, to the powers of great poets and novelists. She herself is a great psychologist, despite her rejection of the technical disciplines of psychology. She is, to use an old-fashioned term, a moral psychologist. She sees the sense, meaning, or pattern, or the underlying rationality, or the disguised but perfectly human aspirations in a piece of conduct or policy that may strike most people as obscure or pointless or that most people may mistake for something else.

It is all the more noteworthy, therefore, that precisely as a moral psychologist, generous or not, she refuses psychological understanding a place in the effort to make sense of the leaders and principal functionaries of totalitarianism. Her position is basically consistent. Whether discussing the Nazi leaders (or Stalin) in *The Origins of Totalitarianism*, or a principal functionary, Eichmann, in *Eichmann in Jerusalem*, she contends, or leaves us to infer, that the unfathomable evil they did is not traceable to a correspondingly unfathomable depravity of their nature.

We must observe, however, that in the preface to *The Origins of Totalitarianism*, reprinted in the second edition but omitted from the last, three-volume edition, she says that with the death camps "an absolute evil appears (absolute because it can no longer be deduced from humanly comprehensible motives)."[7] She is here suggesting a necessary connection between unfathomable evil and unfathomable depravity of nature, as if only some other species than human beings could do the kind of evil inherent in totalitarianism. Her preface is anomalous.

Her extended analysis of totalitarianism in *The Origins of Totalitarianism*, in all editions, does not offer an account of unfathomable depravity. Like the analysis of Eichmann, however, it is unrelenting in the presentation of totalitarianism as distinctively inhuman evil, "absolute" in that sense and hence unforgivable. Inhuman evil was therefore initiated and administered by human beings who were not inwardly unique. The social and technical circumstances of modern Europe proved able to effect the malignant transformation of seemingly ordinary criminality (Hitler and Goering) or of not uncommon thoughtlessness (Eichmann).

Of course some camp guards, entrusted to carry out the daily job of killing, acted with a personal cruelty that in fact was meant to be *excluded* by systemic cruelty. Arendt thinks both that they were clinically normal and that they acted sadistically. She says:

> If we think of these overt acts of sadism as having been committed by perfectly normal people who in normal life had never come into conflict with the law on such counts, we begin to wonder about the dream world of many an average citizen who may lack not much more than the opportunity.[8]

Psychological explanation is pertinent for individual acts. But totalitarianism, whether Hitler's or Stalin's, is more than all the individual acts it spawned. We must go beyond psychology and find as exact a description of the phenomenon as possible. Arendt means to provide us with that description, and the concept of ideology is its center. But because others have already produced descriptions that tend to assimilate totalitarianism to other phenomena, such as tyranny and despotism, and to offer psychological explanations that really do not explain, Arendt sets out to disabuse us of what we think we know about totalitarianism. Only then can we come to know totalitarianism in its reality, in its novelty. We cannot know it as we know other political and social phenomena, even though such modern concepts as nihilism, gangsterism, messianism, revenge, *ressentiment*, terrorism, metaphysical rebellion, and sadism may now and then seem to clarify an aspect of it.

If psychological penetration is one of the most prominent features of *The Origins of Totalitarianism*, the rejection of psychology in the most crucial task of the book, is the most important fact about it. Arendt extends the limits of psychological understanding before trying to establish them, and she claims to have established them unarguably, definitively.

The Burden of Our Times

In arguing for the utter novelty of totalitarianism, and hence for the radical discontinuity between it and all other political and social phenomena, including the pathologies of Europe in the nineteenth and early twentieth centuries, Arendt seems caught in a paradox. Her title indicates that the book will be about origins, as if events that preceded Nazism and Stalinism must be seen as leading to and accounting for them; as if there were no radical discontinuity. (The title of the English edition is *The Burden of Our Times*.) She was aware of the difficulty:

> The book, therefore, does not really deal with the "origins" of totaritarianism (*sic*)—as its title unfortunately claims—but gives a historical account of the elements which crystallized into totalitarianism, this account is followed by an analysis of the elemental structure of totalitarian movements and domination itself. The elementary structure of totalitarianism is the hidden structure of the book while its more apparent unity is provided by certain fundamental concepts which run like red threads through the whole.[9]

This passage is not as clear as it could be, and it must be read together with some occasional sentences in the book itself for Arendt's complex sense of connections and similarities to disclose itself.[10]

Arendt is saying that totalitarianism—at least in its first appearances in the forms of Nazism and Stalinism—happened against all odds; that it was a kind of miracle, a black miracle. She is clear that for happening once a phenomenon may more readily happen again. The hard time is the first time: so hard that the phenomenon—in this case, totalitarianism—must remain inexplicable. Whenever Arendt discusses the human capacity to begin, to start or found something new, to interrupt seemingly automatic and fated processes, she emphasizes her belief that such initiative could not have been predicted. Causal explanation of a phenomenon is not compatible with its novelty and thus with the exercise of human freedom. Totalitarianism, however, is distinct from other novel phenomena in being inexplicable in a double sense. It is not only inexplicable in the sense that all novel phenomena are—not reducible to the "product" of antecedent causes. It is also inexplicable in the sense that it resists the retrospective assignment of some kind of rationality. One can uncover some proximate purposes, but there is no ultimate purpose of a rational sort.

Why does Arendt spend so much time discussing the earlier pathologies, antisemitism and imperialism, in a book on a qualitatively different pathology, totalitarianism? One possible answer is that the book is a work of excess: it contains more than its thesis needs. One can be grateful for the brilliant abundance yet regard it as extraneous, or perhaps as even incompatible with the thesis concerning totalitarianism. That answer is unsatisfactory. Although nothing that happened before totalitarianism led directly or inevitably to it—to the will to do its deeds—much that happened before it helped the initiators and principal functionaries do such deeds. Those who propagated antisemitism and other kinds of racism, those who championed imperialism, those who provided the numbers needed to carry out racist and imperialist policies, and some of those who were victimized by such policies all contributed to the possibility of totalitarianism.

Above all, in the particular case of Nazi totalitarianism, the totalitarian movement before it comes to power and for a time afterward as well, wears the appearance of earlier movements, racist and imperialist, in Europe. The appearance helps to attract segments of a population already susceptible—susceptible for generations—to racist and imperialist notions and fully developed ideologies. (Even Stalinism now and then wears the borrowed clothing of pan-Slavism.) The real continuity between the earlier movements and totalitarianism is found in the readiness of European peoples to think in racist and imperialist categories, to accept the normality of, sympathize with, or embrace ardently such modes of response and half-thought. Arendt does not say that the appearance is a deliberate disguise, meant to take susceptible people in by getting them to believe that a fundamentally new movement is not much more than a revised form of an older one. Although Hitler and Stalin were most likely disposed to evil from the start, the situation of others close to them or somewhat farther down in their respective hierarchies, is not very clear. Thus to describe the early appearance of Nazism and Stalinism as a deliberate disguise would be too crude a rendering of Arendt's meaning.

Arendt does not deny the changing nature of the two totalitarian regimes through time, whatever the fixity of the two leaders' intent to kill. It took time for both regimes to grow ever closer to their essence; and both did so, no matter what the circumstances. But that does not mean that there was a widespread awareness of the *telos* of the two regimes from the start. Thus the resemblances between earlier racism and imperialism and Nazism and Stalinism are outward and rather shadowy.

In addition, Hitler and Stalin learned from racism and imperialism. Arendt says:

For the immediate predecessor of totalitarian imperialism is not the British,

Dutch or French version of overseas colonial rule, but the German, Austrian and Russian version of a continental imperialism which never actually succeeded, and therefore is neglected by students of imperialism, but which in the form of the so-called pan-movements—pan-Germanism and pan-Slavism—was a very potent political force in Central and Eastern Europe. Not only does totalitarianism, nazism no less than bolshevism, owe a heavy debt to pan-Germanism and pan-Slavism in matters of ideology and organization; their expansion program, though global in scope and thereby distinguished from those of the pan-movements, follows the aims of continental imperialism.[11]

In sum, totalitarianism is not conceivable, not conceptually possible, not superficially recognizable, not experientially familiar, not able to receive welcome and adherence and cooperation, without several generations of antisemitism, other kinds of racism, and imperialism (not only in Africa). At the same time, totalitarianism is not their causal derivative or logical outcome.

Arendt's view on the coming of totalitarianism is best seen in contrast to a view that is different, but yet not wholly so, on an another horror. I refer to the famous passage Henry James wrote on the outbreak of World War I. In a letter to Howard Sturgis, he said:

> The plunge of civilization into this abyss of blood and darkness by the wanton feat of those two infamous autocrats is a thing that so gives away the whole long age during which we have supposed the world to be, with whatever abatement, gradually bettering, that to have to take it all now for what the treacherous years were all the while really making for and *meaning* is too tragic for any words.[12]

Arendt is not saying that totalitarianism came when Europe drifted into its fate, but that it, after all, encountered something it had prepared for itself. Even so, it is no wonder that two of the three parts of Arendt's book on totalitarianism deal with racism and imperialism. Totalitarianism is Europe's *responsibility*: that is surely one of the main ideas that Arendt leaves us with, even though she may never put the matter as baldly as that. Yet the fact remains that *The Origins of Totalitarianism* is full of generosity toward those—or at least some of those—responsible, even though they were not members of totalitarian movements or regimes. A large part of the book's tremendous power to instruct comes from Arendt's empathy with racists and imperialists. Her generosity of understanding shows itself in this way: She enlarges our understanding of distasteful, even abhorrent human responses, but she does so without raising our sympathy for them. She shows great daring: After all, she is extending herself to those who bear some responsibility for immeasurable evil and she means to take us with her. She also enhances our understanding of disreputable elements who are only marginally related to totalitarianism.

Two cases of the first generosity are valuable for our general comprehension of totalitarianism and the European world that made it possible. One is Arendt's effort to find out why antisemitism—the eventual core of Nazi totalitarianism—was so prominent in the social and political life of Europe in the last few decades of the nineteenth century. The other case is the response Arendt imputes to white people when they first encountered the black "savages" in the heart of Africa, especially in the nineteenth century. To say it again, she does not arouse, or try to arouse, our sympathy for antisemites and white destroyers of blacks. She does, however, throw light on the inwardness of both species of hostility. By doing that she does *not* prepare us for the relentless murderousness of totalitarian practice; rather, she deepens our sense of the European world in which totalitarian movements could appear plausible because they were familiar in their earlier stages.

ON ANTISEMITISM

Arendt maintains throughout the book that antisemitism played a large role in the political and social life of Europe from the 1880s on. The beginnings of modern antisemitism she dates from the Napoleonic period. The climax of modern antisemitism of course is the organization of antisemitic sentiment in the Nazi movement, where it was the core of Nazi ideology and the subsequent genocide. (Only at the end of Stalin's rule did antisemitism figure in his form of totalitarianism, and he did not live to make it central to his periodic liquidations of whole categories of people. Yet pan-Slavism had antisemitic features.) Antisemitism need not have led to extermination camps; but they would not have existed had not European peoples made antisemitism a regular part of their way of looking at the world.

The astonishing thing is that Arendt asks the question, Why was antisemitism so pervasive and often so deep? And she proceeds to answer it as if it were a question that needed a scholarly answer. She denies to herself and her fellow Jews any self-pity that grows out of self-indulgence. It is not that she hides her grief and feigns stoicism, and it is certainly not that she is a self-hating Jew. On one hand, her book is instigated by both horror and grief. On the other, she affirmed on many occasions with an absolute matter-of-factness—no pride, no shame, no humility, no secret sense of chosenness or superiority—that she was a Jew, as if everyone knew that she was a Jew and what a Jew was. As a Jew, she asks, Why have we been disliked? Why have we been hated?

In her ruthless quest for an answer Arendt vehemently rejects two proffered answers. One is that Jews are scapegoats: a vulnerable minority, sufficiently different from the rest and sufficiently weak to attract the displaced frustration and wrath of people who are confused or in trouble. The other is that there is an eternal antisemitism, that all non-Jews have always been hostile to Jews, and that there are therefore no differences between historical periods and cultures. She insists on making distinctions. The most important distinction is between modern European antisemitism and all previous kinds. She argues that antisemitism could not have become the elemental force that it became, from the 1880s to the destruction of Nazism, unless the Jews themselves had something to do with it. Now and then she goes so far as to implicate the Jews in the responsibility for their victimization.

Now to be told that you are responsible, in part, for your victimization must sound harsh, almost gratuitous, especially in light of the ultimate destination of European antisemitism—genocide. Even if there is some truth in the analysis, some may feel that it is a truth best left unmentioned. Does not tact have a place in inquiry, even if the inquirer is closed to a positive ethnic solidarity? Is there not something suspect about an intellectual generosity that seems to exact such an unpleasant cost from others, the others being no less than the victims (or intended victims) of those being "generously" understood?

Arendt's greatness lies precisely in her honesty. She sweeps aside all that would make her ethnic fellows and herself comfortable, if that comfort is bought by self-deception or half-knowledge. In her judgment, modern antisemitism depends on the character of modern Jews. She never stupidly says that the Jews deserved what they got in the nineteenth and early twentieth centuries. Rather, she is trying to show that given certain patterns of Jewish life, the response of antisemitism was not beyond the realm of normal human meanness or unimaginative resistance to the foreign or the dissimilar. Antisemitism was not quite just what should have been expected, but it was not some strangeness requiring extraordinary modes of interpretation. Yet so painful is the subject that an extraordinary effort is required to see the unobscure truth.

Arendt traces the fate of European Jewry through the nineteenth and early twentieth centuries. That is to say, antisemitism had a constantly changing career tied to a number of salient events. The basic background condition was that a number of Jews were intimately connected to the state authorities in various countries as financiers throughout the eighteenth century and into the nineteenth, and they were thus associated with both wealth and secret power. The irony is that as Jewish influence over the state decreased because the money-raising powers of modern governments grew more public, antisemitism increased. She says:

> Neither oppression nor exploitation as such is ever the main cause for resentment; wealth without visible function is much more intolerable because nobody can understand why it should be tolerated. Antisemitism reached its climax when Jews had similarly lost their public function and their influence, and were left with nothing but their wealth....The Dreyfus Affair exploded not under the Second Empire, when French Jewry was at the height of its prosperity and influence, but under the Third Republic, when Jews had all but vanished from important positions (though not from the public scene).[13]

She drives the point home:

> Only wealth without power or aloofness without a policy are felt to be parasitical, useless, revolting, because such conditions cut all the threads which tie men together. Wealth which does not exploit lacks even the relationship which exists between exploiter and exploited; aloofness without policy does not imply even the minimum concern of the oppressor for the oppressed.[14]

Tocqueville's insight is acknowledged as seminal, but Arendt's development is original and sustained. The further complexity is that Jews suffered all the more from their perceived association with the state, as social classes, in competition with each other, grew more disaffected from the state when they could not bend it to their will.

Against this background of combined wealth and comparative powerlessness (formalized until the movement toward the civil and political emancipation of European Jewry in country after country), certain kinds of oppression and humiliation manifested themselves, and were answered by Jewish adaptation. Arendt is hostile to the two main Jewish responses: assimilation (the response of the parvenu) and reclusive existence (the response of the pariah). Both responses tended to aggravate antisemitism. Arendt is especially attentive to the psychology of the parvenu, the Jew who will accept acceptance on any terms, provided that acceptance permits entry to the most fashionable circles. Her model is Disraeli, on whom she expends some of her most acute analytic ability. But the story of the usual parvenu is more distressing than that of the brilliant Disraeli.

Arendt examines the nature of the social acceptance that awaited the aspirant Jew (the upstart), and finds that the Jew fascinated the upper classes as an embodiment of vice. For society at large, the Jew was a criminal, a traitor, and unreliable because of double loyalties. The upper classes transmuted "crime" into vice and found in acquaintance with "vice" an exotic sensation, a forbidden delight. The result of acceptance on these terms was that the Jew became all the more strange in the eyes of ordinary people. Arendt says:

> Social "philosemitism" always ended by adding to political antisemitism that mysterious fanaticism without which antisemitism could hardly have become the best slogan for organizing the masses. All the *déclassés* of capitalist society were finally ready to unite and establish mob organizations of their own; their propaganda and their attraction rested on the assumption that a society which had shown its willingness to incorporate crime in the form of vice into its very structure would by now be ready to cleanse itself of viciousness by openly admitting criminals and by publicly committing crimes.[15]

In an essay first published in German in 1948, before *The Origins of Totalitarianism*, and titled "Die Verborgene Tradition," Arendt sketches the few responses she does admire:

> Realizing only too well that they did not enjoy political freedom nor full admission to the life of nations, but that, instead, they had been separated from their own people and lost contact with the simple natural life of the common man, these men yet achieved liberty and popularity by the sheer force of imagination. As individuals they started an emancipation of their own, of their own hearts and brains.[16]

The heroes are Heinrich Heine (voice of the innocent, the *schlemihl*); Bernard Lazare (the conscious pariah); Charlie Chaplin (the archetypal suspect); and Franz Kafka (poet of the fate of the man of good will).[17] The only politically relevant response in this grouping was that of Lazare, who courageously agitated the Jewish issue in France. He rebelled as a Jew in behalf of Jewish rights and sought acceptance as a Jew. He thus rejected both assimilation on the terms of non-Jews and a reclusive and civilly dead existence. Lazare was the *conscious* pariah: He would not accept acceptance except on his own terms, and he fought politically to secure those terms. His very commitment earned him the respect of professional antisemites. Arendt's implicit point is that concerted political resistance at the right time could have diminished the poisonousness of antisemitism, just as the wish to be accepted increased it.

Antisemitism is thus a heterogeneous phenomenon; modern antisemitism is bound to the changing relation of Jews to the modern state, the changing relations between the state and the rest of society, the spread of Jewish emancipation, and the efforts at assimilation. Arendt also takes specific historical circumstances into account, including financial scandals and disasters with which Jews had some close involvement. She is painstaking in her effort to make modern antisemitism in Europe an intelligible social and political tendency. The method of intelligibility is the attempt to think the thoughts of antisemites, to study and half imagine the ways in which they saw and felt the world. We do not leave Arendt's writing with added sympathy, but rather with a sense of the mottled humanity of antisemite and Jew alike. Arendt achieves the effect of an impartiality that has overcome pain and aversion.

ON RACISM IN AFRICA

Unlike her exploration of antisemitism, Arendt's treatment of European antiblack racism is perforce a reconstruction of experience that she did not have firsthand, but this does not inhibit her effort to impart the inwardness of white reaction to black natives. She relies in part on literary evidence, especially Joseph Conrad's *Heart of Darkness*. In fact she does not supply much evidence of any kind. One mentions these facts because Arendt's analysis is upsetting to an unusual degree. Mentioning her remoteness from the scene is not an honest way of expressing one's own doubts about what she says, and one's hopes that the situation was not as she says it was. What she says does not have the effect of justifying racist exploitation, not even the effect of raising a little human sympathy for the Europeans. Nevertheless, there is an indigestible quality to Arendt's analysis, to her act of generosity toward the Boers, Germans, Belgians, and other European exploiters and imperialists. What differentiates her treatment of antiblack racism from her treatment of nineteenth-century antisemitism is that the former was accompanied by atrocities on an inconceivable scale, as she herself mentions, while the latter only made possible such atrocities. There was no intervention of time and circumstance between antiblack racism and imperialist atrocities as there was between European antisemitism and Nazi genocide.

The appalling fact is that any effort to render the inwardness of those who engaged in the slaughter, enslavement, or other systematic exploitation of millions of people must appear callous at the least. But Arendt is willing to risk any appearance for the sake of truth. Nowhere in her work does she take more chances—is at greater risk—than in her discussion of European antiblack racism in Africa. (She once said, in conversation, before the publication of *Eichmann in Jerusalem* that she received more hostile response to her essay opposing school desegregation, "Reflections on Little Rock," than to any other piece she had ever done. But that essay is undramatic in comparison to the pages on antiblack racism in *The Origins of Totalitarianism*.)

Arendt is clear that "racism is the main ideological weapon of imperialistic politics."[18] The doctrine of racial inferiority was deliberately used to justify policies initially prompted by other considerations. Arendt follows Hobson and Hilferding in understanding "the scramble for Africa" as instigated by economic pressures. The wish to find a profitable place for the investment of surplus or "superfluous" capital was basic. Joined to this was the desire to find a place to settle for "superfluous" people, the unemployed and the discontented. The stress in Arendt's analysis is on the illimitable nature of late nineteenth-century European capitalism: profits for profits' sake, expansion for expansion's sake, the fevered wish to be forced by the logic of economic conditions to keep constantly in motion, constantly pushing outward, never prepared to draw the line and say enough. She quotes Cecil Rhodes's remark, "I would annex the planets if I could," as emblematic. She sees imperialism as politics denatured into pure power, as politics corrupted by the newly potent bourgeoisie. But such ferocious energy needed a justification, an ideology, and it found it in racism. The pity is that racism had a foundation in fact.

Arendt claims that the first contacts between whites and blacks in southern Africa indelibly affected the whites and provided the factual foundation for a developed racist ideology, which in turn helped to strengthen the imperialist urge by covering it with the semblance of thought. What were these contacts like? Arendt says:

> Race was the emergency explanation of human beings whom no European or civilized man could understand and whose humanity so frightened and humiliated the immigrants that they no longer cared to belong to the same human species. Race was the Boers' answer to the overwhelming monstrosity of Africa—a whole continent populated and overpopulated by savages—an explanation of the madness which grasped and illuminated them like "a flash of lightning in a serene sky: 'Exterminate all the brutes.'"[19]

In what lay the capacity to disgust and madden the Europeans?

> What made them different from other human beings was not at all the color of their skin but the fact that they behaved like a part of nature, that they treated nature as their undisputed master, that they had not created a human world, a human reality, and that therefore nature had remained, in all its majesty, the only overwhelming reality—compared to which they appeared to be phantoms, unreal and ghost-like. They were, as it were, "natural" human beings who lacked the specifically human character, the specifically human reality, so that when European men massacred them they somehow were not aware that they had committed murder.[20]

What Arendt does not say is that the Europeans would have needed some imagination to see the "savages" as human, as equally human to themselves; but there was no incentive to let one's imagination of otherness work. Profit and conquest rested on a complete effacement of this kind of imagination. Arendt oddly excludes the intoxicant role of self-interest in these passages where she tries to view the world as the Boers and others did, even though she is so insistent on the underlying connection between capitalism and imperialism.

How can one be sure in matters like this? It seems that Arendt is too generous in her attempt to make sense of incalculably evil behavior. She perhaps gives too much of herself. In *The Human Condition*, she meditates on the ignobleness of man when he lets himself imitate the rest of nature too well, or when he lets his whole life be spent in the exercise of natural "metabolic" functions. We find that she attributes nearly identical sentiments to the Europeans in Africa. The urgency in her writing drives her close to an identification with the Europeans.

Yet she may be right. The warrant for saying that is the disgust with which she treats the Boers. If she can imagine their feelings when they first saw the blacks, she is also unremitting in describing the Boers' cruelty and their own degeneration into a merely natural, though completely exploitative existence. She shows nothing but a horrified disapproval of the other Europeans and their deeds as well. It is as if Arendt believes that unless inquirers went to the limits of their imaginative powers, inquiry must fail. Some of the worst criminals in human history must be included too, within the grasp of the empathetic imagination. Yet empathy is not to be accorded to the Nazis, because to understand them does not mean understanding their inwardness.

THE ELITE

Arendt enlarges our understanding of the distasteful, even the abhorrent. She also enlarges our understanding of the *disreputable* and engages our sympathy while doing so. In dealing with the main example of this latter effect, we deal with a group to whom totalitarian movements were immensely attractive and who had their roots in the imperialist period and even earlier. But because they did not retain their fascination with totalitarianism once the movement came to power, they were properly part of the Europe that made totalitarianism possible rather than part of totalitarianism itself. As such, they receive Arendt's generosity of understanding. They strain generosity greatly, without making its exercise quite as risky as the antisemites and antiblacks do.

This group is the "elite," the intellectuals who from roughly the latter part of the nineteenth century mounted a campaign of spiritual subversion against the dominant opinions and beliefs of bourgeois Europe. Arendt is interested particularly in "the front generation," those who fought in the Great War and came back permanently altered, permanently disaffected. She labors with great delicacy to show how totalitarian movements (and by implication all extremist movements) answered to a terrific need to see the bourgeois order shaken up, ridiculed, exposed in its real nature. This need led to what Arendt calls "the temporary alliance between the mob and the elite." (The mob is the aggregation from which the leaders of extremist and totalitarian movements came.)

Arendt acknowledges that the pleasure that intellectuals took in extremism is "more disturbing to our peace of mind than the unconditional loyalty of members of totalitarian movements, and the popular support of totalitarian regimes."[21] But she will not call this pleasure "nihilist" if by using that epithet one thinks one has disposed of the matter. The epithet may finally capture the tonality of the elite's attitude, yet there was nothing gratuitous, nothing inexplicable about their readiness to see everything go under.

Throughout the book Arendt does not hide her own severity toward bourgeois culture. In making the mentality of the elite accessible to her putatively skeptical or hostile readers (especially American ones), Arendt is not promoting a view of life she shares. She and the elite look on bourgeois culture with revulsion, but her response is energized by a love of politics and a regard for the integrity of the publicness and impartiality of the state. The European bourgeoisie killed these principles. Most of the elite, contrastingly were fundamentally unpolitical and sometimes antipolitical, anarchic; at least, they no more admired citizenship and the rule of law than they did the bourgeois transformation of public life into an instrumentality of partial interests and domestic obsessions. There is generosity in her account of the elite precisely because her divergence from them is considerably more significant than the fact that they have enemies in common.

In a few pages she makes us feel what the elite felt: that bourgeois society was full of deadening routines and the most pervasive sham. The experience of war in the trenches intensified the critique inherited from Nietzsche or Sorel or Bakunin or Rimbaud. The sense of the rotten hollowness of bourgeois life gained authenticity from the irrationality and destructiveness of the bourgeois war they witnessed and fought in, while the passion to see that life utterly destroyed grew more sharp from the very destructiveness of the war. Arendt says:

> The self-willed immersion in the suprahuman forces of destruction seemed to be a salvation from the automatic identification with pre-established functions in society and their utter banality. These people felt attracted to the pronounced activism of totalitarian movements, to their curious and only seemingly contradictory insistence on both the primacy of sheer action and the overwhelming force of sheer necessity. This mixture corresponded precisely to the war experience of the "front generation," to the experience of constant activity within the framework of overwhelming fatality.[22]

More than anything else, the elite admired the mob aspect of the movements. This aspect represented the surfacing, with earnest, deadly intent, of elements in European society hitherto despised and rejected by the bourgeoisie. The verbal propaganda of the movements, together with the propaganda of the deed—the coercion and violence in resentful acts of "political expressionism"—signified the presence of a genuinely anti-bourgeois group. Two lines of attack on the bourgeoisie especially delighted and enthralled the elite. First, there was the destruction of respectability through the mere prominence and threatened ascendancy of the mob-led movement. Second, the movement's praise of violence and cruelty came as a relief after the hypocritically liberal and humanist pieties of the bourgeoisie. In a passage that seems equally relevant to the mentality of some urban terrorists today, Arendt describes the deepest source of attractiveness in the mob-led movements:

> An atmosphere in which all traditional values and propositions had evaporated...in a sense made it easier to accept patently absurd propositions than the old truths which had become pious banalities, precisely because nobody could be expected to take the absurdities seriously....What a temptation to flaunt extreme attitudes in the hypocritical twilight of double moral standards, to wear publicly the mask of cruelty if everybody was patently inconsiderate and

pretended to be gentle, to parade wickedness in a world, not of wickedness, but of meanness![23]

Arendt goes so far as to say that "aversion against the philosemitism of the liberals had much more to do with this reaction [against bourgeois hypocrisy] than hatred of the Jews."[24] Her rendering of the mentality of the elite opens up the perspective of extremist and totalitarian movements as cleansing, avenging angels. That these movements, when they gained power, crushed the intellectual elite is an irony she underlines. Yet even then, she says, there were a few who saw in the totalitarian repression of individuals like themselves a policy that also answered to a terrific need. She refers to the "perverted selflessness" of some in the elite and connects this disposition to "the totalitarian movements' spurious claim to have abolished the separation between private and public life and to have restored a mysterious irrational wholeness in man."[25]

With brevity and concentration, Arendt makes vivid an era of European sensibility. Her generosity enhances our understanding and may create sympathy for the disreputable. For some, her powers are wasted because they are spent in humanizing right-wing immoralists and esthetes; spent on those who, whatever their talent, lodged their affections in movements they should have known would do far more evil than the whole selfish and hypocritical bourgeoisie ever did. It may be thought that even though the intellectual elite had little or no direct role in the successful attainment of power by the Nazis or by Stalin, they cannot be exonerated. They dishonored their calling just by celebrating the base and the violent.

In truth, Arendt's pages on the elite are a hard test of the reader. But it would be evasive if one refused the encounter that Arendt arranges. The spirits she presents the reader must be studied, and their cruelty seen, finally perhaps, as Arendt would have us see it—as an embittered kindness, an all-consuming fear of the possibility of human suffocation in an atmosphere of falseness, obtuseness, and selfishness. Of course—and Arendt knows it unimpeachably—the cure for bourgeois sickness was itself a worse sickness. That there was a sickness, a pathology, to begin with is the fact that Arendt's pages make it impossible for us to ignore.

Arendt does not extend her exceptional generosity of understanding to all the individuals and groups who appear in her book: Not all emerge with heightened humanity. Yet, because there is so much generosity in the book, its absence in regard to particular individuals and groups is all the more striking. The temptation for an admirer is to say that when generosity is absent, when individuals and groups appear either wholly reprehensible or so imposed upon by others as to resemble something lifeless and plastic, then some are simply beyond the reach of generosity. It would be immoral to present them as ripe for revaluation or reconsideration. Why assume that they are more than they appear?

The only reason to resist the admonition of our hypothetical admirers is that Arendt's analysis may be weakened by an absence of generosity in at least a few instances. Having expanded the humanity of some of the practitioners and

abettors of racism and imperialism, and of some of the friendly observers of
totalitarian movements, she may create distortions when she withholds
generosity from others. The latter may seem all the worse for the contrast with
the former: The former may seem undeservedly better. It may be ungrateful,
perhaps silly, to demand that remarkable gifts be evenly distributed, but the
book's ideal proportions may have necessitated more evenness. A definite view
on this matter is elusive. Reference to two cases may at least suggest the extent
of the difficulties. These pertain to fundamental aspects of Arendt's analysis of
the European society in which totalitarianism was made possible, and of
totalitarianism itself: the bourgeoisie, as the dominant class in Europe, the
main source of values, opinions, and attitudes; and the mob.

THE BOURGEOISIE

All through Arendt's work, not only in *The Origins of Totalitarianism*, there is a
persistent animosity displayed toward the European bourgeoisie. The story of
the bourgeoisie is the story of modern Europe, for Arendt no less than for the
Marxists. For Arendt, however, the story of modern Europe—Europe since
the French Revolution—is the story of pathologies, with Nazi and Stalinist
totalitarianism as the climactic pathology. The European bourgeoisie is thus,
in Arendt's work, continuously responsible, continuously culpable. They are
even denied, except very infrequently, the heroic stature and historical
appropriateness that they achieve in the Marxist outlook.

What, then, is the heart of the story of the bourgeoisie which is also the story
of modern Europe and the story of pathologies? Arendt sees it as "the
nineteenth-century struggle between *bourgeois* and *citoyen*, between the man
who judged and used all public institutions by the yardstick of his private
interests and the responsible citizen who was concerned with public affairs as
the affairs of all." The bourgeoisie pressed private interests "regardless of the
common good."[26] A more abstract formulation is found in *The Human
Condition*, in which Arendt speaks of "the rise of the social" and the victory of
society over the public in the modern world. The gist is that the stuff of politics
is depoliticized; it changes into economics. Economic interests reduce politics
and government to techniques instrumental to "housekeeping," to getting,
holding, and augmenting wealth. The contests between interests are internal
and international. If consumerism, welfare economics, and state regulation
are presently the main content of society's triumph over the truly political,
class struggle to control the state and use it for internal aggrandizement or
foreign adventures expressed society's triumph over the truly political in
nineteenth-century Europe.

The idea of citizenship suffers continuous attenuation. Arendt associates a
regard for the common good with the practice of citizenship. Implicit in her
conception is another theoretical point: the status of citizen when taken
seriously, when taken as at least partly constitutive of one's identity, and
joined to a tradition of citizenly watchfulness over and concern for political life
and governmental activity, is the only real guarantor of a sense of limits, and it
is one of the main sources of rootedness in reality. Where that status is not

understood, or too recent, or unrealized sufficiently in daily practice and reflection, limitlessness and unreality can take over. What is at issue is not the full citizenship of direct, participatory democracy, but the modern citizenship of constitutional representative democracy—a kind of citizenship Arendt praises mostly in the form of civil disobedience, but which obviously is the positive moral center of her writings on modern pathologies. The "political emancipation of the bourgeoisie" is the cause of the decline of citizenship, even though the struggle for enfranchisement is thought to be a sign of bourgeois strength. The tragedy is that their expanded enfranchisement, political power, and influence in general actually resulted in the enfeeblement of citizenship. Citizenship is betrayed, rather than being properly exemplified, by the effort to bend government to a group's or class's economic interests.

Arendt mentions but does not offer a detailed sociological analysis of the gradations within the bourgeoisie. Nor does she give a sustained explanation of the enormous differences the bourgeoisie shows from country to country, especially the differences between the English bourgeoisie and all others, and the lesser but still important differences between the French bourgeoisie and that of central Europe. The English bourgeoisie exhibited some restraints; at least they budgeted their cruelty more carefully. In any case, the European bourgeoisie is the main source of pathology and bears the main responsibility for later totalitarianism.

Unaffected by commitment to the idea and practice of citizenship, demons were unleashed: greed; the logic of capitalist investment; flattering and convenient doctrines claiming that some individuals or groups or races are superior to others, which were propagated by apologists in bourgeois employ; and an unbelievable growth in technical capacities, with a corresponding intoxicated hubris. These were the demons of the upper bourgeoisie. Their arrogance engendered an economic system that produced alongside its wealth a tremendous social dislocation, including unemployment, and an irrepressible tendency to expand outside national borders, sponsoring imperialism in Africa and aggressive inclinations at home. With Europe in constant but confused motion, everything was unsettled. The politics of Europe became increasingly susceptible to irrational or desperate responses, the desperation intensified by the greater scale of things—more people, more demands, increased violence, a greater confidence in the ability to act and find solutions.

The feeling of strength waxed with the feeling of vulnerability. The bourgeois system created the mob; and when its tensions brought on the Great War, it created the masses in war's aftermath, the phenomenon of the mass-man. These were the demons of the lower bourgeoisie. (Even though all classes were represented in the mob and the masses, their dominant orientation was bourgeois.) In the middle was the ordinary bourgeoisie, absorbed by the pursuit of income and willing to yield rule to any strongman who could preserve law and order and the sanctity of property while dispensing favors. They were politically indifferent and made political indifference praiseworthy. These were the demons of the middle. Going together with all this—with the tensions, the racism, the imperialism, the wars—was that bourgeois culture that so disgusted the elite.

The bourgeoisie was the villain that prepared the way for the evil worse than any villainy. The question is whether Arendt has succeeded in disclosing, by an act of empathetic generosity, the inwardness of the principal members of the bourgeoisie, the principal villains. The answer is that she has not tried. The rapacious business mind, on the one hand, and outwardly conformist respectability, on the other hand, she must find too repellent. She closes herself to them; they remain, in this book, closed to us. We have to go elsewhere to glimpse the souls whose economic quest was as limitless as their social behavior was restricted. She hates the upper bourgeoisie for carrying the virus that weakened or destroyed right citizenship and lawful politics. By a perverse esthetic standard, it is good that the book have some, almost deliberate, blank spot to go with such a superabundance of empathetic understanding.

Yet the villainous bourgeoisie is still on the near side of the abyss that separates totalitarian leaders from the rest of humanity. Repeated references to the need to invest "superfluous capital" do not carry enough explanatory weight—that is, if we expect from Arendt the depth of explanation she ordinarily gives us. At the same time, if we left the inwardness of the bourgeoisie aside, the whole account of imperialism as a solely capitalist phenomenon is deficient. It is just as deficient as the account sometimes given—though not by Arendt—of the Great War as a solely capitalist phenomenon. The operation of other passions and calculations in both phenomena must be allowed: geopolitics, dynastic rivalry, vainglory and superstition, dislike or suspicion of otherness, and so on. If the story of modern Europe is the story of modern pathology, there are other sources of villainy than the bourgeoisie as the bearers of social hypocrisy and the profit motive.

THE MOB

The mob figures in Arendt's analysis in two ways. It is represented among those who went to Africa to plunder it and those who were involved in the agitation of extremist and irregular politics like the anti-Dreyfusard tendency, the pan-movements in central and eastern Europe, and most decisively, the Nazi movement up to the Roehm purge. (Hitler came from the mob, but he was not merely the mob mentality magnified.)

Sociologically, the mob was the creation of capitalism. Those who comprised the mob were unemployed, yet only a fraction of the unemployed. Arendt rather shockingly refers to them as "the refuse of all classes."[27] She sees them as the lumpenproletariat, the underclasses, indeed, the underworld. They are an outside class, in part literally criminal, altogether *louche*. The mob is not the working class; it is not the people. It is not the norm, despite the widespread existence of pathologies of every sort in European society. But although the mob is not the norm, it is not an accidental eruption of aberrant individuals. Arendt says:

> The mob is not only the refuse but also the by-product of bourgeois society, directly produced by it and therefore never quite separable from it. They [the historical pessimists] failed...to notice high society's constantly growing

admiration for the underworld, which runs like a red thread through the nineteenth century, its continuous step-by-step retreat on all questions of morality, and its growing taste for the anarchical cynicism of its offspring. At the turn of the century, the Dreyfus Affair showed that underworld and high society in France were so closely bound together that it was difficult definitely to place any of the "heroes" among the Anti-Dreyfusards in either category.[28]

There must be something a bit offensive to a democratic soul in the tone of Arendt's voice. *Refuse* is an unacceptable word to use about people. Its use may be symptomatic of some reluctance to understand that stems from a prejudice not entirely dissimilar from snobbery. If there were (and are) snobs who feel or affect a *nostalgie de la boue* and thus admire the mob, and if there were (and are) snobs who find the mob odious because of its vehement lack of respectability, there are also snobs who look at the mob and fail to master their disgust and therefore fail to see humanity. These latter would be the snobs of virtue or decency. Probably a better way of putting it is to say that even Arendt has to have polemical moments. The mob, after all, provided the leaders, the massed bodies, and the shock troops of totalitarian movements. It instigated totalitarianism. But it must be understood more intimately than Arendt has understood it.

Arendt says, at one point, that the "more gifted were walking incarnations of resentment."[29] With the word *resentment* we are in the conceptual world of Nietzsche and Scheler, where the human traits of envy, frustration, and revenge seize the soul and possess it. But there was nothing secretly subversive in the mob. It fully acted out its negative passions. It therefore escapes the analysis of Nietzsche and Scheler, or at least its central thrust. We cannot append their analysis to Arendt's with the aim of filling it out consonantly to her overall sensibility. The issue is crucial because the mob was crucial to the success of totalitarianism. Arendt does not take us inside the souls of its members. It may be that one writer does: Dostoyevsky. He may provide us with as much help as we can expect. In the character of Pyotr Stepanovitch Verhovensky in *The Possessed*, we may come as close as we can to inspecting the soul of one of the mob, a leader of a mob.

Yet the very word *mob* may obscure our understanding. It heaps together large numbers of people whose differences may matter greatly. To be sure, they acted in concert. But their actions were radically unpredictable and stemmed from idiosyncrasies. The influence of personalities on action was exceptionally pronounced, and action was therefore strange, unaccustomed. That is why we need to know them from the inside.

The Elements of Totalitarianism

In antisemitism and in imperialism in Africa, in the intellectual elite, the bourgeoisie, and the mob, Arendt locates the elements that provided the necessary conditions for the appearance of totalitarianism. She tries to throw light on all these elements. This endeavor is of course preliminary to an examination of totalitarianism itself. We may say schematically that in *The Origins of Totalitarianism* and elsewhere, Arendt studies the phenomenon of totalitarianism by seeking to understand its main constituent elements: the masses, the functionaries, and the leadership.

THE MASSES

Traumatic events destroyed the articulation of a disciplined class structure in the interwar period. When classes disintegrated, people became masses. The term refers to the great majority. Without the masses there would have been no totalitarianism. First: totalitarian movements are possible "wherever there are masses who for one reason or another have acquired the appetite for political organization."[30] Second:

> What prepares men for totalitarian domination in the non-totalitarian world is the fact that loneliness, once a borderline experience usually suffered in certain marginal social conditions like old age, has become an everyday experience of the evergrowing masses of our century. The merciless process into which totalitarianism drives and organizes the masses looks like a suicidal escape from this reality.[31]

Arendt refers to the "indisputable popularity" of Hitler and Stalin in power.[32] She explicitly says that totalitarianism answers to the needs of men. Beyond that, the "mass-man" came into ever greater prominence in totalitarian regimes, supplanting the mob elements. The masses, that is, supplied the personnel, whose unquestioning loyalty and obedience kept totalitarian regimes in motion. They carried out the policies of evil.

Now the masses did not originate these policies; they did not want them, necessarily. They were not drawn to totalitarian movements by the promise of genocide. While genocide was taking place, most of the masses did not know about it with any definiteness or clarity. Arendt is not accusing the masses of murderousness, of willing that totalitarianism be carried to its completely self-consistent conclusion. Once again, Arendt is careful to distinguish the leaders, the givers of orders, from everyone else. But the plain truth, as Arendt sees it, is that the masses accepted some part of the totalitarian outlook on life, and welcomed some part of the translation of that outlook into action and the general disposition toward activism. They did so with some voluntariness: Terror and propaganda were not the sole causes of their acceptance and compliance. And some representative men from the masses carried quite easily the burden of systematic murderousness once the orders were given.

The psychological understanding of the masses must therefore occupy a central place in Arendt's analysis, and it does. Obviously she is not the only one who has essayed an understanding of the masses involved in totalitarianism. But to her analysis should be applied the standard she has made us expect: generosity of understanding. In regard to the masses she meets the standard ambiguously. She does not condemn, except for those who took direct part in genocide; she provides a fresh way of looking at the condition of the masses; but there is a cold abstractness of analysis that precludes a rendering of the pathos of the ordinary person in harrowing circumstances. The conceptualization of the masses is one of the most brilliant achievements in the book: It has the brilliance that a supremely resourceful creation of character has. But is the created character truly that of the masses, or is it rather a construction divorced in some respects from actuality? This is not a question with an answer, but it is not an idle one either.

Arendt works with a cluster of notions: loneliness, superfluousness, uprootedness, lostness. The emphasis is on loneliness, but at times the other notions are used synonymously or to fill out the notion of loneliness. (These concepts have some relation to the concept of alienation discussed in Chapter 5.) In discussing the mob Arendt had already invoked the notion of superfluousness. By becoming the helpless victim of unemployment, some people came to feel dispensable, extraneous. Arendt suggests that this is a historically new feeling. It lay behind the mob's irrational and punitive or exploitative behavior, either in Europe or in Africa. Unemployment continued to engender the feeling of superfluousness and related feelings in the twentieth century, with special sharpness in the period after the Great War. So that trying to account for the invasion of society by those feelings, those experiences, which prepare large numbers of people for totalitarian movements and regimes, Arendt assigns a major role to unemployment.

To illustrate the experience of uprootedness, Arendt takes up the related phenomena of transfer of populations after the Great War, the presence of countless deported or stateless people, and forced or free emigration. The impact on those who suffered these experiences and also those who witnessed them was immense. She says about those who were uprooted: "To be uprooted means to have no place in the world, recognized and guaranteed by others....Uprootedness can be the preliminary condition for super-fluousness."[33] These were the lost souls, without mooring, and prone, in the absence of relief and rescue, to a diminished sense of self-worth that facilitated nonresistance and even acceptance of any treatment. Their plight could not have but imparted a pervasive sentiment throughout Europe of the fragility of human life and, ultimately, of its unreality.

To the Great War itself, Arendt pays scant attention. She does pay exquisite attention to the way the war changed the intellectual elite. But she generalizes the effects of the war into the concept of the breakdown of the class system and the corresponding emergence of "an atomized and individualized mass."[34] The class system represented clear and delimited loyalties, interests, and expectations. These delimitations helped to constitute the self by establishing surety for the self. The war smashed the class system. Arendt says:

> The number of the mass of generally dissatisfied and desperate men increased rapidly in Germany and Austria after the First World War, when inflation and unemployment added to the disrupting consequences of military defeat.[35]

All the elements are named in this sentence. Arendt's analysis, however, does not deploy them and then dwell on each, and then connect them and make them into the very condition of life that begged for a radically novel solution. The loss of ties, the loss of work, the poverty, the sense of nations' shame and mutilation, the erosion of surety, and the inevitable confusion in the sense of self can, together, be called "loneliness." The word still can strike one as remote from a condition that probably requires a description and an analysis with a different tonality from that in which "loneliness" is the organizing concept (or metaphor).

Arendt is clear that when she speaks of masses she is not endorsing the views of those who deplore the spread of education and leisure to the hitherto excluded, and who lament the overall equality of condition in modern society. She strains to purge her discourse on the masses of any reactionary condescension. She explicitly excludes the American people from the category of masses: Indeed, they are less like masses, despite their equality, than any people in the world.[36] She succeeds in not being reactionary. I doubt, however, that she is free of a certain coldness or remoteness that resembles condescension. The masses were victims: She does not manage to convey that thought without faintly discrediting the victims. The fact that many industrial workers resisted the seduction of totalitarian movements shows that humanity is capable of a humane response no matter how desperate the condition. Arendt notices this fact with approval. But surely that cannot be used to relegate the rest to the status of masses, an undifferentiated aggregation of lost and lonely souls.

There is power in Arendt's depiction. What is missing is the sense vividly caught recently in Ingmar Bergman's movie *The Serpent's Egg*—the sense of hopelessness that can come over people when a number of traumas converge, any one of which would be enough to demoralize and unsettle them. The convergence disposed them to welcome a seemingly heroic resolve to save them. To put it flatly: The masses made totalitarianism possible. The flat assertion is true but misleading. If a flat sentence is not to mislead, it must go: The desperate and legitimate needs of the victimized masses made totalitarianism possible. Just as the masses did not choose their misery, so they did not choose a remedy that they knew would lead to the wars and extermination camps of totalitarianism.

Yet I fear that I have exercised a leniency toward the masses that I have no right to exercise. Out of the masses, out of the aggregation of the lost and desperate souls, did come the SS and other murderers. (The Stalinist system is given separate treatment by Arendt.) She says that the original leaders of the Nazi movement and regime were from the mob; but the future, if the Nazis had lasted longer, would have been with the mass-men, not the mob. Himmler was the type of the future leader. Yet Nazism lasted long enough for the mass-men to carry out as subordinates the genocide ordered by Hitler and wanted by his principal functionaries. Arendt does not always say that any member of the masses—anyone from the majority of the German people—could as easily have done what a few did. In the analysis contained in *The Origins of Totalitarianism*, some quality sets off the few from the rest, whether fanatical hatred of the Jews, fanatical devotion to the leader and his plans, some private depravity, or something else. This untypicality was signaled by the fact that for a time only volunteers were used for the policies of extermination. The masses supplied volunteers: That is the inescapable fact. If not all in the majority were eager, all those who were eager came from the majority. No prior experience of desperation in the Weimar period can extenuate, much less excuse, this criminality. If that is so, then any concern to dwell on the pathos of the Weimar period, any wish to penetrate to the inwardness of mass-men, is not to lack generosity of understanding, but to want a mindless exculpation.

The trouble is that by the time Arendt wrote *Eichmann in Jerusalem* (written in 1962 and published in 1963), she had devised an explanation for the administration of atrocities—as distinguished from conceiving and ordering them—that seems independent of the masses and their misery, their loneliness, uprootedness, and superfluousness. Eichmann was not an executioner in his own person; he was not a mere cog in the machine. He was a "desk murderer."[37] In these respects he differed from the average participant in atrocities. Yet he was like them. In Arendt's portrait, Eichmann is without any strong passions or beliefs. He is therefore the average mass-man as philistine. Before *Eichmann in Jerusalem* and even before *The Origins of Totalitarianism* were published, Arendt had sketched the good family man and jobholder as "the great criminal of the century."[38] Of course the experience of unemployment is in the background, but Arendt's analysis focuses on the compatibility of a normal family life and either sexual or dutiful implication in the greatest atrocities. The good family man could be either a sadist or a "regime criminal."[39] The essentially private person, anxious to make a good life for his family and totally lacking in any attachment to the idea of citizenship, is the perfect cog:

> He has driven the dichotomy of private and public functions, of family and occupation, so far that he can no longer find in his own person any connection between the two. When his occupation forces him to murder people he does not regard himself as a murderer because he has not done it out of inclination but in his professional capacity. Out of sheer passion he would never do harm to a fly.[40]

In *The Origins of Totalitarianism*, Arendt presents a similar description but does not make it central. In *Eichmann in Jerusalem* it *is* central. Its thrust is not to trace involvement in atrocities to the masses and their past trauma, to feelings of loneliness, uprootedness, or superfluousness. The phenomenon is altogether different. Eichmann was not able to think: he could not recognize himself in others; he could not act on his feeble and intermittent awareness that Jews were human beings too. Arendt does not, in turn, trace this incapacity for thinking to some further source. She neither psychologizes the incapacity nor offers a broadly sociological explanation of it.

It may be that the description of Eichmann is extendable to most of the executioners.[41] There is a much firmer conceptual link between atrocities and the nearly universal tendency to compartmentalize life than between atrocities and the experience of loneliness.[42] Add to compartmentalization the nearly universal ability to make any activity into a routine that deadens the awareness of what is being done, provided steps are taken to shield the senses to some degree. Only at the start of an activity does shocked response have a chance to deter involvement. But many considerations, many pressures, all work in the direction of absorbing the shock and not letting it guide action. Arendt provides a splendid itemization of these considerations and pressures in the book on Eichmann. If the concept of being unable to think is extendable beyond Eichmann, then the idea of masses seems not to do the work Arendt

wants it to do in *The Origins of Totalitarianism*. On the assumption that the idea
of masses cannot explain the readiness to acquiesce in or to commit atrocities,
it is not an obscene leniency to ask that a psychologist as great as she show
more generosity in understanding those who, because of their suffering, put
their desperate hope in a false redeemer. Why call thoughtless murderers
mass-men? Then, too, why call distressed people masses? Must there be
masses when classes decay?

This is not to say, however, that "civilized" ordinariness in the willing
service of genocide or serious wrongdoing is itself not mysterious. Such
ordinariness may not be depravity or inhuman blackness of heart. It may not
be radical evil in the Kantian understanding: a Satanic disposition "to adopt
evil *as evil*."[43] It may not be Milton's Satan saying, "Evil be thou my Good, "[44]
or Claggart in *Billy Budd* tormented by an innocence he must torment.[45] But it
may be something altogether more strange: a nonhuman blankness. To speak
of Eichmann and others as "terribly and terrifyingly normal"[46] is in fact, to
preserve the mystery: Arendt cannot mean that normality as such is terrible
and terrifying. The phenomenon is not fully caught by such culturally
unspecific characterizations as an inability to think or to judge. I believe that
thoughtlessness of the Nazi sort and scale is possible only in a culture that can
produce and respect a sentence like the following:

> Even if a civil society were to dissolve itself by common agreement of all its
> members (for example, if the people inhabiting an island decided to separate and
> disperse themselves around the world), the last murderer remaining in prison
> must first be executed, so that everyone will duly receive what his actions
> are worth and so that the bloodguilt thereof will not be fixed on the people
> because they failed to insist on carrying out the punishment; for if they fail to
> do so they may be regarded as accomplices in this public violation of legal
> justice.[47]

To think that there is only rigor where there is cruelty; and that a sense of
duty can serve only rigor; is a cultural deformation that precedes the
advent of masses.[48] Whatever other problems remain concerning the
concept of being unable to think, it does not exist in a clear relationship
to masses.

The Essence of Totalitarianism

THE LEADERS AND FUNCTIONARIES

What of the leaders? What of Hitler and Stalin, especially? Do we understand
them better for the principled avoidance of psychological explanation? Arendt
is a generous psychologist much of the time; when she is not generous, she is
nevertheless provocative and instructive. Her acumen, her subtlety, and her
perceptive energies are of the highest order. Yet, in all her psychological
strength, she says that totalitarian leadership is best understood
unpsychologically. We must now look more closely at her concept of
totalitarianism if we are to grasp her view of the leaders.

Arendt's analysis of totalitarianism is principally based on Hitler's regime.
The consideration of Stalinism is secondary, even though it is by no means

casual or introduced for the sake of some convenient symmetry. It may turn out that some features of her analysis, some of its levels or some of its particulars, may not apply to Stalinism. It may even turn out as well that her characterization of Hitler's mentality does not suit Stalin. But I still think that her concept of totalitarianism helps in understanding Stalin's system, not only Hitler's.

What, then, is totalitarianism? First let us see what Arendt says it is not. It is not tyranny, the form of government that it seems at least to resemble and to which it is often assimilated. Ordinarily, tyranny means the absolute rule of one man (although the concept is sometimes stretched to include the rule of a few and sometimes, as by Tocqueville, to include the democratic many). The tyrant aspires to *total* power over his subjects, usually with the aim of enjoying his power. Arendt speaks of tyranny as arbitrary power serving the interest of the tyranny and as being hostile to the interests of the people.[49] She does not say what the tyrant's interest is. But it may be possible to suggest that though she was not sympathetic to the view that mankind has an innate power drive or love of power—power in the conventional sense of command and control over others—she would understand the tyrant as interested in feeling pleasure from making people do what he wants them to do and what they do not want to do. The tyrant is an extreme bully tending to sadism; one who is likely to be bloodthirsty; one who at once seeks to crush all resistance to his will yet delights in the occasional opportunity to experience resistance so that he may crush it. Indeed, he may even provoke it to have the pleasure of crushing it. The tyrant wants to be feared or revered like a god; he wants to stand out as not only preeminent, but as the only one capable of doing things, making things happen; the only one with a public identity.

Pure tyranny is best rendered by Orwell in *1984*, although his rendering may seem not wholly credible and almost impurely to exult in the depicted cruelty. The tyrant is not interested in anything but his own power: its retention, enlargement, and display. He will do anything for power; and it may be that he is especially happy when he must do wicked or evil things in his career of power. He thus combines terrible means with a terrible end. Arendt is saying that neither Hitler nor Stalin was a tyrant. Or at least neither was only a tyrant, even though both practiced some of the immemorial arts of the tyrant. She attributes to neither one the love of power for power's sake: that is, love of power for the pleasure it gives of compelling others to do what they do not want to do, to the point where it seems that it is only because they do not want to do it that the tyrant wants them to do it. At this extreme, perversity is intrinsic to tyranny. Even at this extreme, the tyrant is not to be taken for the totalitarian ruler.

On the other hand, Arendt's analysis points to the conclusion that neither Hitler nor Stalin was what we may call instrumental tyrants or dictators. They were not leaders who would do anything to achieve a purpose that seems describable by reference to utility or practicality—ruthless, merciless leaders possessed of a mission, say, to reform, reinvigorate, mobilize, or modernize, and who seek total power to achieve that purpose, independently of the pleasure of power. She does not see them as great bad men. The temptation is

especially strong to see Stalin in this way—a way best caught by Arthur
Koestler in *Darkness at Noon*. This way of seeing Stalin her analysis would lead
us to deplore and to reject. It tends to a long-term exoneration, which would be
bad by itself, but much worse, it falsely attributes to Stalin an overriding
purpose of utility or practicality. In fact, Stalin, like Hitler, had no such
purpose and enlisted those who had such a purpose for an altogether different
purpose, neither useful nor practical, and, indeed, a purpose that actually
impeded the useful and the practical. Thus neither Hitler nor Stalin was, in
essence, a ruthless dictator in the usual sense.

What emerges so far is that for Arendt neither the aspiration toward total
power nor the possession of total or nearly total power is sufficient to indicate
the presence of totalitarianism. The tyrant intoxicated by the wielding of
power and the purposive leader of complete unscrupulousness—two types
that may often seem more easily differentiated in theory than in the historical
examples that present themselves for analysis and judgment—are not entirely
discontinuous with ordinary human nature. As Plato instructs us, even the
best soul dreams of doing what tyrants actually do. Pride, vanity, egotism, and
megalomania infect us all, even if to greatly varying degrees. We are always on
the verge of seizure by obsession.

On the other hand, normal politics is stamped by an abatement of scruples,
by at least a tincture—perhaps a necessary tincture—of ruthlessness. Thus,
the tyrant and the ruthless leader are each of us, but grossly exaggerated, or
they are rulers, grossly exaggerated. To explain them, if Plato is right, is only
to have recourse to considerations that explain each of us. The point is that for
Arendt totalitarian leadership is not to be explained so. Totalitarianism is a
distinctive phenomenon because the roots of its deeds are not explainable by
any of the usual ways in which we try to make sense of what may disturb or
appall us. Correspondingly, the deeds themselves are also distinctive.

To suggest Arendt's idea of totalitarianism is necessarily to gather together
the various elements she deploys in her work. These elements, which are taken
mostly from *The Origins of Totalitarianism*, can be synthesized as follows.
Totalitarianism is genocide, a methodical genocide "within the frame of a legal
order."[50] Totalitarianism is the methodical killing of certain populations on a
large scale (involving millions) undertaken deliberately and as a matter of
policy by those in power, whose overriding aim is to kill such populations, and
to kill them even though they are not hostile or even dissident, or even
unwitting obstacles to any purpose of utility or practicality, or even in
possession of worldly goods of any sort that their killers need, want, or covet.
To the rational observer, totalitarianism is as gratuitous as it is methodical: It
combines the most extreme proficiency of method with what appears to be a
total absence or emptiness of purpose. Even the word *mad*, used when Captain
Ahab has "some glimpse" that all his means are sane but his motive and his
object are mad, does not capture the totalitarian purpose. Arendt's analysis
takes us far beyond as well the closing pages of *The Protestant Ethic*, where
Weber attaches the extremest rationality of method to a compulsive
pursuit—the aim of which seems almost forgotten or non-existent—a
cojoining he likens to sport, if only half-heartedly.[51] (His real lesson is that

after a certain point a desire to increase rationality of method is a symptom of irrational purpose.)

Any one of the elements of the synthesized definition of totalitarianism, or even some combination of them, may be present in other events or conditions. History exhibits enormous massacres, abundant conquest and imperialism, heartless expropriations, wretched conditions of confinement or servitude, and systems of racial and religious discrimination. Just as it shows many tyrants or near-tyrants and many ruthless leaders, many would-be aspirants to or wielders of total or near-total power or control, it shows countless episodes of systematic cruelty. But Arendt insists on totalitarian distinctiveness: Only under Hitler and Stalin was there methodical genocide within the frame of a legal order.[52] In the case of Hitler, although he was responsible for the deaths of many Poles, Ukrainians, White Russians, and Russians, many more than the number of Jews he had killed, the killing of Jews was the essence and the differentiation of his totalitarianism. He also killed Gypsies as he killed Jews, but all one can say is that there were fewer Gypsies to kill. Of course, from a certain point of view the numbers killed cannot matter; the killing of any one innocent soul is an atrocity.

Arendt's radical thesis, then, is that totalitarian rulers are to be understood in their essence as mass killers of objectively unthreatening populations in an age where mass killing is easily and antiseptically done. If the aim is to understand totalitarianism, we cannot remain content with a structural analysis; we must attend to the actual tendency of policy. A particular policy dictated the structure. The will to kill was the ultimate source of totalitarian structures, structures of total or near-total power or domination. A mere syndrome of the structural characteristics of total power leaves the meaning of Nazism and Stalinism unaddressed.[53] Arendt is saying that the real place of totalitarianism was the death camp: the scene where the true purpose of totalitarianism—extermination—was realized. It was also an experimental laboratory for techniques of total control; a model for society as a whole, one's own or a conquered one, in the near or distant future; and an image of terror by which to discipline and intimidate people outside the camps. She says that the motto of the camps and hence of totalitarianism was "everything is possible."

We might ramify Arendt's analysis and say that in relation to some Hitler was a tyrant and to others a ruthless leader, so that he could be to the Jews (and the Gypsies) a totalitarian ruler. Stalin eludes Arendt's characterization. She is right to say he was not, in essence, merely a ruthless leader. But in relation to all those whose fate he directly affected, he may have been "only" a tyrant. He may have wanted total control because he wanted not only to be number one, but to be the only one, the only man, alone capable of initiating action, and aiming to convert a whole society into his shaping clay. The oriental despot *à outrance*, he could not endure anyone with the slightest dignity or independence, traits that in his *paranoia*[54] he saw as a threat not to his plans, but to his very identity. He was a madman of such bloodiness that perhaps the word *mad* should not be used about him. He not merely preferred policies that would exact an immense human cost, he *defined* policy as that which exacted an immense human cost.

The overarching question is, How could someone order a policy that killed millions of men, women, and children who never opposed him and would have obeyed him had he let them live? In Hitler's case, the obvious answer is that he was a racist. He believed that Jews (and Gypsies) were not only inferior but subhuman—noxious and fit only to be destroyed. Alternatively, he was afraid that the Jews really were superior, and wanted them dead just for that reason. Or he thought the Jews were unassimilable, despite their formal assimilation in Germany, and that so long as any were alive a tradition of criticism, nonconformity, deviance, or corrupt sophistication would continue and thus erode the purity or unity of a people. Arendt mentions all these possibilities.

The problem is to explain how anyone can go from virulent racism to genocide. Arendt says: "There is an abyss between the men of brilliant and facile conceptions [the mid-nineteenth-century theorists of race-thinking] and men of brutal deeds and active bestiality [the death-camp killers] which no intellectual explanation is able to bridge."[55] Those who killed face to face were psychopathological: An "intellectual explanation" does not explain them as it explains the abstract theoreticians. There was also an abyss between these killers and their leaders. We have already said that unfathomable evil need not come from unfathomable depravity. The leaders were not psychopathological. How, then, can they be explained intellectually? A beginning is made when we see that the passion that conceives and initiates a policy need not be commensurate to the scale of that policy. There need not be an inside to match the outside, so to speak. Actually, there *cannot* be an inside to match the outside when the outside is so vast. Activities of any kind, provided they are part of a system and on a large scale, dwarf the instigating passions. The involvement of numerous people as helpers and accomplices does not provide an accumulation of passion—an addition that yields some huge sum, some gigantic passion that no one person has, but that the collectivity does have. To think in this way is to be deceived. There is an accumulation of energy and hence of the power to act, as there may be diverse but compatible purposes. But that is different from positing an immense passion. In guiding thought along these lines, Arendt helps to clear away confusion, so long as we remember what now and then she obscures; namely, that there *were* instigating passions of horrible strength and eventually self-destructive tenacity.

Arendt is willing to toss out some brief characterizations of Hitler and his principal functionaries. She says of the "normal" Himmler: "He was not a bohemian like Goebbels, or a sex criminal like Streicher, or a crackpot like Rosenberg, or a fanatic like Hitler, or an adventurer like Goering."[56] By themselves these labels lead nowhere. There were and are millions of people in each category, but Hitler and his circle were unique. Her emphasis is that they were unique in what they caused to be done, not in what they were.

Arendt says of Eichmann: "Except for an extraordinary diligence in looking out for his personal advancement, he had no motives at all."[57] He was not an Iago or Macbeth or Richard III: He was not a villain. (The characters Shikin and Stepanov in Solzhenitsyn's *The First Circle*, a book Arendt greatly admired, are kin of Eichmann, and their characterization throws light on Arendt's characterization of Eichmann.) On the other hand, Hitler and his circle were evil beyond villainy, and they did have motives. Only, the motive—to destroy Jewry—was not sustained by a passion equal to it, and could not be.

The presence of a motive may distinguish the top circle from Eichmann and his like. Yet Arendt seems at times to draw them all together in a common shallowness, a common "word-and-thought-defying *banality of evil.*"[58] In her reply to Gershom Scholem's criticism of her book on Eichmann, she said that she had changed her mind from the time she wrote *The Origins of Totalitarianism.* She no longer wanted to use the concept of "radical evil":

> It is indeed my opinion now that evil is never "radical," that it is only extreme, and that it possesses neither depth nor any demonic dimension. It can overgrow and lay waste the whole world precisely because it spreads like a fungus on the surface. It is "thought-defying," as I said, because thought tries to reach some depth, to go to the roots, and the moment it concerns itself with evil, it is frustrated because there is nothing. That is its "banality." Only the good has depth and can be radical.[59]

Evil-doing is thus banal even when the initiator of evil acts, not only when others follow. Here Arendt is overworking her thesis. She is in the grip of what she says is one of her main intentions in writing the book on Eichmann: "to destroy the legend of the greatness of evil, of the demonic force, to take away from people the admiration they have for the great evildoers like Richard III."[60] But we should not take her best sense to be that the concept of "the banality of evil" applies to Hitler and his top associates. If unfathomable depths should not be assumed, neither should shallowness.

To account for the leap from virulent racism to the initiation of genocide, Arendt offers in place of psychology a redescription of the totalitarian phenomenon. As her analysis proceeds in *The Origins of Totalitarianism,* totalitarianism is disclosed as the disposition to live a fiction or live by a fiction or enact a fiction or make the world over into a fiction.[61] Totalitarianism is a systematic way of refusing the given reality and remaking it *with an absolute lack of restraint.* The leadership, which initiates and inspires, imagines without restraint; the abettors act as if restraint simply were an irrelevant consideration. An alternative formulation is that totalitarian leaders show the latent murderousness inherent in estheticism: a readiness to sacrifice anything to the "consonance of their own system," or to its " 'beautiful' consistency."[62]

Arendt says that the emotional relation to the fiction varied with the group. The sympathetic outsiders were the only ones who believed "loyally and textually in the Leader's words."[63] They were the ones who most craved an intelligible world, who experienced the void created by the failure of all received ideologies and religions. The ordinary party membership did not believe the propaganda put out for mass consumption, but "it believes all the more fervently the standard clichés of ideological explanation, the keys to past and future history which totalitarian movements took from nineteenth-century ideologies, and transformed, through organization, into a working reality."[64] How about the leaders? The elite did not believe in the literal truth of the clichés. In the minds of the elite resided the greatest cynicism combined with the greatest gullibility. The gullibility, however, was not doctrinal in any usual sense. Arendt says:

The elite is not composed of ideologists; its members' whole education is aimed at abolishing their capacity for distinguishing between truth and falsehood, between reality and fiction. Their superiority consists in their ability immediately to dissolve every statement of fact into a declaration of purpose. In distinction to the mass membership which, for instance, needs some demonstration of the inferiority of the Jewish race before it can safely be asked to kill Jews, the elite formations understand that the statement, all Jews are inferior, means, all Jews should be killed.[64]

Elite gullibility was behaviorial and issued in automatic enactment. They claimed that Jews were subhuman and then treated them in ways that made them subhuman.

An absolute absence of restraint sustained the leaders in the initiation and direction of the fiction. The fiction was the world to come. It was a self-realizing fiction because no restraint stood in the way of the realization. The magical proficiency of coordinated action sustained the absolute absence of restraint. Modern technology contributed to the phenomenon but was not its heart. The few wanted to redesign the world because they could; they could because they wanted to. They were drunk with the possibilities of action.

One point can be added to Arendt's theory. Totalitarian leaders carried beyond all limits a habit of thought commonly present in political action: to transfer the categories of face-to-face action in private life to massive public action. For example, acting out of concern for reputation in everyday life ordinarily excludes force and injury to others; in politics, especially international politics, it ordinarily requires force and injury to others. But the hold of the analogy between personal and organizational action is too great for political actors to care much about the cost of what they do. The change in scale is a qualitative change, but it is barely noticed. Totalitarian leaders carried this murderous abstractness to the limit.[66]

Detached from the inherited reality by decades of war, poverty, and social dislocation, totalitarian leaders jumped over the intermediate desire to restore normality and embarked on the journey to a new world. If there is, at the start, a hatred of the substance of reality for its pain and ugliness, there grows a "contempt" for anything that already is just because it *is*: It has not been made.[67] The only endurable world is a world that owes its being to the enacted fiction. Their model was the secret society, but they surpassed the model. It was no accident that the enacted fiction was murderous. The means were the end; methodical genocide was the *raison d'être* of totalitarianism. The fact that both Hitler and Stalin acted in ways that were conventionally antiutilitarian in peace and war is proof of their enslavement to their fiction. Hitler made war so that he could perfect totalitarian control;[68] he "believed that he would need a war as a smoke-screen for his non-military killing operations."[69] He wanted to commit genocide so that his ideology would be actualized.

But the question persists: Why was the fiction *murderous*? Why did Hitler and his associates want to commit genocide? Arendt is saying that there can be no answer that goes beyond the considerations already adduced. This great psychologist cannot give an answer: not because there are depths psychology cannot reach, but because there are no depths. The answer cannot be psychological, or at least it cannot be psychologically subtle or ingenious. The mystery of evil is that there is no mystery. "Only the good has depth and can be radical."[70]

But can we dispense altogether with psychological exploration? Just as Eichmann's blankness cannot be explained entirely unpersonally, unpsychologically, so Hitler's relentlessness cannot be. Hitler is no mere criminal or "clown" as Arendt in her Brechtian moments says.[71] With the help of Horkheimer and Adorno we can say something she hints at but does not develop.[72] The point is that only a moral or pseudomoral passion makes it possible for a modern European group to embrace and then enact a murderous fantasy—a genocidal fantasy. It is of the essence that Hitler was a racist fanatic. There are limits to the explanatory efficacy of such considerations as the gap between motive and the scale of activity, or the power of abstractness, or the role of clownish criminality. Belief was his animating energy. Arendt does suggest that "scientificality," the pseudoscientific nature of racist ideology, facilitated the deeds of Hitler in an age worshipful of science.[73] But the pseudomoral was and is more potent than the pseudoscientific.

The deepest cause of the Nazi destruction of Jews (and Gypsies) was the conviction that the people put to death were being punished for the worst possible *sin*, not crime. The worst possible sin, Protestantism seems to have taught Europe (and social Darwinism and Marxist materialism echoed it) was not behavioral but ontological, with the sinners deserving damnation all the more because they were not responsible. They could not be responsible, after all, for who they were. The Jews (and Gypsies) were punished for being unclean and hence as unfit to live, as unfit to "share the earth."[74] Nazism was the enactment of a myth (in the Sorelian sense of myth)—a myth of punishment—the most punitive, perhaps, of all myths. The myth is also sufficiently broad to accommodate a wide range of terrifying urges to work revenge on life by destroying anything vulnerably distinctive, as well as able to absorb the loyalty of every sort of banal, conformist, or shallow human type. (Nazi crimes against Slavic peoples, although on a greater scale, need a different and considerably more conventional conceptualization.)

By this account, totalitarianism is an exorcism. But, as always, exorcism is self-exorcism: To kill the Jew in oneself, one must kill all Jews. Of course to say this, however, is only to be led more deeply into perplexity. What is this Jew that must be exorcised? And by extension, what groups might one day be assigned the role of victim in a new ideology, a new myth of punishment? Most of the human race? The best counsel is to remain in perplexity. Such counsel is found in a remark Arendt makes, even though she seems with time to have thought she could dispense with its good sense:

> There is a mystery about the Nazi regime, but it has nothing to do with secrets. It resides solely in a response, humanly unavoidable, that makes us go on asking, "Why—but why?" long after all the facts are reported, all stages of the process known, all conceivable motives considered.[75]

Without Arendt's insistence on the distinctiveness of totalitarianism, we could not begin to take the phenomenon with the gravity it demands. The problems within her concepts and methods count for little in comparison to her achievement.

Notes

1. Hannah Arendt, "The Image of Hell," review of *The Black Book: The Nazi Crime Against the Jewish People, Commentary* 2 (September 1946), 291-95.

2. Arendt, "A Reply," *Review of Politics* 15 (January 1953), 76-84 The reply is to Eric Voegelin's review of *The Origins of Totalitarianism*, published in the same issue together with Voegelin's "Concluding Remark."

3. Arendt, *The Origins of Totalitarianism* (rev. ed., Cleveland: Meridian, 1958), 441. Hereafter cited as OT.

4. Arendt, "On Humanity in Dark Times: Thoughts about Lessing" in *Men In Dark Times* (New York: Harcourt, Brace & World, 1968), 17.

5. Arendt, "A Reply," 79.

6. Arendt, *Eichmann in Jerusalem* (2nd ed., New York: Viking, 1964), 49. Hereafter cited as *Eichmann*. See also "The Concept of History: Ancient and Modern," 51; and "The Crisis in Culture: Its Social and Its Political Significance," 220, both in Arendt, *Between Past and Future* (2nd ed., New York:Viking, 1968).

7. OT, viii–ix.

8. Arendt, Introduction to Bernd Naumann, *Auschwitz*, trans. Jean Steinberg (New York: Praeger, 1966), xxvii. See also "Civil Disobedience" in Arendt, *Crises of the Republic* (New York: Harcourt Brace Jovanovich, 1972), 70-71.

9. Arendt, "A Reply," 78.

10. See the excellent discussion of the structural difficulties of, and intended but unwritten additions to, OT in Elisabeth Young-Bruehl, *Hannah Arendt: For Love of the World* (New Haven: Yale, 1982), 211, 276 ff. Hereafter cited as Young-Bruehl.

11. OT, 505.

12. Percy Lubbock, ed., *The Letters of Henry James* (2 vols., London: Macmillan, 1920), 2: 398.

13. OT, 4-5.

14. Ibid., 4.

15. Ibid., 87-88.

16. Arendt, *The Jew as Pariah*, Ron H. Feldman, ed. (New York: Grove, 1978), 68. This is a posthumous collection. Hereafter cited as *Pariah*.

17. Ibid., 69.

18. OT, 160.

19. Ibid., 185.

20. Ibid., 192.

21. Ibid., 326.

22. Ibid., 331.

23. Ibid., 334.

24. Ibid., 335.

25. Ibid., 335–36.

26. Ibid., 336.

27. Ibid., 155.

28. Ibid.

29. Ibid., 189.

30. Ibid., 311.

31. Ibid., 478.

32. Ibid., 306.

33. Ibid., 475.

34. Ibid., 318.

35. Ibid., 315.

36. Ibid., 316.

37. Introduction to *Auschwitz*, xi.

38. *Pariah*, 232.

39. Introduction to *Auschwitz*, xi.

40. *Pariah*, 234.

41. Arendt extends it to many others in "Personal Responsibility Under Dictatorship," *The Listener* 72 (August 6, 1964), 185-87, 205.

42. On this theme, see the valuable collection of essays, Nevitt Sanford and Craig Comstock, eds., *Sanctions for Evil* (Boston: Beacon, 1972).

43. Immanuel Kant, *Religion Within the Limits of Reason Alone*, trans. T. M. Greene and H. H. Hudson (New York: Harper Torchbooks, 1960), 32.

44. John Milton, *Paradise Lost*, IV, line 110.

45. For those of evil human nature, see Arendt's discussion in *The Life of the Mind* (2 vols., New York: Harcourt Brace Jovanovich, 1978), vol. 1, *Thinking*, 3-5.

46. *Eichmann*, 276.

47. Immanuel Kant, *The Metaphysical Elements of Justice*, trans. John Ladd (Indianapolis: Bobbs-Merrill, 1965), 102. There are bridges between totalitarianism and even a rationalist authoritarianism.

48. Arendt connects Eichmann's obedience to certain tendencies in Kant's thought in *Eichmann*, 135-37.

49. OT, 46.

50. "Personal Responsibility Under Dictatorship," 187. In this essay Arendt says that the word *genocide* does not capture the essence of totalitarianism because there have been mass killings in the past. Totalitarianism, she insists, is a special kind of mass killing: It takes place *legally*. Yet *genocide* is still the appropriate word for our discussion, provided we remember that Arendt is not saying that only Jews have been the victims of mass murder.

51. Max Weber, *The Protestant Ethic and the Spirit of Capitalism*, trans. Talcott Parsons (New York: Scribner's, 1958), 182.

52. In a preface to the third volume of the three-volume edition of *The Origins of Totalitarianism* (New York: Harcourt, Brace & World, 1968), vii-x, Arendt indicates that Maoism may possibly also be a totalitarian system, but she leaves the matter doubtful. Hereafter cited as Preface. Her remark picks up on what she says in the text itself, that "the lands of traditional Oriental despotism" are especially prone to totalitarianism because of their vast populations. (OT, 311.)

53. Occasionally, Arendt uses *totalitarianism* to mean total domination in itself, apart from legal, methodical genocide, and distinguishes it from tyranny, which spares private life from its control. See Preface, ix. I believe this is inconsistent. Let us say that *traditional* tyrannies control less of life because the people are left "underdeveloped" and hence unable to imagine resistance, while modernizing tyrannies try to control all of life because modernization enables resistance. Totalitarianism, at root, is neither kind of tyranny. Arendt usually refers to post-Stalinist Soviet rulers as tyrants or dictators.

54. See Robert C. Tucker, "The Dictator and Totalitarianism," *World Politics* 17 (1965), 555-83.

55. OT, 183; also *Eichmann*, 278.

56. OT, 338.

57. *Eichmann*, 287.

58. Ibid., 252. For earlier uses by other writers of comparable phrases, see Stephen J. Whitfield, *Into the Dark: Hannah Arendt and Totalitarianism* (Philadelphia: Temple University Press, 1980), 212-13. Especially noteworthy is Joseph Conrad's "Author's Note" (1920) in *Under Western Eyes* (1911) (New York: Anchor, 1963). He says about Nikita, "the perfect flower of the terroristic wilderness," that what "troubled me most in dealing with him was not his monstrosity but his banality." (lxi).

59. *Pariah*, 251.

60. Roger Errera, "Hannah Arendt: From an Interview," *The New York Review of Books*, October 26, 1978, 18. Hereafter cited as Errera. The shallowness of the evil-doer corresponds to the inability of the experience of horror to change the survivor's *personality*. "The reduction of man to a bundle of reactions separates him as radically as mental disease from everything within him that is personality or character. When, like Lazarus, he rises from the dead, he finds his personality or character unchanged, just as he had left it" (OT, 441). In mentioning this Lazarus effect, Arendt speaks of the disintegration of the "psyche, character, and individuality" of camp inmates and SS men, although her emphasis is on inmates. "The end result—is inanimate men, *i.e.*, men who can no longer be psychologically understood" (OT, 441). Here is a variation on the theme of the limits of psychology. In this case, as in the

anomalous passage on the inscrutability of those who do "absolute" evil (quoted above), the limits are imposed by the departure from humanity, not from anything that is analogous to shallowness. Yet Arendt does suggest that if one survives the worst that can happen—disintegration—it is as if the worst never happened: so "shallow" is the effect of incommensurably deep suffering that is scarcely describable.

61. Arendt offers a different account in an essay published after *Eichmann*. In "Personal Responsibility Under Dictatorship," she says that the killing was done by respectable people "who more often than not did not even believe the 'words of the Fuhrer,' which had the force of law." (205). She also speaks of "the extent to which the whole people, regardless of party affiliation and direct implication, believed in the new order of things for no other reason than that was the way things were" (205). Also, in a letter written to Mary McCarthy after *Eichmann*, Arendt says in Elisabeth Young-Bruehl's account that "Eichmann 'in the flesh' had taught her that she had overrated 'the impact of ideology on the individual.' She concluded that for Eichmann 'extermination *per se*]was(more important than anti-semitism or racism' " (367). With these formulations she seems not only to call into question the central role she gives ideology, in *The Origins of Totalitarianism*, in regard to the mentality of the masses and to the entire structure of the regime. She also leaves the murderous situation even more puzzling by trying to make it appear so matter-of-fact, so devoid of energy of any kind, so merely a matter of obedience for the sake of obedience. Compare the formulations of Herbert Marcuse when analyzing the system of advanced industrial society as a system of totalitarianism. He says of the prevailing discourse that "the new touch of the magic-ritual language rather is that people don't believe it, or don't care, and yet act accordingly." *One-Dimensional Man* (Boston: Beacon, 1964), 103.

62. Arendt, "Hermann Broch: 1886–1951" in *Men in Dark Times* (New York: Harcourt, Brace & World, 1968), 122-23.

63. OT, 383.

64. Ibid., 384.

65. Ibid., 385.

66. Compare Clausewitz: "The greatest generals speak of war in the plainest and briefest manner....so that the whole tremendous act of war is personalised into a kind of duel....This personification of the whole action of war, is so entirely and completely the right way of conducting war, that in no other but this broad way could anyone attain that freedom of mind which is indispensable if one is to dominate events and not be overpowered by them." Quoted in W. B. Gallie, *Philosophers of Peace and War* (Cambridge: Cambridge University Press, 1978), 45.

67. Preface, xiv; Errera, 18.

68. Preface, vii.

69. "Personal Responsibility Under Dictatorship," 205.

70. *Pariah*, 251.

71. Errera, 18. See also Arendt, "Bertolt Brecht: 1898–1956" in *Men in Dark Times*, 247. She refers to Brecht's play *The Resistible Rise of Arturo Ui* and his notes to the play. The texts can be found in Bertolt Brecht, *Collected Plays* (New York: Vintage, 1976), vol. 6.

72. OT, 465. See Max Horkheimer and Theodor W. Adorno, *Dialectic of Enlightenment*, trans. John Cumming (New York: Seabury, n.d.), 168-208, 236-37, 245-56.

73. "The Image of Hell," 294-95.

74. *Eichmann*, 274.

75. Arendt, "The History of the Great Crime," review of Leon Poliakov, *Breviaire de la Haine: Le IIIe Reich et les Juifs*, *Commentary* 13 (March 1952), 300-304.

Chapter Three

Politics and Absolute Morality

Arendt's exploration of the evil of totalitarianism does not lead her to look for refuge in a public realm where the moral opposites of totalitarianism would reign. To the contrary, she is eager to conceptualize a realm that either is not charged with moral purposes (politics as imagined in the light of the polis) or is made moral only from an indissociable connection to a political artifice, a constitution (modern politics). Her writing continually disparages the transfer of moral preoccupations to political life. She adopts a severe attitude toward absolute as distinguished from ordinary morality, especially activist absolute morality; and she finds only minimal uses for abstentionist absolute morality. This chapter will elaborate on the view suggested in Chapter 1: that Arendt's challenge to absolute morality in behalf of the prestige and freedom of political action, whether Greek or modern, is seriously questionable. Her treatment of it may overlook important considerations. When they are recognized, perhaps absolute morality can have a larger political role than she allows.

Arendt is determined to impeach absolute morality, to take away the aura it may have for her readers, in an effort analogous to and connected with her impeachment of philosophy in *The Life of the Mind* (see the Appendix). She does not try to debunk the concept of absolute morality:to show, for instance, that those who try to practice it are always self-deluded or hypocritical. But she does try to analyze it in such a way as to compromise it. This does not mean that Arendt's analysis is anything but complex. In truth, it has the complexity that comes from the mastery of almost contradictory impulses. The net impression of this, which her whole work gives, including *The Life of the Mind* is not entirely sharp. At the risk of making it sharper than it really is, I would suggest that her main emphasis is to ease acceptance of political action in the face of that resistance to it which comes from some deep or even merely residual attachment to the spirit of absolute morality. (Such resistance is not of course the only sort that Arendt tries to overcome or erode.)

Rejection of the Lesser Evil

Arendt introduces a number of arguments to explain her insistence on the antagonism between absolute morality and the practice of politics. What is curious is that she is not interested in making the standard point that the realm of politics can only be the realm of the lesser evil, and that therefore office-holders and citizens can never aspire to purity, but must be prepared to use any means, to do any kind or amount of evil, provided it is needed to avoid or remedy a greater evil. This sort of calculation, presumably allowed by ordinary morality, is foreign to her for two main reasons.

First, true political action is intrinsically valuable. It is exhilarating and fulfilling; it is the sole or main opportunity for the display or acquisition of certain immensely valuable human characteristics; it helps to differentiate humanity from the other animals; it alone leads, if indeliberately, to mutual understanding and acknowledgment on the part of the group of peers who engage in it; and it prepares the way for individuals to grow reconciled to their existence. Given this conception of political action, the idea of the lesser evil seems to miss the point, to make politics falsely tragic.

Second, even where politics—or what passes for politics—is not practiced according to her ideal, Arendt's objection remains. She finds that doing the lesser evil is never what its practitioners claim it is. It may seem paradoxical that she both reserves little place for absolute morality in political life and condemns the usual conceptual alternative, the lesser evil, as the proper political form of ordinary morality. I do not know how to ease the paradox, except to say that she wants her grounds to be that ordinary morality itself is not compatible with doing the lesser evil, even in political life. Specifically, neither her selective version of ordinary morality nor her notion of constitutional justice (both discussed in Chapter 1) is meant to be compatible with doing the lesser evil.

How does Arendt arrive at this conclusion? The core of her position is that "those who choose the lesser evil forget quickly that they chose evil."[1] Her sense is that no moral idea is more amenable to abuse than the lesser evil. She is willing to allow—more by implication than by assertion—that self-defense is an excuse for "the crime" an individual may commit when in peril. She seems reluctant, however, to see the right of self-defense unproblematically extended from the individual's physical being to the state's allegedly analogous being.[2] In any case, her position seems to allow doing the lesser evil for the purpose of self-defense. To that degree, Arendt allows what ordinary morality allows. The lesser evil is the necessary evil, but only under the strictest definition of necessity; and it remains evil, a "crime," even when necessary.

Arendt knows how conveniently plastic *necessity* is. To be at ease with the idea that one must sometimes do evil guarantees that one will do it when unnecessary. She goes so far as to say that the result will be that "good men do the worst."[3] We faithfully draw out her view when we say that it is wrong to entrust any government with the warrant to do anything it pleases to any individual or group provided the ultimate result can plausibly be described as benefit to the greater number. The whole utilitarian enterprise of calculating harms and benefits is alien to her. That is to say, when the idea of the lesser evil passes into the related idea that one may do evil for the sake of a positive good, all restraint is lost.

Arendt explicitly repudiates the doctrine that the end justifies the means—specifically, that any conceivable political end could justify unrestricted means.[4] Nevertheless, when she discusses founding a political society rather than governing one, she seems to allow that good can, indeed must, come from evil. She gives a matter-of-fact restatement of the "universally applicable tales" of Cain and Abel and Romulus and Remus: "Whatever brotherhood human beings may be capable of has grown out of fractricide, whatever political organization men may have achieved has its origin in crime."[5] Her dread must be that utilitarianism will be made into a habit or the code of daily political conduct. To be sure, she does not elaborate a theory of basic rights as antiutilitarian restrictions on policy. She does not say that a society's constitutional commitment to individual rights is one political form of absolute or near-absolute morality—as in fact it is. Still the tendency of her thinking is in this direction.

But Arendt's main concern is not doing evil for the sake of good, but the way in which Nazi totalitarianism exploited the idea of the lesser evil. First, it created a situation in which those who took part in the policy of methodical genocide could charge those who refused to take part with irresponsibility. "We who appear guilty today are in fact those who stayed on the job in order to prevent worse things from happening."[6] The initial readiness to do the lesser evil "responsibly" provides the energy by which the quantity of supposedly necessary evil is constantly increased. The "extermination of Jews was preceded by a gradual sequence of anti-Jewish measures, each of which was accepted because refusal to co-operate would make things worse—until a stage was reached where nothing worse could happen."[7] Yet the hold of the idea of the lesser evil had become unbreakable.

Arendt also suggests that when the amount of evil is so large as to be "monstrous," the very idea of the lesser evil turns into a lunatic parody of itself. If the idea has any plausibility at all, it can cover evil only on a small scale, just as evil in the particular form of violence is allowable only for a limited purpose.[8] Even so, she spurns the calculation that with "100 victims we shall save a 1,000."[9]

Arendt's cautionary remarks about the idea of the lesser evil are valuable. However, she is too restrictive. Ordinary morality allows a fuller application of the idea than she does. Certainly in the version in which some evil is done to avoid a "clear and present" greater evil, the idea seems indispensable. Obviously the meaning of *evil* is not always clear; but if it includes harming aggressors and wrongdoers, those who threaten or destroy not only life but other rights, then the resemblance of Arendt's position to absolute morality is unexpected and undeniable. As for harming the innocent in order to spare a larger number of innocent, perhaps the only justification is a pseudojustification. From the point of view of an office-holder (or anyone else who must act), calculations must be made. They must not pertain to the sacrifice of rights in daily policy-making: Rights are not to be abridged for the sake of benefit. But when policy does not abridge rights yet still significantly affects interests, then the calculations of the lesser evil are allowable; indeed, exchange of harms and benefits (of "pains" and "pleasures") may be allowable up to a certain point not readily specifiable.

At the other extreme, when a decision is needed in circumstances of extraordinary emergency or distress, the office-holder may well be right in believing that with "100 victims we shall save a 1,000." Nevertheless, in such circumstances there is another perspective than that of the office-holder (or decider). That is the perspective of the innocent victims, for each of whom his life and rights are infinite in value and cannot be entered as a finite sum into a calculation. The great Hobbesian teaching that a criminal is not morally obliged to cooperate with his punishers, and he may even be morally obliged to impede, resist, or escape them, is surely transferable to the seemingly less problematic relationship between an innocent person and his government. There is no way to tell a victim that he is wrong. Unless he gives way, he will be overpowered. But neither is the office-holder wrong. He stands for more than superior strength. The perspectives are mutually exclusive, but they are both right. If that is the case, there is only a pseudojustification for what the office-holder does; but he must do it.

Obviously, the possible existence of a duty to risk death or great loss for others (say, as a soldier) further complicates the issue. But Hobbes's vacillation on the rightness of conscription is exemplary.

It would seem that at crucial moments Arendt fails to make the case that ordinary morality almost completely excludes the idea of the lesser evil. Her scruples sometimes resemble those of an adherent to absolute morality. Better that greater evil happen than that a lesser be deliberately done. Such a sentiment may suit the individual's response to totalitarianism, but elsewhere it may come too close to a self-protecting purity of the very kind that Arendt impeaches. Yet though she fights the lesser evil, and seems to have absolutist moments, she also fights absolute morality. That is the surprise. There are unresolved tensions in her thought about politics and morality. Sometimes, there even seems to be an impossible combination of absolutism and amoralism. The fact remains, however, that her main target is absolute morality. And what *drives* her to challenge it is not really any contrasting conception of political morality, but her whole philosophical commitment to wordliness.

Arendt's great ambition is to persuade us that the source of the wish to act in accordance with absolute morality is almost always one or another kind of self-interest. In order to delineate her strategy, one must answer two questions. First, what does Arendt mean by absolute morality? Second, what is the relation to self-interest?

The Two Kinds of Absolute Morality

It is too abbreviated to say merely that absolute morality is purist about means and methods used and actions done to realize an end or purpose, in contrast to ordinary morality, which does not rule out any means *a priori*. Without using the phrase, Arendt distinguishes between two kinds of absolute morality. The first is Socratic and is summarized in the formulation from the *Gorgias*, which Arendt regularly cites: "It is better to suffer wrong than to do wrong."[10] The second is Christian, and teaches that one should treat everybody, including one's enemies, with love.

By Arendt's account, Socratic absolutism is the morality of conscience:

> the rules of conscience...are...entirely negative. They do not say what to do; they say what not to do. They do not spell out certain principles for taking action; they lay down boundaries no act should transgress. They say: Don't do wrong.[11]

She discusses Christian absolutism, on the other hand, as "active goodness," an "active love of goodness," as "living...for others."[12] The great example of such goodness is Jesus, who is also the great philosopher and teacher of it. He taught what he lived; and what he lived manifested both a willingness to suffer wrong rather than do or return it, and a positive power to perform good works without regard to his own good or even self-preservation.

Nowhere, however, does Arendt say that Jesus is a fuller Socrates. Despite apparent aspects of commonality between them, the very idea of what comprises "wrong" or "harm" or "evil" is not the same—or at least not the same in every significant feature. Joining Socrates and Jesus is a refusal by each to do what ordinary morality allows: to suspend moral limits on acting, on the employment of certain means, when his self-preservation is at stake. But their reasons for such scruples are different, and so is the range. After all, Socrates served as a soldier. Although he never harmed the innocent, in some sense he "harmed" the enemy, even if not for the sake of his own individual preservation. We cannot imagine Jesus using the sword, even for an impersonal end. So, even on the negative elements of absolute morality they differ. What positive element can we attribute to Socrates? Perhaps none. For Arendt he is characteristically a negative figure, a no-sayer, an inhibitor. If a lover, he is a lover of wisdom rather than, as Jesus is, a lover of humanity.

What matters for Arendt is that the two men, if imitated, if taken with the utmost seriousness, make political action as free initiative impossible. Absolute morality in both its forms is in a condition of unrelieved enmity with the world, with the will to worldly action, not merely, not primarily with the encouragements and permissions that a less restrictive ordinary morality bestows on humanity for the sake of preparing our release into the glorious exertions of politics. Our primary concern is with Arendt's critique of Socratic absolutism, the morality of conscience. Her treatment of Christian absolutism, the morality of goodness, appears earlier in Arendt's work than her discussion of conscience, and it may be seen as a prefigurement of it.

Christian Absolute Morality and its Vicissitudes

Arendt has a startling reverence for the figure of Jesus. Her reflections on the quality of his goodness in *The Human Condition* are among her most searching explorations in moral psychology. Yet for all the tribute she pays Jesus in the form of a penetrating attention to his words and their meaning, she is moving in a direction that is not his, that would be opposite to his, if the Devil had not already taken possession of the opposite. Her work is in the service of the world, especially in the specific political sense of the world as the realm of public speech, but also in the broader sense of the world as a culture, as the setting for the public realm. The goodness of Jesus destroys the world; the morality of love destroys the world.

There are a number of ways in which Christian absolute morality may be set in contradistinction to the world, especially the world understood as the public realm. Arendt's way is quite her own. In order to show the incompatibility of Jesus' goodness with worldliness, she dwells on a particular characteristic of deeds done in the spirit of such goodness. That characteristic is the self-unawareness of the doer while he is doing and after he has done the deed. The key formulation is, "Let not thy left hand know what thy right hand doeth."[13] She says:

> Goodness obviously harbors a tendency to hide from being seen or heard....For it is manifest that the moment a good work becomes known and public, it loses its specific character of goodness, of being done for nothing but goodness' sake....Goodness can exist only when it is not perceived, not even by its authors; whoever sees himself performing a good work is no longer good, but at best a useful member of society or a dutiful member of a church.[14]

Thus the very spirit of goodness shuns the world of human appearances. It is at war with all display and with the essence of the wish to display, namely, the wish to do deeds that are memorable. To be at war with display is to be at war with political action, the supreme ostentation. Not to know that one is doing praiseworthy deeds is incompatible with the political will to act memorably—to act in the Greek sense especially, but not exclusively. One cannot be in love with goodness and have any remaining desire or energy for the worldly life of political action. No one can have the character type suitable for both goodness and politics. Respect for goodness is disrespect for the world.

One might think that such an interpretation of Christian absolutism is devious. What is Arendt doing? Is she trying to persuade those who still retain if only a faint allegiance to Christian absolutism—or some nontheistic equivalent—that it is impossible to be good? She quotes the words of Jesus, "Why callest thou me good? None is good, save one, that is, God."[15] Has she not shown the full meaning of these words by her depiction of the dependence of goodness on unawareness, on unintentionality, almost on unconsciousness? Is she not urging, consequently, that those who want to be good but know they cannot be so on these terms stop trying and instead commit themselves to the world? It seems that way.

However, there is almost nothing as bad as the refusal to see that goodness and political action exclude each other and, instead, making the effort to combine them. Arendt reads Machiavelli as saying that "goodness that comes out of hiding and assumes a public role is no longer good, but corrupt in its own terms and will carry its own corruption wherever it goes."[16] With that contention she is in complete sympathy. The burden of her writing on the Reign of Terror in France during the Revolution is that the source of terror is the determination to act in public out of what seems one or another form of love of humanity, out of either compassion or pity. There is no doubt that she is free of reactionary contempt for Robespierre and Saint-Just. She sees them as still in thrall to Christian absolutism, rather than as bloodthirsty madmen. But she is unrelenting in condemning them for the hideous self-betrayal and betrayal of political life that they accomplished out of misplaced feelings and sentiments.

Arendt's strategy is to show that self-interest is almost always the source of the wish to act in accordance with absolute morality. The one time it is not is when a person wishes to be good in imitation of Jesus. This is certainly not to be self-interested, provided one stays outside the political realm. If one knows what Jesus knew, he will never make a system out of his action. He will not think that goodness can ever be an attribute of a structure, of formal and continuously existent relationships. Rather, goodness comes and goes invisibly; it is episodic, irregular, miraculous, and altogether inappropriate for a citizen as citizen or an office-holder as office-holder. Goodness is only for everyday life, for relations where fixed roles do not prevail. It is for life that is hidden or, if not totally hidden, is so at least in comparison with political action, which by its very nature is manifest and is done to be known and recalled. Arendt says:

> Yet what love is in its own, narrowly circumscribed sphere, respect is in the larger domain of human affairs. Respect, not unlike the Aristotelian *philia politike*, is a kind of "friendship" without intimacy and without closeness; it is a regard for this person from the distance which the space of the world puts between us, and this regard is independent of qualities which we may admire or of achievements which we may highly esteem.[17]

(We call such respect, when it is publicly institutionalized, by the name of justice.) So long as these things are remembered and these distinctions preserved, there will be no taint of self-interest in goodness and no mortal danger from its practice.

But goodness may helplessly create catastrophe. Her emblematic figure is not Jesus himself, but Melville's Billy Budd, whose story Arendt reads as a parable on "What tragic and self-defeating enterprise the men of the French Revolution had embarked almost without knowing it." The message of the parable is that "absolute goodness is hardly any less dangerous than absolute evil."[18] Its danger derives from its nonhuman innocence—a quality that Arendt does not attribute to Jesus. Provoked by Claggart, who is evil incarnate, Billy becomes murderously violent. Such goodness is perforce speechless, unpolitical, unmoderated. It can go from angelic serenity to the destructiveness of a natural force, as if all human relations were beyond it, or it was beyond them. Society cannot contain it. Human relations, most especially political relations, reside in the middle; between goodness and evil; they are intermediate. Their essence is to mediate; their medium is speech and the formalities and distances it makes possible. If Melville's story is a pondering of the mysteries of the French Revolution by the creation of a figure larger than life almost a century later, the record itself of that Revolution is seen by Arendt as eloquent vindication of the contention that a politicized love of humanity sponsors appalling ruin in political life.

Confronted with the spectacle of terror, not only in France but in Leninist Russia and elsewhere—although in this context emphatically *not* the terror of Hitler and Stalin—Arendt probes for the explanation. She finds it in the deformation of superior moral sensitivity. At times, she seems to be saying that there was something suspect in the initial sensitivity; but preponderantly she seems to be saying that the revolutionaries were overcome by their sensitivity, or their sensitivity was overcome by the strains put on it. Her analysis constitutes a coherent psychological story in which passions and sentiments work themselves out with a grotesque autonomy, as they sometimes do in Hegel's *Phenomenology of Mind.*

The revolutionaries in France (and later, Russia) were good men. Arendt does not say of course that they were Christ-like. "Compassion and goodness may be related phenomena, but they are not the same."[19] She stresses, however, their superior and unusual moral sensitivity. Apart from their temperamental dispositions, they were prepared for their fate by their susceptibility to Rousseau's instruction. She finds in him the philosophical source of one of the main kinds of wrong interest in the self: an obsessive attention to shifts and changes of mood and to the registry of experiences on the inner observer. She hates the pleasure taken in self-inspection, and derides the activity when she is not denying its reality and equating it with self-mystification. It is as if, for Rousseau, the world existed only so that one may have the raw material for the processes of the inner life. The most interesting inner life is one of conflict. Rousseau made it attractive to have a torn soul, a soul that (by Arendt's interpretation) the observing self divides into a part that aspires to goodness and a part that craves vicious gratification. Each person is torn between the general will and the particular will. The torn soul is in conflict, not in the dialogue of two-in-one. The conflict "engenders passion in its twofold sense of intense suffering and intense passionateness."[20]

The outcome of the conflict should be a condition of selflessness, which Arendt defines as the ability of those who are not miserable to feel for those who are. This is not the active goodness that Jesus exemplified, but it is akin to it in a distorted way. There is distortion because all the while one is glad that one has an internal fight to wage, and therefore glad that the world presents abundant suffering so that one's internal fight can take the fascinating form of overcoming strong tendencies to selfish indifference or to selfish enjoyment of privilege. Certainly Rousseau demonstrates this pattern in its fullness, even though the later revolutionaries under his spell may depart significantly from it while nevertheless showing aspects of it. A reduction of Arendt's thesis on Rousseau is that he was a man who loved the suffering that the suffering of others aroused in him. From such a psychic configuration only corruption can ensue.

Arendt's specific analysis of Robespierre and Saint-Just blends into her words on Rousseau and into that intense meditation on *Billy Budd.* She also introduces some thoughts on the Legend of the Grand Inquisitor. (These two literary works she perceives as the deepest reflections on the French Revolution just because they are reflections on Jesus.) The sense that persists throughout these feverish and tormenting pages of *On Revolution* is that the sensitive person who lets his sensitivity lead him into the life of political action will, when exposed to mass misery—as he was in France and Russia—change convulsively. His sensitivity crystallizes into compassion, which then changes into pity. Pity will show a capacity for cruelty greater than cruelty itself. It will turn cruelty into a *system* of cruelty, that is, a reign of terror.

The distinction between compassion and pity is not lucidly maintained throughout Arendt's presentation. But basically, compassion is fellow-feeling, the suffering one endures at the sight of the suffering of the person present before him. Pity is a generalized or abstract sentiment: It is "to be sorry without being touched in the flesh."[21] Arendt suggests that pity and compassion may not be related at all; but more typically, she sees pity as the perversion of compassion. Compassion can approach pity when the imagination of the revolutionary converts the suffering masses into one immense suffering individual. Both responses are destructive of human artifice and human limits, the spiritual essence of political action. The responses combined, in fact, to destroy the fragile but beautiful beginnings of direct communal democracy in the early days of the French Revolution, one of the rare genuine moments of political action at its ideal best in human history. The nub of the matter is that now stricken by the misery of the Parisian masses the sensitive souls, overwhelmed by compassion or its degraded relative pity, used violence on all those who stood in the way of their effort to ameliorate that misery. Clearly they abandoned their kinship to goodness by abandoning its core: self-sacrifice. Instead, their moral sensitivity licensed unprecedented ruthlessness. Of Robespierre, Arendt says, in words that carry much of the burden of her thought on the paradoxical relations between political action and superior morality sensitivity:

> Even if Robespierre had been motivated by the passion of compassion, his compassion would have become pity when he brought it out into the open where he could no longer direct it toward specific suffering and focus it on particular persons. What had perhaps been genuine passion turned into the boundlessness of an emotion that seemed to respond only too well to the boundless suffering of the multitude in their sheer overwhelming numbers. By the same token, he lost the capacity to establish and hold fast to rapports with persons in their singularity; the ocean of suffering around him and the turbulent sea of emotion within him...drowned all specific considerations, the considerations of friendship no less than considerations of statecraft and principle.[22]

Arendt insists that the alternative to pity, its political equivalent, is *solidarity*, just as the political equivalent of love is respect. Acting out of solidarity with the oppressed and the exploited, the truly political individuals would "establish deliberately and, as it were, dispassionately a community of interest" with them.[23] The sense of suffering cannot guide solidary efforts; only something like an extended sense of human honor or dignity can.

Pity is the real adversary in Arendt's theory. Its effects are ruinous of the possibility of genuine political action, and it always fails when it employs political coercion to ameliorate misery. She is adamant in the claim that poverty has only strictly economic and administrative solutions, never political ones. Furthermore, beyond the ruin and the failure, Arendt finds in the sense of suffering, in compassion and pity, the trigger for further extremisms of response, including the implacable urge to unmask the hypocrisy (real or imputed or imagined) of all those whose position in life automatically makes them suspect. They must be hiding something, some hostility to the Revolution, some resistance to the needs of the people, some incapacity really to feel the sufferings of others as though their own, some silent treason of the heart. The burning desire to unmask may itself hide the very vices to be unmasked in others. Whom can the revolutionary trust to be sincere when his inveterate self-examination causes him to suspect himself? As shown in Chapter 1, Arendt holds that the insistence on disclosing the real self in the political realm is contradictory to the public nature of that realm. Nothing that is innermost in the heart can survive the transition to public disclosure without ineluctably undergoing an unintended transformation of some kind, whether a stylization, a falsification, or an inarticulate display that is either unrecognizable or destructive of further political relations. The heart is a dark place, Arendt says more than once, and light cannot be thrown on it. What appears—the words and deeds of political actors—is necessarily impersonal, even though it is revelatory of something distinctive about each of the actors, just as a writer's style is no outpouring of his heart but is nevertheless indicative of something distinctive about him.

Pity at the end of its journey is rage, "the mode in which impotence becomes active in its last stage of final despair."[24] Arendt's verdict is absolute: "Every effort to make goodness manifest in public ends with the appearance of crime and criminality on the political scene."[25] She places us in the enclosure of Pascal's words: He who would act the angel acts the beast.

In Arendt's moral psychology, then, compassion and pity are the fertile source of political crime and terror. A superior moral sensitivity predisposes toward compassion, if not toward pity. The impulse to project one's compassion as one's best and truest self onto the political world is indissolubly connected to a terrific self-absorption, a perhaps narcissistic interest in one's inner condition. The most consuming interest of the compassionate soul is that there be enough suffering in the world to keep itself torn and hence continuously fascinating to itself as an internal spectacle.

Obviously a long and patient answer is needed to Arendt's indictment. The most insidious element in it is that compassion and pity express self-interest. They seek out what they need to thrive and are happy when they find it. That is, they crave and devour the suffering of others. How does one respond? One can certainly acknowledge the general point; namely, that there is likely to be impurity in any deep human emotion or sentiment and ambiguity in any strong one. This acknowledgment also cuts the other way: Every ostensibly unlovely or hateful emotion or sentiment has something forgivable in it, if you just look long or probingly enough. But are compassion and pity simply disguised forms of self-interest, of that morbid self-fascination that Arendt excoriates? Is that all or most of what there is to them? Not continuously, but for the most part, Arendt says yes. To answer yes, however, is either unsubtle (and that, Arendt never is) or too ingenious (and that, Arendt sometimes is). She is too ingenious in her pursuit of the true, perfect essence of politics.

Encountering what she takes to be emotions and sentiments that weaken or cripple the will to be and shine as a political actor, and, at the same time, to observe and applaud the performances of others, Arendt will try to discredit them. The direct way to discredit them is to say they lead to failure as judged by the intentions of those who act from them. The indirect way, the insidious and more powerful way, is to demonstrate that these emotions and sentiments are not really what they seem. She revaluates them, with Nietzsche as the formal model, although not as the substantive, doctrinal model. In the process, she loses some plausibility because she makes too much of the role of compassion and pity in explaining revolutionary tragedy and too little of the role of undistorted selflessness in explaining compassion and pity.

Second, the greatest amount of cruelty that has been done politically throughout human history has been done out a range of motives that does not include compassion and pity. Rather, the range includes such commonplace inducements to action as vanity, pride, arrogance, fear, greed, fanaticism, duty, adventurism, loyalty, restlessness, lack of imagination, paranoia, virtuosity, and unreasoning cruelty. Those who died in the two world wars and in the labor camps and extermination camps of this century were not killed by compassion and pity that had turned political or by misplaced love of humanity. This number of dead far exceeds the number killed during and right after leftist revolutions—even if the attribution of irrepressible compassion and pity to the revolutionaries is correct to some important degree. That perhaps the most searching and original theorist of political horror in the twentieth century could, as if in self-forgetfulness, accuse compassion and pity as the sponsors of more cruelty than cruelty itself is bizarre, aberrant. Words that are less strong will not do.

Even after we absorb Arendt's concept of the banality of evil and see, if we do, that thoughtlessness rather than an intoxicated sadism was principally behind the day-to-day administration of totalitarian terror, we still do not find that either compassion or pity played any part. She herself says at one point in *Eichmann in Jerusalem* that the problem for those who ran the extermination camps was "how to overcome not so much their conscience as the animal pity by which all normal men are affected in the presence of physical suffering."[26] That fleeting comment is not enough to deter one from finding an inexplicable excess in Arendt's basic presentation. That revolutionaries may have, time after time, chosen to sacrifice the incipient expressions of direct participatory democracy—the reassertion or transmutation of the spirit of the polis in a modern framework—to the hopeless struggle against material misery does not make them history's worst criminals. They are history's worst criminals if we think that the only value that counts is freedom as political action, and that its destruction is the worst crime. But its destruction is not the worst crime, nor does Arendt ever say that it is. The slaughter of innocents is; or perhaps the slaughter of the guilty, or any slaughter, is the worst crime. You do not speak out of compassion or pity when you say that, but out of feelings more common.

The third point is that although Arendt has much to teach on the bad tendencies of raw passions (including compassion) or self-induced emotions (including pity) in political life, the moral energy that these passions and emotions provide political actors seems indispensable. Without them, any ameliorative movement in human affairs could barely get started. The pressure often begins with the tenderness of the few: Arendt is clear on that point. If later there are more massive pressures, they are instigated and set in motion by that sense of suffering—care for the suffering of others—which Arendt reproaches. Terror and rage may follow, and when they do, the effects are enormous and dramatic. But there is also the long-term and quietly maintained labor to better the human lot. There is no strictly economic and administrative solution, despite what Arendt says. It must be undergirded by political will, which in turn is formed and sustained by many things, and surely one of them is the sense of suffering. I do not know with what warrant she says that, "As a rule, it is not compassion which sets out to change worldly conditions in order to ease human suffering."[27] The hope is to find ways of disciplining that sense, of making it suitable for public appearance, without diminishing its efficacy. Also, solidarity is not the political equivalent of the sense of suffering. The corruptions of solidarity are great. No doubt, following Arendt, a positive appeal to human honor or dignity is worthier than a naked materialist humanitarianism that would settle too easily for bodily ease and security while letting everything else go, including participatory freedom. But cannot that point be made without impeaching the sense of suffering?

Next, when Arendt grants that something other than self-interest lies behind compassion and pity, she is expecially incisive on the harm that the men and women of compassion and pity *do themselves* when they enter the political realm as violent revolutionaries and radical reformers. In circumstances of great risk, uncertainty, and resistance, the best, most noble traits may wither or change into the worst, most base traits. Only lilies fester; weeds do not. Those who decline seem lower than those who were always low, so appalling is the discrepancy between the original and the latter state. But if the sensitive stay cloistered, what meaning could their moral sensitivity have? The ingredients of tragedy are present when the best natures undertake action under the most dangerous circumstances. Arendt includes the danger to the revolutionaries themselves: the psychological and moral danger. If only she had lamented it more and had not placed so much weight on the unconditionally unpolitical quality of their native disposition.

Last, we may grant that Christian absolutism, goodness in strict imitation of Jesus, is essentially nonpolitical, indeed antipolitical. But it is a miscalculation to sever it utterly from political life. One would insist, overriding Arendt's ambiguity, that Christian goodness is not only related to compassion, but is its ultimate source, historically and existentially. She seems to say as much when she remarks that the deepest thought about the French Revolution is thought about Jesus, the thought poetically luminous in Melville and Dostoyevsky. Christian absolutism changed the world without being realized in it. A distant ideal had the power to engender lesser ideals that could be realized, but though lesser, they were still profoundly different from those that preceded them. Somehow the tension must be kept alive: Christian absolutism is not of this world, but the world cannot do without it in some "demythologized," "revaluated," attenuated condition. It cannot do without the politicized love of humanity.

Let us now look at negative or Socratic absolutism and its politics of conscience.

Socratic Absolute Morality and its Vicissitudes

"Politics of conscience" is not an exact phrase and does not refer to a narrow range of activity. Nevertheless, common opinion includes within its scope such modes of political response as passive resistance, evasion, or noncompliance; "blowing the whistle"; principled resignation from office; conscientious objection; selective conscientious objection; selective secret lawbreaking; civil disobedience; disobedience of an order; massive nonviolent endeavors. Each of these phrases, in turn, does not lend itself to tidy or unambiguous use. Conscience is (or seems to be) the common element; but conscience, too, is various in its meaning. Yet for all the indefiniteness, we would probably agree that the solitary individual, or the succession of like-minded individuals, or the organized group, or the spontaneous group, or the movement, who or which engages in any of these modes is saying no, is refusing to go along with public authority or public officials on the basis of some overriding or especially compelling moral reason. (Perhaps some kinds of official lawbreaking could be seen as examples of the politics of conscience as well.) One could exclude all kinds of politics in which there is no restriction on the means. Violent revolution, guerrilla warfare, and protracted resistance are not suitably included in the politics of conscience, nor is "incremental" politics, since the end has no special moral urgency.

The politics of conscience may occur under all forms of government. Under repressive regimes it may be a heroic undertaking. Arendt admires such heroism without reservation. Her analysis makes problematic the role of conscience only when the resistance or refusal is selective (to use a word that appears in the names of some of the modes); that is, when it takes place in a context of acquiescence in or approval of the political system as a whole (ordinarily, a democratic constitution). Although Arendt is silent on the issue, part of the moral pain the conscientious may feel comes from the contrast between selective refusal and general acceptance, as the larger part comes, naturally, from the deeds of office-holders. Henry David Thoreau, who figures in Arendt's analysis as a model of selective conscientious resistance, is not easy to describe. He protested slavery when the Constitution allowed it. He was therefore not simply selective in his refusal: "Its [the state's] very Constitution is the evil."[28] He said that if a revolution over taxes was justifiable, all the more so was one to abolish slavery. If slaves were morally allowed to use violence to become free, the free could use violence to help them. But if violence was justified, obviously nonviol;ent resistance was, too. Hence his refusal to pay the head tax can be seen as an individual act of nonviolent revolution. Yet Thoreau had no ambition for a new constitution. He would have been satisfied with the Constitution once it had been amended to abolish slavery. Indeed, the spirit of the Constitution enabled his resistance to its radical deficiency. He is a mixed case, but we will take him as Arendt does—selective in his refusal.

Of particular concern is Arendt's thinking on one of the modes of the politics of conscience; civil disobedience in America. However, to study civil disobedience, in particular to study Arendt's thought on civil disobedience, including her confrontation with Thoreau and *his* essay on civil disobedience, is to involve oneself with almost all modes of the politics of conscience. That is so because she offers an overall political critique of conscience, at least within the framework of a nonrepressive form of government. It is highly profitable to follow her thought on this matter, even though one may finally reject it. Moreover, not only does she help to perplex and enrich our views on civil disobedience and on almost all modes of the politics of conscience, she leads us on to the overall theory of political legitimacy. In her profound unconventionality she disturbs some of the standard ways of thinking about conscience.

A preliminary point is that a strong connection exists between Socratic conscience and Christian goodness. The latter not only sponsors the revolutionary and reformist politics of compassion and pity but also has come to reinforce the Socratic sponsorship of the characteristically negative politics of conscience. This affinity to Socratic conscience is probably more true to the spirit of the Gospels than any political activism. There is thus a Christian conscience as well as a Socratic one.

Arendt deals only casually with Christian conscience. She tends to dismiss it as merely subjective, as if its invocation were always a private claim to have God's special inspiration. The Christian conscience, by this account, is anarchical because it always commands that we should obey God, not man; yet God is always at the mercy of individual definition.[29] Arendt does not do this matter justice; she slights both the reference to scriptural authority and the frequently universalist claims present in assertions of Christian conscience. But these shortcomings in her analysis need not concern us, except as a small sign of a larger ambition—to impeach the kind of conscience that she identifies with Socrates. Her work implies that in the modern age those who act out of conscience are, knowingly or not, acting in imitation of him.

Arendt presents an immediate obstacle to the usual way of considering civil disobedience by saying throughout her essay, simply called "Civil Disobedience" (which first appeared in *The New Yorker*, September 12, 1970, and later reprinted in *Crises of the Republic*), that it is not properly seen as one of the modes of the politics of conscience. This essay marked her abandonment of her earlier view that active civil disobedience is a mode of the politics of conscience. And it was a notable contribution to the discussion of what only a few years ago seemed so urgent an issue, and doubtless will seem so again. One could say that there was an efflorescence of writing on civil disobedience,[30] and a good deal of it was faithful enough to its requirements to remain permanently relevant to thinking about fundamental questions of political theory. The writing keeps its freshness.

In the midst of this efflorescence, in the midst actually of vehement contention, Arendt proceeded to defend civil disobedience. This fact should not be passed over too lightly. Indeed, there are probably fewer inhibitions in Arendt's essay than in many other works that were written to justify civil disobedience. In fact, her lack of equivocation is somewhat surprising. One did not think to connect her praise of the early moments of revolutionary spontaneity in *On Revolution* (published seven years before) to her praise of those who were now committing civil disobedience. One thought that Arendt owed student activists some acknowledgment. After all, they seemed to come closer to fulfilling her theoretical expectations concerning political action than anyone else did.[31] But of course not all student activism was civilly disobedient; thus to take satisfaction in activism need not have extended to celebrating civil disobedience. Yet that is what Arendt did. Only, she was emphatic in severing civil disobedience from conscience. So that if one could feel surprise at the very fact of her advocacy, one had also to feel surprise at her conception of civil disobedience. One can still feel surprise, or at least a strong initial disapproval, even though one can now see that there was something inevitable about her repudiation of conscience, especially as a continuous instigation to protracted activity. Such repudiation is the affirmation of politics. More narrowly, the affirmation of civil disobedience purged of the infiltration of conscience is the affirmation of politics. Her strategy is to show that Socrates and his American heir, Thoreau, are not to be seen as teachers of civil disobedience. As men of conscience, they are inactive until they feel compelled to be reactive. But civil disobedience is not mere reaction, but genuine action. Arendt also traces conscience to an unexpected root. She thus aims to place the prestige of conscience at some risk and to show its essential irrelevance to civil disobedience.

It is not for any deed of Socrates that Arendt makes him the great archetype of conscience. Her analysis does not have its center in Socrates' conscientious dissent as a councillor in the Athenian democracy; or his conscientious refusal to execute an order from the Thirty tyrants that would have resulted in the unjust death of an individual; or his hypothetical refusal to desist from philosophical conversation; or his conscientious acceptance of an unjust death sentence in preference to an illegal escape. Her interest in him is directed instead at the formula he enunciates in the *Gorgias*, "It is better to suffer wrong than to do wrong," or "It is better to be wronged than to do wrong." and to the reasons he gives to support it. All his conscientious acts she claims, are subsumable under the formula of the *Gorgias*: in these cases he risked, then accepted, wrongfully inflicted death rather than inflict harm or wrong or evil on either individuals or the laws.[32] One must notice, however, that Socrates claimed to be agnostic on whether to have to die was to be harmed, and he also said that a good man could not be harmed. To recollect these things is not of course to impugn his courage. What matters to Arendt is the naked proposition and the supporting reasons.

Just as Arendt works over compassion and pity so that they come to reflect a convoluted self-interest, so she traces Socratic absolutism to another kind of self-interest. She never tries to "revaluate" the love that Jesus had: She turns against only the derivatives, perversions, or semblances of such love. But she addresses herself reductively to the Socratic formula itself. And once again, when she criticizes it, she does not content herself with making the conventional objections against it. She certainly does not abstain from making them: She repeats the point that it is only against comparatively decent adversaries that anyone less heroic than Socrates would dare try to put some version or other of the Socratic formula into practice. But that point is only incidental. She also undertakes no direct and lengthy critique of the several theories that fill out and justify the formula. It is as if tracing it to its source was sufficient to analyze it and demystify it. Much of the energy behind Arendt's impeachment and demystification comes from the disinclination to act, the aversion to full-bodied citizenship, the turning away from the world, which a commitment to the Socratic formula signifies. She is battling a character type more than a doctrine.

To persuade young Americans that they misconceive themselves as civil disobedients when they claim they act at the behest of conscience, Arendt tries to show what conscience really is. She takes the chance that those who say they act at its behest may not initially recognize it or themselves in her analysis. Her claim is that we know what conscience is only if we go back to Socrates and if we see Thoreau, a hero to civil disobedients, as reenacting the Socratic pattern. How, then, does she expound the Socratic idea and connect it to self-interest?

The self-interest Arendt sees here is much less compromised than that which she sees as infecting compassion and pity. The key is found in a remark by Socrates in the *Gorgias*:

> It would be better for me that my lyre or a chorus I directed should be out of tune and loud with discord, and that multitudes of men should disagree with me rather than that I, *being one*, should be out of harmony with myself and contradict me.[33]

On this remark Arendt builds her exposition.[34] Because Socrates *thinks*, because he is constantly holding an internal dialogue, because that dialogue concerns among other things his own past conduct, he knows that if he were to do wrong to another he would suffer the merited pain of self-reproach. Such pain is what makes it impossible to live harmoniously with himself. Since he is double, he can be one only on the terms of absolute morality. Arendt's sense of Socrates could be translated into the proposition: It is better for me, because it is less painful, to suffer the wrong that others do me than the pain I inflict on myself when I wrong others.

In the two incidents reported in the *Apology*, Socrates refused to carry out orders he received as an office-holder or citizen. At the risk of harm to himself, he refused in one case to harm the innocent and in the other to cooperate with a circumvention of legal process. He engaged in two acts of *direct* civil disobedience, disobeying a substantively unjust act of state, not in *indirect* civil disobedience, where the disobeyed law or command is not unjust in itself, but related in an ancillary or symbolic way to injustice. The additional assumption, found in the first two books of the *Republic*, must be that wronging others includes retaliation in kind or in some other way against those who have wronged you as a private person or individual citizen.[35] So that Socratic conscience in its fullest sense entails moral absolutism, the absolute prohibition of harming others where harm is seen as *any* private or individual retaliation; or as involvement in unjust or irregular public retaliation (that is, unjust or irregular state-imposed punishment). At least this is what harm seems to mean in the *Apology* and here and there in the first two books of the *Republic*. It is *not* what it becomes in the *Gorgias*: impairment of the capacity to be virtuous. Arendt's thesis thus proceeds without reference to the insidious change effected in the rendering of Socratic absolutism in the *Gorgias*.

By extending the notion of harm to include what ordinary morality defines as merited pain, Socratic conscience bars the effort to use just laws, or to act within them, in order to settle scores or to act punitively. The prohibition of private retaliation is distinct from a prohibition of private lawlessness. In sum, Socratic conscience in its *fullest* sense goes beyond the requirements of ordinary morality in two ways. First, it prohibits more acts, and second, it asks for the readiness to be harmed (as the world understands harm) even unto death, rather than violate the prohibitions. It is of crucial importance to see, however, what Arendt overlooks. In regard to the two acts of refusal in the *Apology*, apart from the general formulations that appear there and in the *Crito*, harming others is exemplified *only* by harming the innocent or those threatened by improper legal procedure. Absolute morality here has no content beyond ordinary morality, and it has only one differentiating characteristic: Its practitioner risks extreme harm, as the world understands harm. The practitioner is holding the state only to the standard of ordinary morality. He never asks of it that it be prepared to be self-sacrificing, that it abstain from the lesser evil, or that it extend the notion of harm as he does, for his own conduct, when he refuses to retaliate against personal injustice by escaping his capital punishment.

In Arendt's analysis the self-interest of the Socratic person is thus the avoidance of self-reproach. His harm is internal, and only he can inflict it on himself. He says to himself such things as, If I did what I am expected or told to do, I could not live with myself; or, Unless I make known my objection to a certain policy or condition, I would sicken. By Arendt's definition, the Socratic person says these or similar words to himself when the result of his obedience or acceptance would be involvement in the initiation or continuance of some great wrong, some atrocity, not some commonplace imperfection. His disobedience or noncooperation withdraws him from the wrong and thus diminishes its strength by that much. He is characteristically interested only in not doing wrong, in not transgressing certain limits. In the absence of atrocity or its possibility, he remains inactive. As a citizen, he rarely acts; and when he acts, all he does is say no, and then carry through on that response as economically as possible. Withdrawn from wrongdoing, he does not organize resistance to it. Although Arendt calls him the good man, he is of course not the actively good man who imitates Jesus in private life.

Let us be clear that Arendt never makes the mistake of likening the Socratic person who usually abstains from action to Pontius Pilate.[36] Pilate was one who gave in too easily to the wrong he could have prevented, and he sought by a ritual gesture, not by a teacherly and self-sacrificing act, to express and secure his innocence. He is a symbol of either ineffectuality or cowardly irresponsibility joined to a concern to be understood by others as guiltless. However, Arendt does say that it matters less to the Socratic person that wrong is being done than that he can believe that he is not responsible for it; that the possible pain of self-reproach is more important to him than the actual pain of others.[37] But I do not see how anyone could say that he would feel intolerable pain if he harmed others, unless he had an exceptional sensitivity to the pain of others. This sensitivity is independent of his own pain and hence of his own self-interest, no matter how rarefied. When Arendt discusses those few who self-sacrificingly refused collaboration with the Nazi policy of extermination, she says that their refusal stemmed from their fear of self-abhorrence. Although, in that context, she does not suggest anything but admiration for their refusal, she nevertheless diminishes their heroism by concentrating so exclusively on their inner dialogue. She does not depict them as overcome by horror at the wrong done others, apart from the role they were called on to play and refused to play.

Arendt does not mean us to see Socratic self-interest as a taint. But no doubt those who initially admire Socrates would probably see it that way if they were persuaded that Arendt's analysis was correct. There is also no doubt that self-sacrificing Socratic persons do often refer to their internal disquiet when justifying a conscientious act of disobedience or noncooperation. It is implausible, however, to convert Socrates' statement into a sufficient psychological account, as if the determining motive in every real case of conscientious resistance at whatever cost to the resister were dread of having to account for oneself to oneself. It is more likely that where this dread, this prospective guilt, is felt acutely it coexists with a powerful inclination to transgressive behavior that often prevails even if in displaced or sublimated fashion, and that paralysis, not resistance, may result. There is something more than odd in suggesting that those who show the courage to say no, even unto death, are more sensitive to their own possible future pain than to the suffering and wrong they see or anticipate. Once again, Arendt is too ingenious. Or one might rather say that she has not been ingenious enough, because she does not allow for the fact that a proponent of Socratic conscience—perhaps Socrates himself—might try to seduce us into accepting his position by an appeal to refined self-interest, while he himself is unmoved by such a consideration and expects anyone else who comes to live by such a conscience eventually to see through this initial appeal.

It is hard not to believe that for Socrates himself the passional source of his absolutism was something akin to samaritan neighborliness: not love of all, but perhaps sorrow at their vulnerability. (If he loved all, he loved as a teacher loves students, not as a mother loves her children or a priest his flock.) This passion was perhaps guaranteed by unworldliness in a conventional sense: He found the goods and prizes of the world to be not much, found life itself not much. He resembled Silenus, as Alcibiades says in the *Symposium*. To lose all, therefore—to be harmed as the world understands harm—hardly signified. The good person cannot be harmed. Of course anyone with Arendt's commitment to the world must fear this distaste. Perhaps the natural bond—if that is what it is—between Socratic conscience and unworldliness (*not* otherworldliness) should be the real object of demystifying analysis. But then again, there need be no such bond, in the case of others who bear a Socratic conscience.

The notion of conscience as self-interest incorporates yet another element that Arendt uses to question conscience further. She suggests that what one person finds he cannot live with, another may find morally permissible or even required. Subjectivity is intrinsic to Socratic conscience: It contains no principle that can be "generalized."[38] Arendt's failure to put Socrates' two acts of refusal at the center of her analysis misleads her here. In his defense of these acts, Socrates invoked nothing beyond either the spirit of the laws of the democracy or a specific law of the democracy. His reference to his inner voice adds nothing to the simple assertion that Athenian office-holders (tyrants or democrats) were acting unconstitutionally. That his disobedience may have struck his conformist contemporaries as odd shows that he was an infinitely better democrat than they. Naturally, that his kind of disobedience was unusual or even unprecedented indicates a rare moral energy. There are times when extraordinary risks have to be taken for ordinary morality, for the avoidance of surplus evil. He was a true "subject," but that did not make his acts the emanation of something subjective.

Arendt takes some of the general impeachment back when she says that the Socratic kind of self-interest is rare. The remark is all the more telling for being so casual. But it is precisely the Socratic person who is least likely to be consoled by what he or she would take to be flattery. Such a person must wish either that the concept of self-interest is being misused when it is made to apply to the dread of self-reproach; or that almost everybody, not only a few, share this self-interest to some degree or other, and that to lack it altogether is to lack one of the constitutive features of being human. Arendt makes conscience at once idiosyncratic and self-interested, and this transformation must be resisted for the sake of truth, as well as for the sake of the prestige of Socratic conscience.

Given that Socrates made such demands on himself, can we say that he has any place in a discussion of civil disobedience? Arendt insists that he cannot be a model for the civilly disobedient, even though many think he can be.[39] She wants to remove him from people's thought on civil disobedience. Yet he has a place, which is roughly analogous to that which Jesus has in the field of continuously ameliorative endeavors. Socrates has a place in thought about civil disobedience, not only in thought about "personal responsibility under dictatorship." He is a sponsor of the will to say no, to resist complicity in the oppression of the innocent, especially in a democratic society that commits atrocities or tolerates (with a hideous inconsistency) institutionalized atrocity or a pattern of atrocious policy. He is major for the democratic ideal in a way that another classical no-sayer, Antigone, is not. In dealing with Socrates on his two explicit occasions of refusal, we are not dealing with the clash between two bodies of law or between higher law and lesser law; just as we are not dealing with any absolutist extension of the notion of harm or wrong. The content of his two refusals are within the bounds of ordinary morality. We are faced with a man who is adamant in his compliance with the spirit of the laws of the democracy, the spirit that only democracy then aspired to make practical. He stands for the idea that the democracy should not forget its difference from other forms and proceed to imitate their systemic cruelty. As for the tyrants, he reminded them of the real meaning of the system they had for the moment abolished. (That democratic Athens was cruel in its policy of imperialism was, in its way, hideously inconsistent. We have no way of connecting Athenian foreign policy with the Socrates of the *Apology* and the *Crito*, the "only" Socrates relevant to this discussion.)

Socrates differs from modern civil disobedients in one significant way: He is willing to risk harm *unto death* to avoid participation in the harming of the innocent or of those whose guilt will not be properly determined. This aspect of absolute morality, of Socratic conscience, is present only in an attenuated form among civil disobedients. They are willing, certainly, to endure some punishment. However, the punishment is often but not always slight, and it is known beforehand to be slight. But otherwise Socrates is a model. To challenge Arendt's imputation of rarefied self-interest to him, and to others of self-sacrificing conscience, is to try to retain him as model, and to retain conscience as a more than marginal political concept.

Conscience and Civil Disobedience

Examining civil disobedience in America, consider the antislavery and antiwar movements. Consider those who engaged in direct civil disobedience—breaking laws that had to do with war-related taxes or the return of fugitive slaves before the Civil War, and with war-related taxes and draft induction during the Vietnam War—and in such indirect civil disobedience as acts of trespass during the Vietnam War. (I exclude civil rights protest, as Arendt does, because it involved breaking laws that were invalid, or presumably so.) We find, as Arendt knows, refusals defended on grounds of conscience. What is this conscience? It is a moral seriousness similar to that of Socrates: the intensity of people who—to borrow an idea from Erik Erikson's *Young Man Luther—meant it;*[40] who tried to stay true to what everyone professed but office-holders failed to practice, with the acquiescence or active support of the majority; and who were willing to risk varying degrees of punishment.

Arendt and others have distinguished the civil disobedient from the conscientious objector in the technical war-related sense. If there is any basis to the distinction, it must be that the conscientious objector is usually a pacifist—to leave aside *selective* conscientious objectors, who are much like civil disobedients. The conscientious objector appeals to a general principle, but it is not a principle accepted by all. In fact, he asks the state to act toward other states in accordance with the Socratic principle in one of its statements: Never inflict harm, no matter what is at stake, even your own self-preservation. That is, the state should never engage in even public, regular, defensive retaliation.

The principle in Christian terms is resist not evil (especially when resistance means killing), without necessarily going the length of loving even your enemies. The conscientious objector in his pacifism subscribes to an extreme form of negative absolute morality—more extreme than Socrates because it is applied to interstate relations. Civil disobedients do not. They appeal instead either to the common sense of atrocity, and hence to the condemnation that ordinary morality (not only absolute morality) would pass on the condition or policy; or to the spirit of the Constitution when some actual feature of it taints it; or to the common sense of constitutional violation, where the Constitution is acknowledged by the civil disobedients to be free of the taint of injustice.

Ordinary morality may allow certain categories of public action under exigent circumstances, while absolute morality prohibits them under all circumstances. But ordinary morality retains a requirement of proportionality that makes the concept of atrocity something other than an arbitrary term of disfavor; and ordinary morality is committed to the defense of the absolute rights of all. One did not have to be an absolutist to oppose slavery or the war in Vietnam. One had only to reject surplus evil. One had only to take seriously what others said they believed but chose not to act on. They did not *mean it*.

Conscience as *meaning it* is not the same as subjectivity. Of course there are cases in American judicial and political history when individuals or groups were radically subjective in their invocation of conscience. That is, they claimed some privilege or exemption on grounds that cut them off entirely from general moral principles available to the whole society. They maintained that they were special in their lineage or inspiration; if not better, then different and unassimilable. They sought tolerance, not full acceptance. They did not expect to convert many others, if any at all. At most, they may have thought they would be granted some larger vindication in the future. The possessed individual or the ingrown sect fits this rough description. But surely Thoreau did not; nor did those in antiwar and student movements. When one of them said something like, I could not live with myself if I went along, or did not make my objection known, he or she was saying, in effect, no one could if they gave the matter some further thought. Characteristically, there was an appeal to a general principle, not to a private scruple, and that principle was one that was supposedly accepted by all and was therefore neither esoteric nor novel. The appeal to the people, in Thoreau's formulation, is from them to themselves.

Then, too, *meaning it* is not exhaustively defined by depth of feeling. Segregationists broke the law out of depth of feeling, but to say, as Arendt does, that their appeal to conscience (if indeed they made it) was as justified as that of those who broke the law to protest the Vietnam War is absurd. Political conscience is inseparable from principle, from justice. The inwardness that goes with political conscience is not subjectivity, but self-examination. Its purpose is to be as certain as possible that one is not mistaken or obdurate. The process cannot be like what Arendt describes as imagining the thinking of others, because too many others seem not to be thinking. It is, rather, independence or thinking or judging for oneself,[41] but always in accordance with the principles commonly professed. No matter how many individuals come together to commit a joint act of civil disobedience, each must be understood as having first thought things through for himself or herself, especially when individuals serially commit direct acts of civil disobedience.

When practitioners of civil disobedience insist on their nonviolence, they do not have to do so in behalf of absolute morality. It seems that in a constitutional democracy the idea of civil disobedience commits its practitioners to nonviolence. Their sense of moral limits that calls forth their resistance to office-holders also governs their choice of methods. They are not revolutionaries or criminals. They may of course be inclined to nonviolence out of prudence or, contrastingly, out of some affinity to pacifist absolutism. But neither of these two motivations is conceptually appropriate for the normal range of civil disobedience.

In sum, the appeal to conscience that civil disobedients typically make is not rightly understood as a result of a special self-interest, nor is it dependent on the two imputed accompaniments of that self-interest: first, the assertion of subjectivity against the generality, and second, the rejection of ordinary morality in favor of absolute morality. (Although the pacifist conscientious objector holds to absolute morality, he, too, should not be seen as driven by a special self-interest or as substituting subjectivity for reasoned dissent.) To speak of the civil disobedient as a conscientious person is only to say that the person is, at least for the while, and at least on one gravely important issue, more serious morally than most other people.

One could concede that if a civil disobedient put the matter in this way he or she may strike some as self-righteous or vain and therefore infected by a feeling worse than the special kind of self-interest that Arendt makes so much of. Indeed, the worst criticism that could be made of this way of looking at civil disobedience is suggested by Justice Thurgood Marshall in his opinion for the Supreme Court in *Gillette v. United States*, 1971. The case dealt with the claim of an individual to be exempt from a particular war on the ground that the war (the Vietnam war) was unjust. Marshall wrote:

> The fear of the National Advisory Commission on Selective Service, apparently, is that exemption of objectors to particular wars would weaken the resolve of those who otherwise would feel themselves bound to serve despite personal cost, uneasiness at the prospect of violence, or even serious moral reservations or policy objections concerning the particular conflict.[42]

Underlining *serious moral reservations* emphasizes the point that some may be conscientious obeyers: They may hate the policy or condition but think that the principle of equality requires them to defer, in some disputable cases, if not in all, to the laws and policies that emanate from a legitimate because constitutionally democratic procedure.[43] They, too, may try to invoke Socrates. After all, he conscientiously obeyed an unjust democratic command—his death sentence. But they would not strengthen their case. His obedience made him the agent of a wrong done to himself, not to another. They have a case without the help of Socrates.

This is the most troubling aspect of describing civil disobedients as *meaning it*, as morally more serious than the majority. The conscientious obeyer may usually be mistaken in ranking obedience to the law as morally more necessary than dissent on any specific policy or condition, especially when he is asked to be the direct agent of what he suspects is injustice. But that he is mistaken need not diminish his moral seriousness. If only out of respect for the conscientious obeyer, the civil disobedient (the conscientious disobeyer) must reserve some anguish for the fact that he thinks himself morally compelled to break the law even while the conscientious obeyer may feel obliged in general to obey laws and policies enacted by a legitimate government. His good faith toward the conscientious obeyer also requires that he show courage, so that his act not be seen as privileged self-exemption from danger or from personal defilement. Courage can be shown either in the acceptance of a duty equivalent to the one foresworn, or the acceptance of punishment, or perhaps the acceptance of physical risk or unpleasantness in the very acts of disobedience. At the same time, there are limits to this argument. It cannot be right that one who refuses to be a direct agent of injustice *deserves* punishment. He is wronged by being punished, even though the punishment comes from a legitimate government. But, "It is better to be wronged than to do wrong."

Civil Disobedience and Group Action

If Arendt's critique of civil disobedience as a mode of the politics of conscience is open to doubts, her own view of the proper self-conception of the practitioners of civil disobedience is rather flat and uninspiring. It is curious that the one kind of public politics of the modern age—apart from debate on a new constitution or the extraordinary occurrence of spontaneous democracy in the early moments of revolution—that contains a good deal of the existential meaning which Arendt finds in the politics of the city-state should elude her powers of vivification. She does celebrate the public happiness that members of the student movement and the antiwar movement found in the rediscovery of participatory politics, including their acts of civil disobedience. She thus establishes a link between her ideal conception of politics and the recent manifestations.

Accompanying this motif, however, is a different dominant line of argument. Arendt works to conceptualize civil disobedience as pressure politics:

> We are dealing with organized minorities, who stand against assumed inarticulate, though hardly "silent," majorities, and I think it is undeniable that these majorities have changed in mood and opinion to an astounding degree under the pressure of the minorities.[44]

She is clear that the pressure politics of the civil disobedients is not in behalf of self- or group-interest in the economic sense, and hence it is to be distinguished from the usual lobbying. Concerning the usual lobbying, Arendt speaks with extreme harshness in *On Revolution*, comparing the tactics of the lobbyists with blackmail and equating economic interest with private interest pushed in disregard of the legitimate interests of others.[45] But her tone changes in the essay on civil disobedience. She now is willing to see economic interest and pressure groups as voluntary associations, as the free and regular cooperation of individuals who act together for a common purpose. That they are economically interested and hence automatically foreign to the nature of ideal politics becomes less salient in Arendt's analysis. They formally resemble civil disobedients, and the formal resemblence decreases the relevance of the substantive differences, especially the difference between acting for an interest and acting for an opinion.

Arendt is trying to Americanize civil disobedience, and in the course of doing so she Americanizes herself. If only for the occasion, she tolerates the pressure politics of economic interests, as if that mode of politics alone could be American. She is trying to gain respectability for the civil disobedients. The cost of that effort, however, is to reduce and flatten both the actual practice and the self-theorization of those who committed civil disobedience.

In her flight from what she holds to be basically unpolitical, the motivation of conscience, Arendt hastens toward an understanding of politics—politics as pressure in behalf of economic interest—which one would have thought she could never countenance. But she seems to prefer the latter even to the former. Conscience is even more remote than economic interest from true politics. At least, however, she preserves some distance between the groups of civil disobedients and the other voluntary associations. The former represent an opinion that they are willing to act for, even to break the law for. Indeed, she detects in the antiwar movement the intimations of an acceptable opinion on the justifiable recourse to civil disobedience, and she proceeds to fill out those intimations in a highly suggestive manner.

Roughly, Arendt says that the lawbreaking that the American civil disobedients do is not a light affair at all. Naturally, the example it gives to the potentially criminal is unfortunate, and it makes it all the easier for an unscrupulous man like Spiro Agnew to lump together the civilly disobedient and the criminally disobedient. Apart from the disturbance of that basic order which any society must have, civil disobedience is problematic because it takes place in a polity in which the systematic provision for dissent creates consent to the basic rules, the Constitution as a whole, and hence to the laws made under it.

Arendt scorns those who think that the majority of the people actually rule in a representative democracy. She has no patience with the effort to derive a general obligation to obey all laws from what she calls the "fictitious" consent of universal suffrage.[46] At best, the people rule their representatives, in the sense of setting some limits on their conduct. She uses a formulation to describe the constitutional monarchies of the eighteenth century that I believe informs her thought on twentieth-century representative democracies. She says that the social groupings

> represented particular private interests but left the public concern to the monarch, who, in an enlightened despotism, was supposed to act as "a single enlightened person against many private interests," whereby it was understood that in a "limited monarchy" these bodies had the right to voice grievances and to withhold consent.[47]

In modern times the civil disobedients are precisely those who guard the limits on the conduct of office-holders; those whose voiced grievances have gone unheeded and who withhold consent to unconstitutional policies. Their obligation is to the Constitution as a whole, which is a codification of the limits. When those in authority attack the Constitution, *and* when judicial review is denied, citizens may apply irregular pressures, including lawbreaking, to defend it. She does not say that when those in authority attack the Constitution, as say Lyndon Johnson and Richard Nixon did, they have forfeited their offices and hence their enactments have lost validity and obligatoriness. Rather, in present-day political circumstances, when the usual procedures are futile, irregular politics will tend to be the most efficacious. Civil disobedience is "basic dissent" in a polity in which the right to dissent is fundamental.[48] Arendt goes so far as to say in *The Life of the Mind* that "disobedience is the most common and least harmful mode of dissent."[49] The matter could be put in the form of a seeming paradox: Civil disobedience is most in the spirit of constitutional democracy, yet it is supposed to be needed there least.

Arendt thus offers what could be described as a purely political way of regarding civil disobedience and perhaps some other modes of the politics of refusal. But there are a fair number of difficulties with it. On its own terms, the characterization of representative democracy as not really democratic at all needs to be qualified. If in broad outlines the people rule; if their rule of their representatives means that they choose office-holders in such a way as to guide policy; if in other ways like town meetings, party caucuses, and the powers of referendum, initiative, and recall, they approach some regular, direct participation, then the idea of consent, and therefore of the direct rather than derivative obligation to obey the laws, must be looked at again. This consideration need not lead to stricter standards for justifying civil disobedience. It may simply make the task of conscientious scrupulousness, political self-examination, more extensive.

Arendt's theory should not, however, be taken on its own terms. A purely political way of regarding civil disobedience is not in accord with the experiential meaning of civil disobedience in modern America, and probably elsewhere. Her account is anemic. It appears all the more anemic just because she makes every effort to stress the robustness and participatory and solidary joy of the civil disobedients. It strenuously misses one large fact—the moral outrage felt and expressed at the atrocities committed by the United States in Vietnam. That the war was against the spirit of the laws, that it was surely anticonstitutional if not formally unconstitutional, is all to the point. But the judgment of "unconstitutional" bespeaks dispassion, a great virtue, and one that even may inspire passionately direct action. It may even be that the best political action begins in dispassionate judgment.

But even if one can get over the dissonance created by combatting a higher illegality with a lesser one—think of those who want to allow illegally obtained evidence into courts of *law*—there still remains something spectral about the sense of unconstitutionality as a sufficient motivation to extraordinary *citizenly* action when the object of protest is a war of cruelty. Other matters will of course lend themselves more suitably to the kind of constitutional emphasis Arendt advocates. But even that emphasis can never be narrowly understood. The moral essence of the American Constitution is crucial to the motivation of the action done to defend it. The stake is not only government lawfulness in itself, apart from the content of the Constitution and the laws.

Arendt herself relents into a more conventional understanding. In two works published shortly after "Civil Disobedience"—*On Violence* and "Thoughts on Politics and Revolution"—she praises the moral intensity of the student movement and speaks of ordinary self-interest as if it were the only kind of self-interest, and she speaks of it denigratingly. She says, "Nothing, indeed, about the movement is more striking than its disinterestedness."[50] She illustrates disinterestedness by, of all things, compassion, and by the passion for justice; and attributes these qualities to all revolutionary leaders, including Marx and Lenin.[51] She says that the student rebellion is "almost exclusively inspired by moral considerations."[52] All these things she says approvingly. Correspondingly, she mocks the pseudorealist concept of enlightened self-interest: "Self-interest, when asked to yield to 'true' interest—that is, the interest of the world as distinguished from that of the self—will always reply,

Near is my shirt, but nearer is my skin." [53] We should not cling to these statements. Taken all together, they still do not allow conscience a place in political life. Such disallowance is Arendt's distinctive emphasis.

But the element of conscience cannot be theorized out of civil disobedience or out of political action, even action as conceptualized by Arendt. What is this conscience, finally, if not the anguish felt at the wrong done someone else? Wanting to act to ameliorate or end such wrong is not primarily wanting to end one's own anguish felt as spectator or agent. It is wanting to end another kind of anguish, the anguish of those to whom wrong is being done. The conscience of the civil disobedient is the imagination of suffering, the ability to imagine what it must be like to go through suffering while one is not suffering.[54] Instigated by it to act energetically and unconventionally, alone or with others, is to be a democratic citizen in the modern age. Unnecessary breaches of moral limits, surplus evil, exaggerated ambitions, and atrocities are a constant possibility, especially in foreign affairs. The negative politics of conscience goes well with the structure and values of constitutional democracy: limited and divided government and a regular politics of dispute and contest. It goes better than ameliorative politics.

The ultimate sources of conscientious politics must include the great moral absolutists, the figures of Jesus, Socrates, and closer to our time, Thoreau, Gandhi, Martin Luther King, Daniel Berrigan, and others. The sponsors of the conscientious actor are those whose lives and teachings transcended the moral world of civil disobedience or any other mode of the politics of conscience. Some were martyrs; some extended the range of obligatory actions for themselves. In such transcendence they made room for the lesser form of conscience that inspires all kinds of conscientious political acts, and some kinds of reformist politics as well. Perhaps in Thoreau we find the most instructive modern distillation.

Thoreau is relentless, excessive. His writings on politics as well as *Walden* contain sentences that seem to champion a radical subjectivity with a corresponding lack of sociality; a contempt for ordinary political action combined with a detestation of the very notion of government; a claim to autonomous judgment that seems to make any living together impossible; an appeal to self-sacrificing moral absolutism that strangely does not exclude an acceptance of violence and does not include a patient willingness to use regular procedures of social change. Such sentences express his strongest temptations and are therefore necessary emanations, although easily misunderstood. They are sentences only for himself. There are other sentences that make his true sentiments as a writer for others unmistakable, and these sentiments are unmistakably political.

Thoreau is saying one must think for oneself; one must not be enclosed by the system of conventions, must never live *dans le vrai*. One must make sure that one does not abet injustice by inattention; a fact must be called by its right name. Living a life does not necessarily lead to continuous citizenship, but if citizenship means anything, it means that the citizen will object and resist when the collective power to which he or she contributes is used atrociously.

Martyrdom is not asked for, but some discomfort is the unavoidable price of conscience. Resistance will take the form either of a luminous act (an act potent to instruct in itself), or an exemplary act (a symbolic act that lends itself to being written about and memorialized). One condemns only by the standard of ordinary morality. One must stay awake to awaken others or to learn from others.

The guarantor of this watchfulness is self-watchfulness, a "doubleness" that precludes ever losing oneself in anything unself-consciously.[55] Not being at one with society requires that a person not be falsely at one with himself. A person is falsely at one with himself when he is at one with his role or function in society: in the sleep of bad faith, in the sleep of unconscious or studied *mimesis*. This doubleness is not the Socratic internal dialogue of me and myself in retrospect, after the fact, the two-in-one that Arendt places at the source of conscience, but rather a continuous division in the acting self, although there are similarities between the two concepts. The desired mode of action is that of detached engagement, austere passion, and all-consuming scruples.

Thoreau himself must be seen as embracing the extremes. He mocks conscience because conscience condemns the world for its evil instead of loving it for its beauty. [56]He paradoxically raises beauty over goodness by saying that "the perception of beauty is a moral test."[57] He eases his way beyond good and evil by professing that the "impression made on a wise man is that of universal innocence."[58] Yet he extends the sense of moral responsibility to the point where a taxpayer in a free state is personally responsible for the continuation of slavery. He is alone, yet he stays alone because his love of others is so intense that their deficiencies unsettle him. His lack of domesticity does not remove him into solitude, but it intensifies his public nature, his citizenship. He seems so cavalier toward the noise and clamor of public life. Yet "at the time of the John Brown tragedy, Thoreau was driven sick. So the country's misfortunes in the Union war acted on his feelings with great force: he used to say he 'could never recover while the war lasted.'"[59] His role in life is not universalizable, but it is nevertheless indispensable. He, like the other great sponsors, is a model only in the sense that he inspires. "Let the judge and the jury, and the sheriff and the jailer, cease to act under a corrupt government—cease to be tools and become men."[60]

Not to be imitated, but rather to be kept in mind while the conscientious person acts, Thoreau makes it possible to conceive civil disobedience and other forms of conscientious politics as ideal politics: nonviolent, nonroutine, nonselfish, episodic, perhaps philsophical. By the standard of power, some forms may seem trivial, distracting, or self-indulgent. We may be struck especially by the immense discrepancy between civil disobedience when it consists in breaking a minor law like trespass and the scale of cruelty of an unjust war. But one power all forms have, either as individual or group acts, either as direct or indirect refusal—the power of annunciation, first to make a matter hard to ignore, and then to make it urgent. If this politics is not the most heroic or the most esthetically impressive politics, then it is nevertheless as heroic and beautiful as nonmurderous politics can be. Arendt fights Thoreau all through the pages of her essay on civil disobedience, but finally he overcomes even her immensely resourceful and provocative attempt to purge politics of conscience.

Notes

1. Hannah Arendt, "Personal Responsibility Under Dictatorship," *The Listener* 72 (August 6, 1964), 185-87, 205. Hereafter cited as " Personal Responsibility."
2. Despite her seeming reluctance to accept the analogy between the preservation of an individual life and the preservation of a state, Arendt praises Lincoln for saying that he would preserve slavery if that were needed to preserve the Union. She mistakenly assumes that Lincoln meant what he said in the letter to Horace Greeley in 1862. Lincoln's whole career was dedicated to preserving the Union only on certain terms, which he thought could eventually be secured: first, the containment and then the abolition of slavery. If his concern had been to preserve the Union on *any* terms, he would not have been as uncompromising as he was. He, and people who thought like him, placed the Union at risk. See Arendt, "Civil Disobedience" in *Crises of the Republic* (New York: Harcourt Brace Jovanovich, 1972), 61. Hereafter cited as CD.
3. Quoted in Elisabeth Young-Bruehl, *Hannah Arendt: For Love of the World* (New Haven: Yale, 1982), 374. Hereafter cited as Young-Bruehl.
4. Arendt, "The Ex-Communists," *Commonweal* 57 (March 30, 1953), 595-99.
5. Arendt, *On Revolution* (New York: Viking, 1963), 10-11. Hereafter cited as OR. On another occasion she seems to deal sympathetically with the Machiavellian idea that "If you do not resist evil, the evildoers will do as they please. Though it is true that, by resisting evil, you are likely to be involved in evil." But she calls this an "argument against morality," as if the lesser evil were merely evil. Arendt, *Lectures on Kant's Political Philosophy*, Ronald Beiner, ed. (Chicago: University of Chicago Press, 1982), 50-1. Hereafter cited as *Lectures*.
6. "Personal Responsibility," 186.
7. Ibid.
8. Arendt, "On Violence" in *Crises of the Republic*, 151. Hereafter cited as OV.
9. Quoted in Young-Bruehl, 374.
10. Plato, *Gorgias*, 469.
11. CD, 63.
12. Arendt, OR, 76; *The Human Condition* (Chicago: University of Chicago Press, 1958), 76. Hereafter cited as HC.
13. Matthew, 6:3.
14. HC, 74.
15. Luke, 8:19.
16. HC, 77.
17. Ibid., 243.
18. OR, 77.
19. Ibid., 78.
20. Ibid., 75.
21. Ibid., 80.
22. Ibid., 85.
23. Ibid., 84.
24. Ibid., 107.
25. Ibid., 93.
26. Arendt, *Eichmann in Jerusalem* (2nd ed., New York: Viking, 1964), 106. Hereafter cited as *Eichmann*.
27. OR, 82.
28. Henry David Thoreau, "Civil Disobedience" in Walter Harding, ed., *The Variorum Walden and the Variorum Civil Disobedience* (New York: Washington Square Press, 1968), 351. Hereafter cited as Thoreau.
29. CD, 66.
30. Arendt provides an extensive range of references. Two essays seem especially to guide her conceptual analysis: Marshall Cohen, "Civil Disobedience in a Constitutional Democracy,"

The Massachusetts Review, 10 (Spring 1969), 211-26; and Wilson Carey McWilliams, "Civil Disobedience and Contemporary Constitutionalism," *Comparative Politics* 1 (January 1969), 211-27. Her discussion of Socrates is indebted, she says, to N. A. Greenberg, "Socrates' Choice in the *Crito*," *Harvard Studies in Classical Philology* 70 (1965). Another useful reference is A. D. Woozley, "Socrates on Disobeying the Law" in Gregory Vlastos, ed., *The Philosophy of Socrates* (New York: Anchor, 1971), 299-318. I would add that the idea that civil disobedience is an expression of fidelity to the spirit of constitutional representative democracy is well pursued in Elliot M. Zashin, *Civil Disobedience and Democracy* (New York: Free Press, 1972).

31. Such acknowledgment came in "Thoughts on Politics and Revolution" in *Crises of the Republic*, 202-4. Also in OV, 117-28; and Arendt and others, "The Impotence of Power" in Alexander Klein, ed., *Dissent, Power, and Confrontation* (New York: McGraw-Hill, 1971), 190-91. And, of course, CD. Most succinctly, she says, "To the often-heard question who are they, this new generation? One is tempted to answer, those who hear the ticking." OV, 120.

32. It is of course possible that, in the abstract, avoiding wrongdoing need not carry the risk of being wronged. One could be spared the risk while still confronted with the occasion to do wrong with *impunity*. (Recall Gyges' ring.) The formula from the *Gorgias* would then be a statement of preference as between two causally unconnected possibilities. Its meaning would be that one preferred one's inner harmony (which would be destroyed by wronging others) to all the goods and prizes of the world (that could be gained, at least in part, by wronging others). In a letter to Gershom Scholem, Arendt expresses a related sentiment: "Wrong done by my own people naturally grieves me more than wrong done by other people" quoted in Young-Bruehl, 344. Her remark resembles an earlier one by Thoreau on the duty of protesting the war with Mexico: "What makes this duty more urgent is the fact that the country so overrun is not our own, but ours is the invading army." (Thoreau, 346.) Arendt's discussion, however, assumes throughout the causal connection: The law or office-holders command wrong, and the person of Socratic conscience refuses and therefore risks being wronged himself by unmerited punishment.

33. *Gorgias*, 482. Arendt's translation.

34. Compare Arthur Koestler's dramatic treatment of the inhibitions that the inner dialogue places in the way of acting in *Darkness at Noon* (1941), trans. Daphne Hardy (New York: Modern Library, n.d.). Arendt treats Koestler unjustly in "The Too Ambitious Reporter," review of *Twilight Bar* and *The Yogi and the Commissar*, *Commentary* 1 (January 1946), 94-95.

35. This latter element is exemplified by Socrates' *obedience*, by his acceptance of unjust punishment *for himself*, rather than avoiding it illegally and thus supposedly wronging the city. Apparently, the city is innocent, and to escape in violation of the law would be to harm the innocent. Only the demagogues are guilty, and they do not morally count in Socrates' decision.

36. Matthew, 27:24. Pontius Pilate figures derisively in Arendt's discussion of Eichmann. See *Eichmann*, 135.

37. CD, 62-63.

38. Ibid., 64.

39. Ibid., 58.

40. Erik Erikson, *Young Man Luther* (1958) (New York: Norton, 1962), 210.

41. See Arendt's praise of those few who resisted complicity with Nazism. "[They] were the only ones who dared judge by themselves." "Personal Responsibility", 205.

42. 401 US 437.

43. Compare Thoreau: "The broadest and most prevalent error requires the most disinterested virtue to sustain it....Those who, while they disapprove of the character and measures of a government, yield to it their allegiance and support, are undoubtedly its most conscientious supporters, and so frequently the most serious obstacles to reform" Thoreau, 350. There is some irony here. His (and the Emersonian) tendency is to scorn institutional reform, especially when undertaken by unreformed—unvirtuous—individuals.

44. CD, 98-99.

45. OR, 273.

46. CD, 89.

47. OR, 179.

48. CD, 76.

49. Arendt, *The Life of the Mind* (2 vols., New York: Harcourt Brace Jovanovich, 1978), vol. 2,

Willing, 201.
50. OV, 125.
51. "Thoughts on Politics and Revolution," 204-5. Also Arendt, "On Hannah Arendt" in Melvyn A. Hill, ed., *Hannah Arendt: The Recovery of the Public World* (New York: St. Martin's, 1979), 310-11.
52. OV, 130.
53. Ibid., 175.
54. On imagination in general, see Hannah Arendt, Lectures, 79-85.
55. *Walden* in Thoreau, 101-2.
56. Henry David Thoreau, *A Week on the Concord and Merrimack Rivers* (New York: Crowell, 1961), 85-6.
57. Quoted in Joseph Wood Krutch, *Henry David Thoreau* (1948) (New York: Morrow, 1974), 176.
58. *Walden*, in Thoreau, 240.
59. *The Writings of Henry David Thoreau*, F. B. Sanborn, ed. (Boston: Houghton Mifflin, 1906), vol. 6, 337.
60. Ibid., Bradford Torrey, ed. vol. 12, 365.

Chapter Four

Modern Democracy

In the body of her work, Arendt pays only reluctant attention to the practice and theory of representative democracy. She also gives it scant praise. Most important of all, she never says or suggests that representative democracy is a genuinely distinctive political system with special moral claims. By her reckoning, it has some undeniably good effects. But wherever the realm of the public is not really the people's realm, wherever there is no direct democracy, discriminations among the forms of public life, among forms of government, do not seem to have major *theoretical* importance.

The trouble is that the subject of representative democracy cannot be slighted without hurting one's sense of the sufficiency of a given political theory in modern times. Political theory must deal with representative democracy in earnest, if for no other reason than that it is one of the two main forms of existent government (along with dictatorship), and the only form preponderantly accorded legitimacy. That it should be accorded legitimacy is of course open to serious dispute. Nevertheless, its ideal nature and its diverse realizations provide the initial matter for the reflection of most contemporary political theorists. In saying, therefore, that Arendt slights this theme, one is also saying that if there is no other point of vulnerability in her thought, then surely there is this one. But Arendt's own theory not only requires that full attention be paid to representative democracy but also that it be given a measure of praise, praise for its distinctiveness. We cannot expect her to judge it as "the ideally best polity": Love of participatory citizenship (separate from offices, from professionalism) forbids such a judgment.

The fact remains that some other things Arendt praises or values depend in modern times on the existence of representative democracy. Without this form—and realized of course in more than a merely formalist way—there would be more of the things she dreads and fewer of the things she celebrates. That representative democracies have themselves engendered some dreadful things, that they have engendered atrocities like the Vietnam War, does not settle the matter. Only in representative democracies can resistance to atrocities be regularly counted on, because of the very spirit of their form. Furthermore, Arendt is quick to insist that concerted response to atrocities, and to lesser kinds of wrongdoing inflicted or tolerated by government, can be not only the instrument of redress but also the occasion for the reappearance of the thing she celebrates most—real political action.

Thus the spirit of representative democracy keeps resistance alive and allows it to shape itself into the latest expression of direct political participation, civil disobedience. It has been noted that the positive moral center of *The Origins of Totalitarianism* is the character type conceptually associated with citizenship in representative democracy, and that Arendt makes almost nothing of this fact. This chapter explores this reticence and discusses as well some of the theoretical arguments that she constructs and that work with a largely disparaging effect on the assertion that representative democracy is a distinctive and praiseworthy political system. The most important point is that Arendt's own political theory must make much more room for representative democracy, if only as "second best"; not, of course, the second best as an imperfect approximation of the best, but as valuable despite its structural dissimilarities with the best.

The Play of Interests

If Arendt wants to free politics from the claims and constraints of conscience and goodness, she certainly does not want to do so for the sake of theoretically easing the way for interest, self-interest, domination, expansion, conquest, or any other ambition that the world—but not Arendt—considers as proper for the ends of action. The world's worldliness is not Arendt's. Throughout her work she expresses a fairly steady distaste for what common opinion holds to be the stuff of politics. This distaste comes out in her first and main characterization of the politics of representative democracy, found in *On Revolution*. In effect, what she finds when she looks at the daily life of representative democracy is an obsession with economic interest. Apart from the gross fact that representation in itself is not compatible with participatory politics, the arrangements and procedures of representative democracy are used to advance aims that she also deems not compatible with the true aims of political action. Even earlier, in *The Human Condition*, Arendt condemned modern politics altogether because of the tendency of the "social" to invade the public realm; specifically, for the tendency of the programs and details of welfare capitalism to absorb all public attention and energies. The administration of social and economic life "has overshadowed the political realm ever since the beginning of the modern age."[1]

There is no doubt that the popular nature of representative democracy ensures that economic concerns will be publicly central. This is an indication that representative democracy, at least on domestic policies, is substantially faithful to popular wishes. It would be hard to believe that any political system meant to be responsive to the people could fail to give priority to economic issues. In modern life, a different priority can only be imagined. One might say that Marcuse's *One-Dimensional Man* is a heroic effort to *imagine* such a world. Yet that book does not present itself as a work of the imagination, but rather as an angry indictment of a society that is supposed to manipulate its people into an exclusive addiction to production and consumption. Marcuse never says what is simply the case: Advanced industrial society coincides with immemorial yearnings for material abundance, even if this society is not the "necessary" outcome of such yearnings. People crave not only material sufficiency—enough is not enough—but abundance, in order to escape the confinement, the curse, of having to be careful about every penny. On the other hand, Arendt knows deeply that advanced industrial society is faithful to the inescapable ordinariness of human beings in almost all times and places. Therefore, insofar as representative democracy is popular government, it will be dominated by economic issues. Economic well-being will be privately pursued and publicly sustained.

Why does Arendt resist and rebel against this gross fact? The reasons are not always clear, but two main considerations, sharply contrasting in character, shape the insistence that economic issues are not proper subjects for the discussions and debates of the public world.

First, at one extreme, is the view that the effort of economic interests to promote themselves by means of the electoral system falsifies the nature of politics by forcing on it essentially private or social purposes. One might say that when economic interests are the substance of political action a component of human life has moved out of its appropriate place and invaded a place that is not its own. One kind of game has taken over the field of another and displaced the rightful possessor. Arendt laments this nearly universal transgression. Her regret may sometimes appear as if it were esthetically induced; as if she found the world guilty of esthetic ignorance or confusion—of not knowing what game to play where and when, and consequently abolishing the best but most fragile, most rare game, political action. But her sense of loss goes deeper. She is convinced that where the typical motives associated with the rough play of economic interests are present the existential potentialities of political action are not fulfilled. A selfish concern with oneself or one's partial group cannot be a source of the great revelatory effects of political action.

Second, at the other extreme, Arendt believes that the disinterested effort, made by those who hold public office, to remedy the condition of the disadvantaged, is not proper political activity. Rather, it is to be understood solely as technical or administrative activity. It thus has a kind of rigidity or even necessity that proper political activity does not have. It lacks open-endedness, indefiniteness, free and uncertain choice. It is not only the heroic and self-destructive effort made by the Jacobins and Bolsheviks to solve "the social question" that Arendt judges as inimical to the preservation of the genuinely political. She also finds that when the energies of political life go into devising plans for gradual social amelioration political life is lost.

For Arendt, then, the enemy of politics is economics. At once responsive to popular pressures and the vehicle of popular involvement, representative democracy consummates the triumph of economics over politics, the triumph in the public sphere, for the most part, of the private and self-regarding over the impersonal and the worldly. A word on each of these two main considerations is in order.

In regard to the fact that much of the political energies of representative democracy are absorbed by the play of economic interests, anyone must concede that self-interest, both crude and subtle, is unleashed. Conventional political science has insisted for several generations that the usual motives of political constituents—whether influential individuals, officials of corporations and other organizations, or leaders of various associations and pressure groups—are narrowly purposive, and that the techniques of persuasion used on public officials often resemble bribery or intimidation or, to use Arendt's word again, "blackmail."[2] The very notion of a public or common interest seems to vanish in this greedy roughhouse. Equally important, public officials are disposed to satisfy the claims of interest groups, even if conflicts of interest ensure a never-ending supply of dilemmas for those who must painfully decide which interest they will favor and which they must at least for the time being turn away. The "political culture" keeps public officials close, as a matter of course, to interests in society.

This normal condition is one that Arendt does not hesitate to call "corruption."[3] Those who seek and those who respond are involved in a pervasive corruption . She seems to be saying that when the domination of economics over politics takes the form of the democratic politics of interest, the corruption is intrinsic. Sometimes she places her emphasis on the ability of some interest groups to gain advantages at the expense of others. A sense of these impositions leads her to advocate that "The public realm....be shielded from the private interests which have intruded upon it in the most brutal and aggressive form."[4] But the deeper corruption she finds does not reside so much in selfishness as in self-regardingness. That is, the promotion of interest may be the promotion of legitimate interest and without hurt to others. Yet this conversion of politics into an instrument of something self-regarding is corrupt in itself, corrupt in an old civic or republican sense. One could say that such corruption is even innocent. But the more innocent it is, the more difficult it becomes to tell society that what it normally does is to extinguish true political action.

Arendt's aversion to the dominance of economic interest carries her to the extreme of suggesting, with Jefferson, that it could well be "dangerous" to give everyone the right to vote when most remain inexperienced in the *raison d'être* of politics. Voting is conceptualized by Arendt as "power....given to the people in their private capacity."[5] Toward the close of her meditation on Jefferson's barely sketched ward system of politics and the analogous council system, she goes so far as to advocate that a new republic be formed as a network of freely created and self-selected councils and grassroots political organs:

> To be sure, such an "aristocratic" form of government would spell the end of general suffrage as we understand it today; for only those who as voluntary members of an "elementary republic" have demonstrated that they care for more than their private happiness and are concerned about the state of the world would have the right to be heard in the conduct of the business of the republic.[6]

This is Arendt's only utopia: a new frame for public happiness. She never again goes so far in abandoning representative democracy, but the distaste never leaves her.

Arendt's distaste does not derive from an uncharacteristic fit of moralizing. Her plea for public happiness is scarcely a plea for any kind of altruism. We have seen how strong her fear of (absolute) goodness is when it interjects itself into politics. The politics of selfishness, as well as the larger politics of self-regardingness, is bad because it is unworldly. It is unworldly because it is unconcerned with the survival of the world, which is understood especially as the place where political action is possible. The aim of politics is to perpetuate itself, to immortalize itself—not only in the sense that individuals aspire to say and do imperishable things, but in the enfolding sense that all who act act for the sake of preserving future possibilities of action. The common interest is the preservation of the frame of action, a constitution. Those who act in the proper way are those who act with the feeling that others will come after them to take their place on the stage of action. She says, "If the world is to contain a public space, it cannot be erected for one generation and planned for the living only; it must transcend the life-span of mortal men."[7]

Relatedly, the concept of the public signifies that the world as the place of action must be "common to all of us and distinguished from our privately owned place in it."[8] It not only permits what is best in each to disclose itself, but it is separate from each. It vanishes when it is owned or possessed just as much as when it is ignored. The politics of selfishness and self-regardingness are no more consonant with true politics than either psychological self-absorption or a religious concern with eternity. The misfortune is that representative democracy, in its unyielding actuality, is in Arendt's judgment little more than the consecration of selfishness and self-regardingness. And that little more is too often a concern with economic necessity.

In some remarks made not long before her death, Arendt presented a different contrasting conception to selfishness and self-regardingness. Not worldliness as concern for one's own immortality or that of the public world, but impartiality is offered as the proper spirit of public participation. She presents *impartiality* as a kind of worldliness, but she changes the existential coloring. The political institution in which impartiality is the presiding principle is the jury. In an earlier conversation with colleagues at a conference devoted to her work (November 1972), she had spoken of the jury as "the last remnant of active citizen participation in the republic," and, like the town meeting, one of "the very few places where a non-spurious public still exists."[9] She had never before considered the jury as a truly *political* institution. Impartiality had rarely appeared before in any itemization of *political* virtues.[10]

Arendt's last remarks on the jury enrich her conception of political action. Yet it still is a bit strange that an occasion as essentially reactive, not to say passive, as service on a jury should strike Arendt as one real model of political life. In any case, what matters is that the qualities of engagement expected of jurors are contrasted sharply with the qualities enlisted in the normal politics of representative democracy:

> Jurors are equalized by the task and the place....They must deal with something which is of no private interest to them at all: they are interested in someth ing in regard to which they are disinterested. What jurors share is an interest in the case—something outside themselves; what makes them common is something that is not subjective.[11]

Arendt's sustained antithesis to this worldly impartiality is the pursuit of economic interest. She insists that there is "an intrinsic conflict" between all interests (as conventionally defined) and an interest in the world. Indeed, she makes sacrifice of private interests an inevitable feature of fidelity to the well-being of the public world—perhaps its very sign.[12]

In regard to the other way in which economics crowds out politics—namely, the determination to ameliorate the condition of the disadvantaged—Arendt is similarly unrelenting. Of course, it is not that she wants the disadvantaged to be ignored. Certainly in recent times the capacities of amelioration have grown far beyond what they were when Robespierre and Saint-Just tried to practice the politics of pity. Arendt is hostile to capitalism not only because it now subjugates capitalist societies (and by the radiation of its influence, socialist societies too) to unappeasable consumerism, but also because she associates it historically with the intensification of misery. The "unchained, unbridled 'private initiative' of capitalism [has] in the absence of natural wealth....led everywhere to unhappiness and mass poverty."[13]

Arendt's theoretical contention is that the project of amelioration, although by no means guaranteed success, can proceed only in an administered manner. For that reason, if this project comes to be seen as the central focus of public life, the understanding of the nature of public life is lost. Thus capitalism in its successes and failures, in its opulence and in its misery, accentuates the departure from the truly political. Ideally, there would be no misery. Given its extent, attention must be paid to it. Arendt's hope would be that such attention would be paid only by those who know how to deal with the complexities inherent in the condition of the disadvantaged. These complexities should not be politicized. Only then would the field of public life be left open and reserved for the truly political.

Arendt offers two convergent arguments. First, the effort to politicize administration injures administration. Second, the effort to politicize administration injures politics. Her underlying premise is that wherever a question of policy has one and only one right answer it ceases having one of the traits that are necessary for a question to be appropriate for discussion in the public place, for it to be the pretext or instigation for action as revelatory speech. "Public debate can only deal with things which—if we want to put it negatively—we cannot figure out with certainty."[14] There must be room for citizenly variety to manifest itself in expressed differences of response, and thus for persuasion. Arendt hence suggests that political life thrives only on indeterminacy. She never says or implies that the range of valid opinion is indefinitely large, or that we should withhold the words *right* and *wrong* altogether from the opinions put forth in public discussion and debate. There is a distinction between a confined indeterminacy, so to speak, and an absolute insolubility. The model of the jury figures in her remarks on indeterminacy. After telling the gathering of her colleagues that she had "great delight" in serving as a juror, even though temperamentally averse to political participation in general (who else could praise action as she does but one who only watches?), she says that a jury's questions "are somehow really debatable." She adds:

The jury was extremely responsible, but also aware that there are *different viewpoints*, from the two sides of the court-trial, from which you could look at the issue. This seems to me quite clearly a matter of *common public interest*.[15]

In contrast, reformist and welfarist measures are not basically debatable. They need experts for their comprehension and implementation. "There are things where the right measures can be figured out. These things can really be administered and are not then subject to public debate."[16] Arendt gives as an example the question of how many square feet of floor space every person needs in order to have decent housing. When pressed (by Albrecht Wellmer) to give one example of a social problem that is not also a political one, she acknowledges that every such question has a "double face."[17] What she seems to mean is that there can be debate as to whether public housing should be integrated, but not as to whether every person is entitled to decent housing. In effect, she rules out two sorts of question from the sphere of indeterminacy and therefore of debate: first, whether every person has basic entitlements, and second, how to satisfy some of these entitlements materially. Strictly, her overall theoretical position requires only that the second sort be ruled out. The first sort, the issue of entitlements or rights is surely debatable. Despite the concession on the "double face" that issues may have, it emerges that Arendt has not really granted much. Her conception of political action at its best simply does not accommodate the dailiness of reformist and welfarist politics, and such politics is, in turn, a principal part of the politics of representative democracy.

What can one say in response to her account of the actuality of representative democracy? If its actuality were mostly selfishness and self-regardingness (with some managerial attention to the needs of the disadvantaged), Arendt would be right to withhold praise. It could not make distinctive moral or existential claims. If we assume that her depiction is right, the best we can do is to say that both the rough play of economic interests and the efforts undertaken in behalf of the disadvantaged show "signs and traces"[18] of real political action. Both may involve action on a large scale; specifically, in the American setting, action in the national (or state) places of politics. Unlike the several sorts of activity (mentioned in Chapter 1) that we may contemplate from a political perspective, even though they do not unfold in national places or are not strictly public, a fair amount of the politics of economics is carried on by national public actors, by national officials, elected and unelected. In dealing with these officials, private citizens are necessarily active in the national places of politics. Correspondingly, some large part of the interests or the concerns pursued have wide importance; their affairs have grave consequences and implications.

To deal with economic matters is often to deal with matters of the highest seriousness, even though anyone who takes politics itself seriously must wish that people were less obsessive about economic matters than they are, that they would more usually find other pretexts and instigations for political action. One wishes that selfishness and self-regardingness (on the one hand) had, and that concern for the misfortune of others (on the other hand) could morally have, less of a role. Yet the fact remains that both main modes of the politics of economics have at least one of the characteristics of political action at its best. That is a kind of agonistic quality. Although not all her analyses of the spirit in which the participant acts include competitiveness or the wish to excel, at least one does: action as virtuosity in performance. Her Greek conception, in general, emphasizes the agonistic.

A case could be made for the idea that both the rough play of interests and the efforts of amelioration often elicit a dramatically intense pattern of action—stirring, instructive, and sometimes dignified. Moreover, for many of the actors the involvement has a quite self-conscious agonistic aspect: The politics of economics turns into a purer politics. The desire to prevail is abstracted from economic content, and sometimes even, antagonists mainfest a greater joy in involvement than in victory. In a formal sense, capitalism is a political system. Not only is its essence economic competitiveness between firms and entrepreneurs (an important moral fact in itself), but also the connections between firms, entrepreneurs, and pressure groups (on one side) and elected and unelected officials (on the other side) are agonistic—as are the rivalries between firms and entrepeneurs for the favors and support of officials, who themselves are also impelled into agonistic relations by their constituents.

In all these respects, this play resists the drag toward centralized passivity that Arendt so dreaded. Even though the unit of action is often an organization, the politics of economics provides a vivid spectacle of nonorganizational action. By this spectacle, representative democracy as a system challenges the prestige of the idea that the only possible form of purposive and intelligent action is bureaucratic. To challenge the all-sufficiency of bureaucracy is to retard the emergence of routine thoughtlessness and hence of atrocity, among other praiseworthy results.

To some interesting degree, speech is the medium of this action. The politics of economics rarely produces great speech; its speech is too often technical or too close to a real or an affected sense of necessity to be edifying. But we must also remember that when Arendt talks about the fine politics of councils she pays no attention to rhetorical power and beauty. This more humble form of political action at its best is full of its own business, its own unglamorous dailiness. Heroic it surely is, and far more heroic than the exertions of economic actors. It is liberated and liberating. But it need not be more esthetically compelling or more capable of attaining the revelatory effects that Arendt posited for political action especially in her Greek conception.

The actuality of representative democracy, even if seen as primarily the politics of economics, is political enough in its agonistic aspect to earn for itself the designation of political—in some way not too attenuated or distorted. If this is true, it becomes less acceptable for one of Arendt's outlook to avoid a direct theoretical confrontation with representative democracy. An approximate kind of real politics is found in its normal actuality, even though not the highest kind. To allow this argument, however, is still not to reach the point from which we could then try to show that representative democracy is a genuinely distinctive political system with special moral claims, and a system that should lead someone of Arendt's outlook to praise it, if only as "second best."

Representative democracy is distinctive and praiseworthy because it sponsors, in a way and with an intensity peculiar to itself, commendable moral and political phenomena. For one with Arendt's outlook the most important of these phenomena must be the disposition to dissent, to resist, to say no. One main political form of this disposition is the politics of civil disobedience. It is not of course the only form of resistance. Arendt singles it out and praises it as the latest example of true political action. Behind her praise there is also a moral admiration for the very fact of resistance to a war she found odious. She calls civil disobedience an American invention, but she does not explain why it began in America and not elsewhere. The reason has a great deal to do with the fact that the United States is the most fully realized representative democracy, the most free of vestiges of contrasting or antithetical political systems, at least in the public realm.

In addition, civil disobedience and related forms of political resistance, by their very existence, demonstrate that other political endeavors are housed by representative democracy than the manifold exertions of the politics of economics. Significantly, they are often free of selfishnss and self-regardingness and of the impress of the technical. One must add that other noneconomic aims enter the national, state, and local political scene in America, and they do not express themselves, at least at first, in movements of illegal resistance, but rather of publicity, agitation, demonstration, persuasion, and the heightening of consciousness. Such movements offer legal naysaying, legal resistance to government policy. The issues of ecology, abortion, women's rights, and the rights of diverse minorities created movements that figured importantly in Arendt's lifetime and still figure today. Because almost all these issues are at least partly constitutional in nature, they can be nicely accommodated by Arendt's modern conception of political action. Similar movements may be expected to continue to appear, just as they always have in America. These movements are not only necessary to the working of American politics, they are emanations of its spirit. Yet they often move against the tide. They comprise the shapely amorphousness of citizenly involvement. (Of course, other representative democracies contain comparable tendencies, and obviously not always because of the force of American example.)

Thus, one may reasonably complain that Arendt did not give enough attention to the abundance of noneconomic political movements that were all around her. The politics of representative democracy has always shown a genuine and vibrant political life besides the economic agon. And though this life is conceptually linked to the spirit of representative democracy and practically linked to its basic institution, the electoral system, it is a parallel political system to the formal one. For many, citizenship is not confined to voting, even though its more dramatic engagements can be only episodic, and perhaps singular in and discontinuous with the rest of the lives of those engaged. The all-absorbing politics of the polis or the councils is not reproduced by these movements. However, they may be as urgent and revelatory as, say, the politics of the councils, even if characteristically negative and reactive. And though negative and reactive, they are not limited in creative passion.

If that is the case, it follows that Arendt's depiction of the actuality of representative democracy is seriously incomplete. She does not take in what her own outlook should have highlighted. The crucial result is that when she theorizes issues connected to representative democracy, she produces a stimulating set of reflections, but she does not bestow on representative democracy itself a moral status that it deserves. It is as if the system were too coarse in its dailiness to be a fit object of theoretical embrace. Furthermore, Arendt leaves it at the mercy of a "thin" theory of obligation—a thinness that answers to her general distaste for a system that she virtually identifies with the politics of selfishness and self-regardingness, as well as with the confusion of the political and the administrative.

Consent to be Governed

How, then, does Arendt approach representative democracy theoretically? The leading texts are *On Revolution* and "Civil Disobedience," but *The Human Condition* also contains some relevant considerations. She introduces some conceptual changes from the earlier texts to "Civil Disobedience," published in 1970. Also, only in the latter essay does she make a direct contribution to the theory of political obligation, a basic component of the theory of representative democracy. The general tendency of her work is remote from concern with political obligation, despite the political emphasis she gives to the idea of the promise. The associative bonds she idealizes lack the distance, the strains and reluctances, the degree of alienation, that always accompany associative bonds conceived as bonds of obligation.

Arendt would think it foreign for a comparatively small group of citizens, whether in the polis or town meeting or councils, to imagine that they were held together by a sense of obligation, or even by a sense of duty. Obedience to agencies outside themselves, to enactments they do not make for themselves, does not define their relationship, which is that of mutuality. A positive commitment, sustained by continuous participation, makes obligation or duty look pale, out of place. Yet the vicissitudes of representative democracy impinge: She eventually works out a theory of obligation when the issue of disobedience becomes stark. Without civil disobedience it is doubtful that Arendt would ever have turned to this theme, even though *The Human Condition* and *On Revolution* certainly offer some intimations.

The fundamental matter is that Arendt conceives of representative democracy as a system that works by means of an essential passivity, the passivity of the large mass of individuals who live under it. That they live *under* it is only another way of saying that they do not live the system: Their continuous and direct relations do not constitute the system. She relegates representative democracy to a status radically severed from direct democracy, and she nearly assimilates it to all nontyrannical systems, even if they are nondemocratic systems: especially to limited monarchy.[19] The irony is that she sees passivity not in spite of, but because of, the obsession with economic affairs. The energies of selfishness and self-regardingness derive from political passivity or inertness. All that furious activity comes from a dead core. Representative democracy thus contributes to that unmaking of man that Tom Paine condemned the ancien régime for, and which he thought that representative democracy would remedy much more suitably than "simple" democracy.

Arendt in effect rejects Paine's judgment. Representative democracy allows people to unmake themselves, even while they think themselves whole and free. Whenever the pursuit of happiness is the declared principle, and happiness is understood as private rather than public, and understood as "getting and spending" rather than as achieving a public identity through action, the reign of passivity is established, and with it and as part of it the confirmation of human isolation.[20] One might say that for Arendt selfishness and self-regardingness are deplorable not so much because they are immoral or show indifference to others, but because they condemn people to an existential lack, the inability to live intensely, to acquire individuation. Yet representative democracy is, as it were, the voluntary renunciation of such a possibility.

The devotion of life to the pursuit of (private) happiness creates the willingness to be governed. The willingness to be governed is the sacrifice of active citizenship. Let us notice certain things Arendt indicates about governance. First, she is not a philosophical anarchist. She never even toys with the idea that a society could exist without government (in the executive, bureaucratic sense). Her only conceptual dread is that a government will claim sovereignty over its people. (She celebrates the American theoretical avoidance of such governmental sovereignty).[21] Second, she is sympathetic to the concept of authority, and she is prepared to praise the institutional embodiment that, for example, republican Rome and constitutional America have given it. The only proviso is that *political* office-holders must not claim authority over their fellow citizens and thus reduce them to children.[22] Last, she is not swift to denounce all those governed peoples who have never had the chance to imagine or to practice political action at its best.

For all the weight of these things, Arendt is insistent in her assertion that representative democracy is the forfeiture—at least half deliberate—of the opportunity to escape the condition in which people are *only* subject to government and do not also reserve for themselves the regular practice of participatory politics: the various activities of discussion, deliberation, and persuasion that lead to decision-making. The political passions present in democratic revolutions of the eighteenth century did not survive their initial success, the founding of new political systems. Either the new system failed by design to create a regular way of enlisting those passions (as in America), or it succumbed to the claims of necessity (as in France). The passions, we can say, were deflected by either the politics of economics (in America) or the politics of pity (in France). The moment was lost. The story of this loss is told in *On Revolution*.

What matters theoretically is the philosophical argumentation that facilitated or rationalized the abdication of active citizenship, the conversion of the promise of freedom into a voluntarily accepted and therefore more efficacious system of *governance*, a system largely devoid of the opportunity for ordinary people to practice citizenship.

It should be noted that Arendt casually distinguishes between *ruling* and *governing*. The distinction is not elaborated or systematically applied; but it does work in favor of representative government, at least in America and Britain. Her most direct statement is found in remarks she made at a roundtable discussion in 1969:

> Now you can rule over willing subjects and unwilling subjects. To the extent that you rule over willing subjects, you can say that they have consented to be ruled. And this was in a way true for all medieval forms of government. But it is not our concept of government. Our way is that we form the government and we elect our representatives who then govern, but do *not* rule.[23]

Because representatives do not rule, citizens do not resignedly *obey*, but actively *support*, the laws. At least, their obedience is never unquestioning, and it is certainly never the childish obedience of man to man.[24] "Under conditions of representative government the people are supposed to rule those who govern them."[25]

Yet Arendt speaks of the dilemma of representation. If the representatives are bound by their constituents, they cannot engage in original, spontaneous action, and if they are not so bound, "the age-old distinction between ruler and ruled which the Revolution had set out to abolish through the establishment of a republic has asserted itself once again."[26] In the first case, the office-holders are reduced to experts and agents, and thus their action is reduced to something like administration. In the second case, the people are reduced to the condition of subject, free only on election day. Arendt says that the latter is "somewhat closer to realities."[27] In saying that, however, she is implying that the office-holders are true citizens not because they rule the represented. Her emphasis is on the genuinely political relations of discussion and deliberation within the group of elected office-holders (to leave aside the question of whether the content of their talk is genuinely political), rather than on the relations between office-holders and the mass of politically inactive individuals.[28] That is, ruling even in the form of making rules (laws) for others, not only in the form of administering rules over others, is a relation of unequals. We therefore can call it true action only if we sever it from its very nature and actual effect; only if we ignore the fact that in their discussion and deliberation, the representatives have made laws for others—the people—to obey. (Not that the lawmakers are above the laws, of course.)

What matters most, however, is that *if the people go along unquestioningly*, representative democracy retains the network of ruling and being ruled, with all the existential loss sustained by the great majority who never hold office or seek participation. The distinction between being governed and being ruled tends easily to effacement. Not until the appearance of civil disobedience in the 1960s does Arendt say that modern citizenship can also exist outside of offices, whether the offices of representative democracy or the informal offices of councils.

The philosophical argumentation that facilitates or rationalizes this free alienation by most of the people is found in the theory of consent as embodied in contract. Arendt develops this theme in *On Revolution*. Her treatment is undeniably rich, and it uncovers aspects of the theory that are ignored by most commentators and readers. She manages, once again, to refresh a subject that had grown wearisome and over-familiar and had therefore suffered an undeserved diminishment. Yet her analysis is not always acceptable, and some of her conclusions are certainly not acceptable. Later, in "Civil Disobedience" she revises her analysis of contract and, at the same time, so reworks her understanding of consent as to rehabilitate this concept, even while disconnecting it from the regular institutional workings of representative democracy. In the first discussion, as well as in the later one, she theorizes with the effect of disparaging representative democracy's claim to distinctiveness and praise.

Arendt's basic thesis concerning the nature of representative government, as presented in *On Revolution*, is that:

> Even if there is communication between representative and voter, between the nation and parliament—and the existence of such communication marks the outstanding difference between the governments of the British and the Americans, on one side, and those of Western Europe, on the other—this communication is never between equals but between those who aspire to govern and *those who consent to be governed* (emphasis added).[29]

The cardinal notion seems to be "consent to be governed": representative democracy is a system in which the people give their consent to be governed. Arendt has deliberately taken an ambiguous phrase—"consent of the governed"—and changed it so as to reduce it to an essentially passive meaning. She finds in the practices of limited monarchy the source and earliest embodiment of consent, even if it is consent to be ruled rather than governed. Therefore, from the point of view of provision for ture political action of the people, representative democracy hardly marks an advance over the more moderate regimes of centuries past. Evidence of consent to rule consists in "the right to voice grievances and to withhold consent":[30] which rights were held at the king's discretion by incipient parliamentary bodies that could say yes or no but not really act, not initiate. Of course, modern representative democracy is not so dominated by the executive; and the executive is not hereditary. Ruling is not the same as governing. Still, Arendt means to draw limited monarchy and representative democracy closer together than almost any other political scientist would hazard to do.

Although she does not explicitly link her discussion of representative democracy in *On Revolution* to her consideration of theories of contract, it seems that Arendt wishes to suggest that the philosophical foundations of representative democracy are in a certain tradition of contractual theory. Whatever the theoretical contribution made by the practices of limited monarchy, one theory of contract in the seventeenth century and later has been decisive for the articulated self-understanding of representative democracy. Against this theory of contract Arendt plays off another, which she prizes; and in her prizing of it, the contrary theory, associated with representative democracy, is necessarily reproached.

The contract (social contract) Arendt prizes creates a body politic on the basis of mutual promises made by equals. The model is the Mayflower Compact. The disseminated examples are the towns and counties and other political units of colonial America. She is passionate and eloquent about the political novelty shown by the untutored genius of the English settlers. Confronted by the perils of a new world and thrown back on themselves, they found salvation in mutual trust. They bound each other by freely given promises and lived up to them. The continuous political institutionalization of the original declaration of mutuality was a daily, participatory politics: The forum of decision-making was the town meeting.

Arendt pays little attention to magistracies, executive functions. She says too quickly that these new political bodies "were not conceived as governments, strictly speaking."[31] She must take the necessity of magistracy as a matter of course. What signifies is that there existed something besides magistracies and something in place of an alienating representation. The political life of early America—without which the urge to declare independence and fight a war to secure it would have been unthinkable—was, then, the realization of the best political life. Society originated in the voluntary and binding agreement of the interested parties; and inherent in the agreement was provision for "a new power structure" of equal participants continuously active deliberatively.[32]

In contrast to the prized theory of contract is the philosophers' conceptualization of the social contract. Not only Hobbes but also the "innocent" Locke is enlisted by Arendt in the tradition of consent as solely consent to be *ruled*. (In *On Revolution* she never *explicitly* fits consent to be *governed* into a contractual theory.) She says that only the contract of mutuality contains the republican principle *"in nuce."*[33] Any political system of consent, whether to be ruled or to be governed, signifies popular abdication to one degree or another. Of course, no tradition of theory can be seen as the sufficient or prepotent source of the creation and perpetuation of political institutions. Still, theory provides at least a rationalization that bestows an artificial intelligibility on systems in being or in the process of formation, and by doing that, strengthens them and may even in time bring them more nearly to resemble their theoretical shape. Perhaps that is the intellectual pattern Arendt posits: theory eased the way for Americans after the Revolution to abandon the colonial political "treasure," and to pursue, instead, private happiness, while erroneously claiming to be free—free, in the true sense, not merely liberated from oppression. The cunning of the theory of consent is that it hides existential subjection.

Arendt is saying in *On Revolution* that the theory of Hobbes and Locke is a theory of contract between "a people and its ruler," or between "a given society and its ruler," in return for protection.[34] Present in Hobbes and Locke is only a confused notion of a contractual founding of a society by individuals. Arendt says that the real substance of the contract in both writers is the consent of individuals to live under a government and obey it. She speaks as if the government were an already existent entity that bargained as a moral equal with each individual, or alternatively with the people. There may, in truth, be elements in the theories of Hobbes and Locke that lend themselves to this interpretation, despite the explicit rejection by both of the validity of envisaging a contractual relationship between government and the individual, or between government and the people.

In passing, one may notice that Hobbes allows for a convenant between an individual and his conqueror who becomes his sovereign after the expressed readiness of the conquered individual to acknowledge him as such. Locke's provision for an express oath of allegiance—that is, for the explicit and voluntary act of joining a proper political society by an individual—is made to the king. But even these elements fall short of a contract *with* government. The plain fact is that this contract is a feature of the parliamentary Whig tradition. For both Hobbes and Locke—and it is always a cause for suspicion when a commentator joins them in a common position—the contract simply establishes that there will be a government, its form to be decided by majority vote.

If Locke is taken as the exemplary theorist of representative government, the point is that his sense is strong and constant that government issues from the agreement of the people; that it has no claim to moral equality with them, much less to moral priority; that it is their servant. It exists by permission and on sufferance. Its temporary absence because of resistance to it is less awful than its absolutist and overpowering presence. Locke makes no explicit provision for direct participation, universal suffrage, or even automatic common citizenship. Neither representative nor participatory institutions are strict moral entailments from his basic moral principles, although a representative legislature is certainly desirable. If he is a democrat, he is a silent one. But all this is not equivalent to the theoretical rationalization of individual (or popular) passivity that must ensue from deploying the un-Lockean idea of a contract between government and the individual (or the people).

The conclusion is that consent of the governed does not mean consent to be governed (in Arendt's pejorative sense), much less consent to be ruled. No philosophy of representative democracy can rest on the idea that rightful government is coeval with the people, either literally or metaphorically, and that it therefore is their moral equal. The moral essence of representative democracy is precisely that all government, even representative democracy, is morally dubious, morally inferior. (When such an assertion is made, the executive power is the principal object of indictment.) Beyond that, Locke cannot be taken as the exemplary theorist of representative *democracy*. Although not a rationalizer of passivity, he is still not a robust, unequivocal defender of representative democracy. He should be seen more as an antecedent to the theory of representative democracy than as an actual principal.

Just by discrediting the idea of a contract with government, he works with an undeniably great force as an antecedent. But we must look to such figures as the Levellers, Paine, some anti-Federalists, American democrats of the nineteenth and twentieth centuries, and to J. S. Mill, among others, for the true articulation. When we do, we find a conceptualization (in various forms) that stresses the dynamic qualities of the notion of the consent of the governed (whether or not the idea of contract is deployed). There is no thought of a contract with government and, consequently, none of the passivity that goes along with it. (It is disturbing that Arendt sometimes lapses and speaks *approvingly* of a "contract between a people and its government," as in pre-revolutionary America.)[35] To make a claim for the praiseworthy distinctiveness of representative democracy, as against Arendt's denigrations in *On Revolution*, we must recapture some of the arguments found or implied in this conceptualization.

The heart of the matter is that an electoral system changes the nature of political authority. Even though only a comparatively small number of citizens hold elective office, and most are thus not regular participants in the political system, filling the main nonjudicial offices by (contested) election qualitatively changes the relationship between government and the people. The first way of describing the change is to say, following suggestions made by the Levellers, that every time there is an election to fill national offices the government is being made anew, being reconstituted. The electoral procedure itself—the constitutional rules specifying the offices and the mode and time of filling them—may remain constant, but the offices themselves are held only temporarily and can be filled only by regular election. They would remain unfilled otherwise. No one person or group can claim them as a matter of right. No individual has any title to office other than what successful contest gives him. He owes what he has to the choice of the relevant constituency. An individual who votes in an election renews his membership in society and thus affirms his voluntary membership. An election is a form in which each individual says to the rest that he is still one with them and with their common purpose, which is to live together on certain terms, and implicitly to acknowledge the necessity of having a government or political authority. At the same time, the group of individuals as a whole reexpresses its voluntary corporate character, and as a whole, it does what only the whole can do: It periodically reconstitutes political authority. This is the most important meaning of consent of the governed. That there must be disagreement for an election to be contested, and that offices are not filled by unanimous vote, does not affect the claim here made. Political authority can have no other existence but a periodically renewed one; just as society itself is not a prison, not a conquest, but a freely willed creation. The electoral procedure thus provides a way of acknowledging the autonomy of every individual and of the people as a whole.

Whatever the actual or fictional nature of an original creation of society by the consent of contracting individuals, the electoral procedure is a method for making the continuation of society the result of such consent. On the assumption that without a government no society could long endure, the act of filling the offices of government is in itself the re-creation of society. Thus, by this view, we argue for the reality of the consensual character of society by reference to the form of government, rather than beginning with an original act of creation of society and then, by a doctrine of necessary human rationality, deducing the form of government. Of course, participatory democracy (the only form Arendt accepts as truly political) achieves the same effect. But representative democracy does too. Since it does (if it does), it cannot be associated with passivity, or at least not in the measure that Arendt suggests. How can there be a mere consent to be governed implicit in the workings of the electoral procedure? How can one think that where there is an electoral procedure the moral equality and equal standing of government with the people, or even worse, that a contractual relationship between "a people and its ruler" is being proclaimed? Representative democracy in its innermost meaning is at war with any such reification of political authority, any intimation that the people may be understood as having permanently alienated their involvement in the constitution of political authority, just as it is at war with the idea that a reified society is above its members, greater in its dignity and morally and metaphysically superior in its interests and purposes.

A further moral consequence may be asserted. The regular workings of the electoral procedure comprise a *chastening* of political authority. By its dependence on the will and choice of the people, political authority loses all majesty. The mystique of *étatisme*, with all the punitive and regulative horrors it spawns, withers. The result is a heightened readiness to resist authority, to resist government, when office-holders forget who they are, when they forget that they are servants of the people. All kinds of authority in a society that has a genuine electoral procedure are chastened, robbed of their majesty, by the force of the transparent public example of chastening undergone by public authority. But Arendt is largely averse to a democratization of authority relations outside the public sphere—as, for example, in the work place or in schools. So we must confine ourselves to the public sphere. When we do, we must say that the phenomenon of civil disobedience is almost entirely the moral result of the changed attitudes toward public authority induced by the electoral procedure (and by its proper accompaniment, a system of constitutional restrictions on the exercise of such authority).

Civil disobedience flows from the spirit of constitutional representative democracy. It supplies an episodic and circumstantial chastening of political authority when office-holders fail to acknowledge or show they are aware of the meaning of the regular workings of the electoral procedure. It adds an episodic and circumstantial chastening to a constitutive, not to say a ritualistic, one. What must be emphasized is that without the initial sense that the electoral procedure is a continuous lesson in the meaning of political authority, civil disobedience could not be conceptually prepared for. Nor could it be psychologically or experientially prepared for.

By common understanding, civil disobedience is an act of resistance against moral atrocity or official lawlessness, or both at once. From the time of Paine and Burke forward, representative democracy itself has been theorized as a system of resistance—benign, non violent revolution institutionalized. The talents and energies democratic revolution elicits and enlarges are, in Paine's account, regularized and made civil by the regular workings of the electoral procedure. Although Paine stressed citizenly vigilance against a mistrusted executive power, he suggested something more. He expected animated disagreements over public policy and thus the readiness on the part of some to resist the decisions of others by raising questions and forcing compromises.

Effort and resistance and counterresistance are intrinsic to the system. The modes of adversariness are multiple: individual versus government, people versus government, group versus group, office-holders versus office-holders, individual versus society acting through government. (Adversariness is related to the agon of economic politics.) Naturally, the public understanding of political authority is dramatically altered when political authority is so unrelentingly caught up in such contention, such disagreement, such readiness to oppose and resist, to claim and contend. That is not to say, as Arendt in fact does, that civil disobedience is basically another form of group politics. Rather, the regular political life of representative democracy, whose skeleton is the electoral procedure, is a constant invitation to challenge political authority and, if need be, to resist it.

To have said all this is perhaps to have said the main thing in regard to Arendt and her theoretical relation to representative democracy. This system of government is the only one that inspires, fosters, or encourages popular resistance to itself when it fails to be itself. Not even direct democracy does that; its solidary nature prevents it. "The law is only a memorandum," said Emerson in his essay "Politics." It is also true that groups of civil disobedients are a memorandum to the law-makers and other office-holders. If, as Emerson also said, "Good men must not obey the laws too well," because the law sullies what it commands just by commanding it, it is then also the case that good men will not obey profoundly bad laws or be accomplices in bad policies. The whole being of representative democracy impresses these sentiments or strengthens them. If one large part of Arendt's life's work is to disclose the nature of political atrocity and to praise whatever it is that offers discouragement to its emergence or resistance to its unfolding, then we have a right to expect that she regard representative democracy with a kinder eye.

Arendt says at one point that "during the Hitler and Stalin era, entirely new and unprecedented criminality [was] almost unchallenged."[36] It is fair to say that in some representative democracies the words "almost unchallenged" could not be applied to atrocities. That representative democracies should commit atrocities may perhaps be thought a much larger fact than that they are challenged. Indeed, some of the atrocities may derive from the passions encouraged or unleashed by popular political involvement. Yet if no society is incapable of atrocity, only a few are capable of mounting steady resistance. And only in representative democracy is such resistance a mode of allegiance to the spirit of the form of government. That constitutional guarantees make resistance comparatively unhazardous must of course be acknowledged. To resist, therefore, becomes obligatory. The absence of resistance becomes blameworthy. Also, to cooperate with or be reconciled to one's own victimization runs counter to its spirit and is also blameworthy: again, another effect that should have commended itself to Arendt. How can we associate passivity with representative democracy?

Obligation and Obedience

The other main analysis that Arendt makes of issues closely connected to representative democracy, her theoretical account of civil disobedience, is also marked by avoidance and subtle denigration. We have taken up her analysis of civil disobedience as political action and the considerations that she thinks properly animate it. Here we should examine the way in which the phenomenon of civil disobedience in America leads her to general reflections on obligation and obedience, consent and law. Once again, her exposition is stimulating, but it is also unsettling to anyone who wishes to hold on to representative democracy as at least the "second best" form, and perhaps as better than that. Notice at the outset that in "Civil Disobedience," Arendt is no more willing to trace the readiness to resist atrocity to the spirit of representative democracy than she is in *On Revolution*.

Obviously many who have thought about civil disobedience have begun with the sense that it is a morally questionable activity because it involves lawbreaking: thus all lawbreaking, whether or not from personal impulses, is deemed suspect because the status of a law or laws is that they exist to be obeyed. Some say that whatever may be the status of the law in oligarchies or party or military dictatorships, it surely deserves to be obeyed in representative democracies—more exactly, in constitutional representative democracies. The form of government makes a difference to the status of the law and hence to the philosophical treatment of the question of disobedience. It does not seem that Arendt thinks that the law's status is affected by the form of government from which it issues. That disobedience takes place in a representative democracy is of no special importance. It acquires a *special* importance in America not because its government is representative, but because it is constitutional. It acquires a *general* importance because Arendt thinks that wherever law exists as something regular and rational it must be obeyed if life is to have some certainty amid inevitable change.[37] Our concern is with her view that civil disobedience is especially morally problematic and philosophically interesting because America, the first and only true home of civil disobedience, has a constitutional order. Arendt writes as if the existence of the electoral procedure were a matter of nearly total indifference.

Arendt is willing to work with the notion of consent in "Civil Disobedience." But consent now means something other than the mere consent to be governed (in exchange for protection, for the right to pursue private happiness). It is linked to the obligation to obey the law. It is also linked to one of two main kinds of political contract, indeed to a Lockean contract that Arendt had earlier associated with political passivity or abdication. She is clear that she wishes to find theoretical support for the obligation to obey the law, not simply an undefended or reflexive readiness to obey. Or at least she is now willing (for the most part) to employ without reluctance the categories of obligation and obedience. To put it more accurately: She suggests that if there is consent, there then will be an obligation to obey. She insists that the notion of consent is difficult to elaborate and defend plausibly and coherently; she also knows that contract as the modality of binding consent is itself a troublesome concept. But her reflections on civil disobedience indicate a new commitment to deal strenuously with lawbreaking, and if finally she is determined to defend lawbreaking in the form of civil disobedience, she will do so only after reasoning with concepts that seem remote from the theorization of political action at its best. Despite her strenuousness, the upshot of her discussion may nevertheless be to take the matter of lawbreaking too lightly.

If there is consent, there then will be an obligation to obey the law. Questions arise. Who consents? To what is consent properly given? Why does consent oblige? What justifies the temporary renunciation of the obligation to obey and thus the performance of acts of civil disobedience?

WHO CONSENTS?

Arendt's unit of consent, so to speak, is the individual. Individual self-binding consent is given by means of a contract with others. Arendt endorses the view that we should understand society as the result of a contract made by individuals. She is aware of the conventional reproach that the social contract is a fiction. But she is persuaded that though this reproach may be correct "legally and historically" it is not correct "existentially and theoretically."[38] Certainly American experience, beginning in colonial times, imparts an experiential veracity to the idea of social contract.

Although Arendt says that there are two main kinds of contract (mentioning a third, the Biblical covenant, which is not actively present in her analysis), the kinds are described in a different manner from that of *On Revolution*. She uses the terms *vertical* and *horizontal* to designate the two contrasting contracts. As in *On Revolution*, one kind of contract is prized while another is seen as a theoretical expression of a disturbing reality. But there is no doubt that she has changed her understanding of what theorists of "aboriginal" contract in the seventeenth century and later intended. In truth, she has more than changed—she has engaged in a sort of reversal. The vertical contract, which she now associates with Hobbes only, is summarized in the language she had used in *On Revolution* to depict the contract that registers consent to be ruled, and that she had attributed to Locke as well as Hobbes. In the vertical contract "every individual concludes an agreement with the strictly secular authority to insure his safety, for the protection of which he relinquishes all rights and powers."[39]

The horizontal contract is Locke's theoretical contribution. It creates society, not government. The horizontalness consists in the mutuality of contracting individuals who agree henceforth to live together on certain terms. Arendt says that the Lockean contract is one of promises: a people freely creates itself out of individuals rather than clustering together on a basis of "historical memories or ethnic homogeneity," or simply succumbing to Leviathan's superior force.[40] After the social contract, in a separate step, individuals "contract for their government."[41] Although in *On Revolution* she had found in Locke's conceptualization a sense of mutuality codified by promising, she thought that Locke had disregarded this aspect in favor of a larger purpose. That purpose was to establish a government for the sake of protection, a purpose that she believes is not compatible with envisaging society as a political body composed of equal participants, whose loyalty to each other is memorialized in the original agreement.

Locke is now, however, the master theoretician. More than that, American political thought and experience must be seen by reference to his horizontal contract. American society is founded by a social contract of equals. There is no contract between a people and its government. It would seem that, from the point of view of one trying to assert the praiseworthy distinctiveness of representative democracy, Arendt had made some advance toward accommodation. But that is deceptive, as becomes apparent when we look at her answer to the second question.

TO WHAT IS CONSENT PROPERLY GIVEN?

Another way of asking the question is, What should each individual expect to come out of the entire consensual process in both its steps? What kind of society and what kind of government are suitable objects of expectation? For those denied the opportunity of explicit creation because they are born into a settlement, what kind of society and what kind of government, by their very nature, clearly manifest their origin in proper consent? What institutions would deserve to be created if they did not already exist? Arendt's answer to these equivalent questions is a proper constitution. That is, even though she sometimes says there are two separate steps, indeed two separate contractual steps, her main answer is that the content of the social contract is a constitution, with the will of individuals to live together as a society necessarily implied.

The founding generation in America needed only one step: All at once the population decided on a new constitution (to replace an earlier, looser one), which created a new society continuous with the old. But two steps are certainly conceptualized by Locke. As for individuals in generations after the founding, the question of voluntary membership is ideally answered by reference to whether the constitution is worthy of support. Altogether, Arendt helps us see that a written (and formally amendable) constitution gives reality to the idea of social contract (explicit terms of agreement), just as the worthiness of the constitution gives reality to the idea of any particular individual's subscription to the contract (voluntary membership).

Arendt does not give a schematic rendering of the term *constitution*. Nevertheless, her understanding of a constitution develops by accumulation as well as by implication. Her intellectual inspiration throughout is the American Constitution. She means that a constitution stands for a general lawfulness, the rule of law, and that in addition it guarantees the right of individuals and groups to dissent. She also indicates, by reference to the plight of black Americans, that individuals and groups must be included in the tacit welcome or acceptance that society grants to succeeding generations. Thus a constitution is lawfulness, the right of dissent, and full acceptance of each person by the rest. Where these conditions are met, Arendt would say that a society originated in a horizontal contract of freely consenting individuals; but more important, it endures because of the consent of the individuals who comprise it. The constitution obliges to obedience and to something more robust than mere dutiful obedience—to support. This support "is but the continuation of the consent that brought the laws into existence to begin with."[42]

One question that arises is, Do these conditions taken together in fact establish what she is looking for, the politics of consent: the continuous renewal of an individual's consent to society, the serially given consent of individuals as they come of age, and the regular consent of the people to what government does? It seems not. How could we say that a society rests on consenting membership, and that it was worthy of doing so, unless we saw in its political workings the involvement of the supposedly consenting individuals? How could we say that a people "supports" (in an active sense) the laws unless they took part in their making? The electoral procedure of representative democracy is a way of periodically renewing the social contract by reconstituting political authority. But the electoral procedure attains another result pertinent to the concept of consent. The procedure by which offices are filled through contested elections is *eo ipso* the procedure that helps to determine the broad outlines of public policy and the broad limits of allowable governmental conduct. One necessary condition for saying that a society originated in consent and endures by consent is that political authority is regularly reconstituted. Another necessary condition is that the people actively help to set fundamental outlines and limits. The usual view is that the electoral procedure of representative democracy meets these two conditions. Put another way, the only valid social contract is one that creates or issues in a democratic constitution. In fact, Americans contractually created a society by creating a democratic constitution, even if imperfectly democratic originally, and still.

Individual consent to society is a different sort of consent from popular consent to public policy and governmental conduct. If individuals did not consent to society, there would either be anarchy or conquest. The choice to consent is shadowed by unattractive alternatives. The whole point is to make the choice to consent to society as real as possible by making society be more than the desperate avoidance of anarchy; and to make it resemble as little as possible the systemization of conquest. On the other hand, popular consent to governmental activity is not shadowed by unattractive alternatives. If the people do not consent, if they disagree, their citizenship can be used to induce change. If they agree, their consent is not mere assent or acquiescence: The possibility of dissent enhances the meaning of consent. And their consent is not mere assent or acquiescence for another reason. The electoral procedure makes their consent active, makes it even more than "support." It makes consent into a politics that works to determine the content of consent. The people give titles to offices, but not blanket permission; office-holders cannot say, "take it or leave it."

What the electoral procedure does so far as outlines for and limits on official conduct are concerned is create the people as a new unit of consent (besides the individual). Membership in society must be voluntary for every individual;

ideally, any proposal that effected a radical change in the terms of the social contract would require the consent of every individual; every individual must be politically included through suffrage and other political rights; and every individual may be said to retain a moral right of veto in all matters threatening conscience. Autonomy requires all these, as well as the largest possible area of individually determined conduct. But in regard to the more normal laws and policies enacted, in regard to the dailiness of representative democracy, the individual can no longer be thought of as the relevant unit of consent. The establishment of society by a social contract creates, at least for some theoretical purposes, a people: the group of governed, those whose obligation to obey laws and policies is a derivation of the social contract.

The law is not a singular imposition on a particular individual; it is made to be the same law for all. The unit of obligation is always the individual, even though the unit of consent is the group. An individual's autonomy is abridged not when he must obey a law he disagrees with (except in cases of conscientious disagreement), but when he is not allowed to vote or denied other political rights. His obligation is, in any case, independent of agreement and disagreement. If he agrees, he may not feel the obligation. His wishes and his obligation may coincide. But he is not merely doing the thing he wants to do when he obeys a law he agrees with, but doing what all must do. Individual agreement with a law or policy does not make obligation otiose, any more than disagreement nullifies obligation.[43]

A people's autonomy, on the other hand, is abolished when it must obey laws and policies imposed on it without the use of the electoral procedure (in the absence of direct democracy). The key consideration is that government not do what it wants on its own. Its independent will would make the people heteronomous, whether or not they agreed with its laws and policies. If laws and policies are made by consent, they are made by the consent of all the governed, the corporate people. For any particular enactment, the consent of the governed must mean the consent of the constitutional majority. Disagreement and division, the signs of the good society, are to be expected, not unanimity, which on almost all matters would be a sign of homogeneous sickness. Hence the people's autonomy is not perfectly analogous to an individual's. Obviously many laws and policies are made without citizenly involvement before the enactment, or without citizenly judgment after it, or they are made at the behest of a few only, for good purpose or bad. A people's relation to its consent is therefore not as steady as an individual's to his. Representative government undeniably establishes distance between the people and what it has consented to. In that distance, both individual obligation and the strain on it grow—although even where the people make the laws directly, the concept of obligation is still in place.

The ever-changing majority must have its (constitutional) way because the principle of equality requires it; not because, as Arendt opaquely says, "the principle of majority is inherent in the very process of decision-making."[44] The only alternative is morally unacceptable, inegalitarian, minority rule—a result not compatible with the social contract. This kind of consent, this consent of the governed concerning normal laws and policies, cannot exist outside democracy, direct or representative. The claim is that it not only exists in direct democracy but also in representative democracy because of the latter's electoral procedure. Arendt says, that "Consent, in the American understanding of the term, relies on the horizontal version of the social contract, *and not on majority decisions.*" (emphasis added.)[45] The truth may be rather that a system of majority decisions helps to demonstrate the plausibility of a horizontal contract.

Arendt's theory of the politics of consent proceeds altogether differently. She is surely ingenious:

> We all live and survive by a kind of *tacit consent*, which, however, it would be difficult to call voluntary. How can we will what is there anyhow? We might call it voluntary, though, when the child happens to be born into a community in which dissent is also a legal and *de-facto* possibility once he has grown into a man. Dissent implies consent, and is the hallmark of free government; one who knows that he may dissent knows also that he somehow consents when he does not dissent.
>
> Consent as it is implied in the right to dissent—the spirit of American law and the quintessence of American government—spells out and articulates the tacit consent given in exchange for the community's tacit welcome of new arrivals.[46]

In one stroke Arendt renders the form of government a matter of indifference. She eliminates the form of government from the set of conditions that have to be met if we are to say that the consent of individuals creates and re-creates a society and that group consent keeps it in motion. She makes a brilliant move in claiming that it is dissent that makes an otherwise tacit consent explicit. In regard to young dissenters, whether or not they are civil disobedients, she is saying that their first political word is no, and this no is also their first explicit *yes.* This move is only one example of a fine resourcefulness manifest in the essay. But the fact remains that Arendt leaves no place for the electoral procedure in resolving the question of obligation by giving reality to individual and group consent.

As we saw, Arendt is willing to allow that consent of the governed in America is not consent "in the very old sense of mere acquiescence, with its distinction between rule over willing subjects and rule over unwilling ones, but in the sense of active support and continuing participation in all matters of public interest."[47] However, her pervasive implication is that support and participation are expressed only through unstructured associative activity, including its "latest form," civil disobedience.[48] She makes no mention of the simple fact that such activity is not purely *ad hoc.* Without the existence of the electoral procedure, supportive and participatory activity would have no starting point, no framework, no source of articulation, no coherence, no focus, no ultimate object of attention, passion, and aspiration. One might say that she willfully omits the structural *sine qua non* of action she admires, just as she willfully omits its psychological *sine qua non.* The electoral procedure of constitutional democracy gets no credit. This omission also makes her approach to our next question seriously detrimental to representative democracy and hence to some considerable part of what she values.

What is involved here is the consent given by each individual to the social contract; that is, one's voluntary membership. Arendt argues, and correctly, that such consent is the only kind that is morally required for a general obligation carried by each individual to obey the laws. But to require individual consent or agreement to every law is to misunderstand law as a singular imposition. Obligation is not created *ab initio* every time a law or policy is made. A law or policy possesses its status as law or policy only because it is the result of some established political structure. The social contract (or acceptance of a constitution) creates consent to all future (valid) laws and policies, understood as the results of an established political structure, a government. It would lack meaning if it did not signify the expectation that everyone would, in future, obey. Yes, the individual must consent to be governed, must consent to be obliged. He need not stay in a society under a democratic constitution; but if he freely stays, he is obliged.

But why does consent oblige? Why is it not only necessary but sufficient for obligation? Arendt simply says, "*pacta sunt servanda.*"[49] She elaborates:

> The moral content of this consent is like the moral content of all agreements and contracts; it consists in the obligation to keep them. This obligation is inherent in all promises. Every organization of men, be it social or political, ultimately relies on man's capacity for making promises and keeping them. The only strict moral duty of the citizen is this twofold willingness to give and keep reliable assurances as to his future conduct, which forms the prepolitical condition of all other, specifically political, virtues.[50]

Such an argument is right only for particular transactions. The argument is formalist, and a formalist argument cannot establish the binding quality of the *social* contract. There surely must be more "moral content" to the social contract than its own contractual nature. Its content is a constitution. Arendt herself has set down conditions for a constitution, the political instrument that, as of right , should be created by the social contract (or after it is made). But we must go farther. We may speak of an individual's proper consent, and hence of its binding force, only if he is guaranteed political rights as a citizen who may take part in the politics of the process by which the governed share in the making of laws and policies. Although his involvement may count for little (and that is up to him to some degree), the *system* of popular consent counts immeasurably for him, not only for his well-being, but for his identity and status as a person.

Arendt's constitution comprises too scanty a provisioning of the consent of the governed. When consent means consent to an all-inclusive commitment like membership in society, it can be inferred only when, by some strict definition, there is something worthy of being pledged to. The worthiness is defined in some significant part by reference to the very principle present in the insistence on grounding membership in consent: autonomy as self-imposition of obligation.[51] Of course, one is not directly exercising autonomy just by being a member of an autonomous people, whether in direct or representative democracy. But is it not true that one's autonomy is abridged if the people, of whom one is a member, do not guide and instruct law-making and policy-making? The two kinds of autonomy go only together. To insist that original individual consent is morally necessary requires us also to insist that continuous group consent is morally necessary, even though individual autonomy is conceptually distinct from group autonomy. The social contract goes consistently only with democracy.

The danger of a narrow conception of the bindingness of consent (even if the conception is not merely formalist) is that it all too easily allows casual complaints that the social contract is meaningless. The idea that one could make an irrevocable commitment and thereafter be prepared to meet indefinitely great demands to comply and to sacrifice, with no guarantee that the source of those demands will be a government periodically re-created and periodically instructed by the people, is an incredible one. Consent without democracy does not oblige; it cannot be understood as consent. But we have only representative democracy available to us.

Another aspect of Arendt's thought works with a similar tendency to dissolve obligation by severing laws and obligation. She sees laws in a certain way: "All laws are ' "directives" rather than "imperatives." ' They direct human intercourse as the rules direct the game."[52] But can a law imposing, say, conscription really be seen that way? Furthermore, in *On Revolution*, Arendt seems to endorse the Roman view that authority was not vested in the laws, but rather "incorporated in a political institution, the Roman Senate." She also says that the Founding Fathers were unwilling "to endow with authority a branch of the legislature... The true seat of authority in the American Republic is the Supreme Court."[53] I think that she has been unambiguous about American constitutional understanding when only a far more equivocal argument should be offered concerning the location of authority in American political life.

Of course, the Supreme Court has the (provisional) last word on the meaning of the Constitution; and the Constitution is, among other things, equivalent to a social contract and hence the authoritative formulation of the terms of the original understanding. But a thousand different laws and policies have been made and will be made by Congress and other agencies. These, too, are authoritative enactments. They are enactments of legitimate authority (subject always to constitutional scrutiny). The idea of law or policy is inextricably joined to a law-making or policy-making body. Of course, there must be an investment of authority in government, not only in the Supreme Court, the Constitution, or the people, despite the right of the Court (basing itself on the Constitution) and, ultimately, the right of the people to constrain and inhibit political authority, and despite the right of the people to guide and instruct it by means of the electoral procedure. How could we speak of an obligation to obey the law in a modern society unless we posited the existence of *political* authority?

Furthermore, how could we speak of civil disobedience if there were not authoritative enactments that were normally obeyed? Civil disobedience, from the nature of the practice itself, is a special medicine that would turn into poison if it were used continuously. If its continuousness were morally justifiable, we would be in a situation in which something more drastic than civil disobedience would be morally justifiable, namely, revolution. It is only against a background of something like legitimacy (politically institutionalized) that civil disobedience (on the American model) can truly exist.

WHAT JUSTIfiES CIVIL DISOBEDIENCE?

In the absence of the idea of political authority, the status of this question becomes uncertain. What are individuals or a group doing when they disobey the law? How serious is noncriminal, nonselfish lawbreaking?

Arendt suggests that lawbreaking is wrong because it signifies that one has not kept one's original promise to obey. As we have seen, she believes with an unusual intensity that not keeping one's word is a grave offense. One harms all other parties to the social contract; one harms one's fellow citizens. The harm lies not only in injurious consequences but also in the inherent injustice of not keeping one's word, the injustice that consists in preferring oneself, in thinking oneself better than others.[54] I would gladly subscribe to this conceptualization in order to avoid any possibility of finding the wrong of lawbreaking in *lèse majesté*, in harm done political authority. Government (to give political authority its more familiar name) is not a separate entity with entitlements: as Paine reminds us, contra Hobbes, government has no rights, only duties. One could of course say that if we expect office-holders to feel obliged to act by and within the laws and the Constitution, we must, for consistency's sake, expect the same of citizens. But can we sustain that sense without trying to show as persuasively as possible, in regard to citizens, that not only is one's lawbreaking a violation of the social contract but also, on any specific occasion, a violation of the majority principle (constrained by constitutional limits)?

To violate the majority principle, where it is appropriate, is to reject human equality, understood as equal human worth. To break a law is thus not only to break faith with all those with whom one is freely tied in a contract. It is also to show one's contempt for their moral status as one's fellows. The majority principle is inherent in the consent of the governed, consent entailed by the social contract. But it also has independent standing. Equal human worth is conceptually distinct from an equal right to autonomy: To count for one and no more than one is distinct from being equally entitled to join or refuse to join with others in a horizontal social contract. The obligation to obey therefore has a double source: the social contract and equal human worth. Lawbreaking is both a contractual violation and a direct violation of respect for others. It is a double offense.

Quite casually, Arendt says:

> It is often argued that the consent to the Constitution, the *consensus universalis*, implies consent to statutory laws as well, because in representative government the people have helped to make them. This consent, I think, is indeed entirely fictitious; under the present circumstances, at any rate, it has lost all plausibility.[55]

Is she saying that if representative government were truly representative she would grant the double nature of lawbreaking, or that the closeness of government action to public will is theoretically immaterial? The proper assumption would be that where representative government approximates to the will of the constitutional majority, in its laws and policies, and does so not by a mere process of ratification, but by a genuine process of guidance and instruction politically received, lawbreaking implicates one in a complex wrong. Even if violating the law of trespass is a small offense, when large numbers do it, it turns into a large political fact and therefore into a general influence in society, for good and for bad. More important, the small offense is understandable only as a way of rejecting and impeding a law or policy that (at least, by rebuttable presumption) results from the procedures of constitutional majority decision.

This is not to say that Arendt takes lawbreaking lightly. To the contrary. Her sentiments are not in question; only the ability of her theory to deal with a fundamental issue. Breach of the original contract, apart from its political entailments, does not appear to be sufficiently weighty theoretically or psychologically to discountenance lawbreaking morally. Arendt leaves us with too thin a theory of obligation.

In any case, Arendt places the emphasis on her justification of civil disobedience on the failure of the American government to abide by the Constitution. By the Constitution, she means two things in this context: the rule of law and the right of dissent. She finds in the Vietnam War lawless executive conduct, the lawlessness of which she illustrates by reference to the waging of an undeclared war, encroachments by secret agencies, invasions of First Amendment rights, and executive disregard of the Senate's proper role.[56] Civil disobedience is the last resort against official lawlessness. When Congress acquiesces, and the Supreme Court abstains from exercising judicial review, civil disobedience is the way to protest and impede. Arendt does not fully ponder the irony of responding to lawlessness with lawbreaking, although it is not foreign to her analysis to suggest that to support lawless decisions is to be in complicity with the initial lawlessness, and that it is only by refusing complicity with a lawless pattern of activity by outwardly illegal conduct that one obeys valid law or stays faithful to the spirit of the laws, to the spirit of the Constitution, to the terms of the original contract. There is an echo of the Lockean assertion that bad rulers are the real rebels.

I have said, in the preceding chapter, that there is something anemic in confining, as Arendt does, the justification of civil disobedience during the Vietnam war to considerations of the unconstitutional or anticonstitutional behavior of office-holders. The basis is too narrow; it excludes the kind of horror or indignation that people feel at the commission of atrocities, apart from constitutional violations. But if the passional basis is too narrow, the overt specification of general reasons that Arendt gives is, contrastingly, too broad perhaps. This broadness is facilitated by her rejection of the view that laws and policies ultimately emanate from the (constitutional) will of the majority, from the consent of the governed. Believing that we are obliged to obey the law only because we have all given a general promise to do so, and that keeping promises is indispensable to most of what is precious in life, she nevertheless is rather permissive in her vindication of principled lawbreaking:

> Civil disobedience arises when ... either ... the normal channels of change no longer function, and grievances will not be heard or acted upon, or that, on the contrary, the government is about to change and has embarked upon and persists in modes of action whose legality and constitutionality are open to grave doubt. ... In other words, civil disobedience can be tuned to necessary and desirable change or to necessary and desirable preservation or restoration of the *status quo*—the preservation of rights guaranteed under the First Amendment, or the restoration of the proper balance of power in the government.[57]

One worry is the formulation, "tuned to necessary and desirable change." It is too loose and permits the introduction of self-interested or self-regarding motives; it threatens to substitute for the lawful and authorized resolution of necessarily disputed issues a continuously irregular and finally illegitimate mode.

Arendt's permissiveness culminates in the suggestion that the American legal system and perhaps even the Constitution itself (by a new amendment) "find a recognized niche for civil disobedience in our institutions of government."[58] She agrees that "the law cannot justify the violation of the law,"[59] but she insists that finding a niche is not the same as legalizing illegality. She goes so far as to say that finding a niche would be an event "of no less significance, perhaps, than the event of the founding of the *constitutio libertatis*, nearly two hundred years ago."[60] It would be preferable if she had recommended a general leniency on the part of the authorities when they are dealing with, say, trespass as a tactic of protest, of indirect civil disobedience. But such leniency is one thing; a more formal niche is quite another. Not only would a less inhibited citizenry loosen further the inhibitions of office-holders in regard to obeying the law and the Constitution, but a regularization of civil disobedience would dim the meaning of the activity, render it less serious, less heroic, less potent as a method of chastisement of authority and instruction in the future. But more important yet is the violation done the majority principle by a lawbreaking that strays beyond the strictest moral and/or constitutional necessity.

Obviously there is nothing morally problematic in any act of *direct* civil disobedience: the refusal to obey a law or policy whose content is clearly criminal. What authority never had the right to command, no one has a duty or right to do; and to punish such disobedience doubles the criminality. Arendt's main interest is in indirect civil disobedience, and as she suggests, the moral complexities of civil disobedience arise in connection with it. I think the central source of complexity is not the harm done by, say, those who trespass, but the readiness to believe that for vague reasons one can break some law or other without defaulting on the general obligation to be law-abiding in a representative democracy.

Only if it could be shown that representative democracy is not a democracy at all, or is a facade for oligarachy, or is only feebly or remotely or infrequently a democracy, could such an attitude toward disobedience be acceptable. Arendt does not accept the radical critique of representative democracy in any of these versions, except in a casual way here and there.[61] She simply reasons with scant reference to the impact of the electoral procedure on the status of laws and policies. The result is as theoretically threatening to representative democracy as the radical critique. Arendt's theory works indeliberately yet consistently to loosen the plausibility of the sense of obligation.

Imperfect Legitimacy

For all that could be said in behalf of the idea that the electoral procedure is a way of making laws and policies that obliges to obedience, the argument is itself seriously problematic. Even if we left aside both the radical critique and Arendt's passing judgment on popular consent as "fictitious," the plain truth is that laws and policies are expressions of the will (and judgment) of the constitutional majority in at best an approximate way. Often we could not speak of approximation, but we would have to say that the connection to the people is tenuous and sometimes nonexistent. The total picture is heterogeneous and shifting. Some of the causes of this partial remoteness are *structural*: for example, the very fact of representation establishes some discontinuity between government and the people; clearly office-holders have a large amount of discretion and the preponderant amount of initiative. Another major structural cause is unequal political power and influence among citizens, traceable to unequal economic and cultural power. Some of the causes are *substantive*: Many areas of policy, but especially foreign policy, ultimately the most important area, are not easily amenable, if amenable at all, to the play accommodated by the electoral procedure. Some of the causes are *circumstantial*: For example, particular office-holders may be transgressive or lawless, unresponsive, needlessly secretive, successfully corrupt.

The net result is that the most we can say is that representative democracy is only to some degree the system of popular rule or the system of the consent of the governed. From that analytic result it may follow that the obligation to obey laws and policies is, at all times, only imperfect—as imperfect as the system *qua* system of consent is. The first two sorts of causes of remoteness loosen obligation; the last sort may suspend it on particular occasions. Of course, all laws that codify basic morality and all laws that merely create morally indifferent conventions, such as traffic regulations, are not touched in their bindingness. But many laws and policies are neither morally categorical nor merely expedient. They are disputable, discretionary judgments. They present themselves as equally binding, but the process of their making imperfectly manifests the politics of popular consent. The more active government is, the more difficult the problem of legitimacy becomes, no matter how successful its policies—just as the more purposive politics is, the smaller the role of citizenship becomes. Mere disagreement does not entitle an individual or group to disobey just because the process is imperfect. We could say, however, that the sense of obligation needs to be reinforced by something else; namely, a sense of duty. If a general obligation derives from rationally imputed personal consent to a good social contract, duty derives from a less well-defined claim on oneself.[62]

The point of saying this is that if Arendt is not strict enough in defining obligation, there are limits to how strict anyone can be, if not in direct democracy, then certainly in representative democracy. But if we believe that representative democracy is distinctively praiseworthy and therefore deserves support and loyalty, we may want to add, if we can do it with propriety, a sense of duty to a sense of imperfect obligation. The hope is—it may be either quixotic or theoretically unallowable—that duty will compensate for the deficiencies of obligation and yield, among other things, a disposition to consider all laws and policies, except wicked or evil ones, as binding. What must be shown is that representative democracy deserves the effort to execute the strategem.

From Arendt's perspective we could say that representative democracy deserves support and loyalty—and hence a general law-abidingness that rests on more than a promise contractually given, as it were once and for all—because it inculcates the spirit of resistance to atrocity and hence to itself when aberrant. To keep that spirit alive we must keep representative democracy alive. To keep it alive we must act as if it were completely legitimate, as if its politics were purely the politics of consent. We must consider its laws and policies as authoritative, as coming from political authority guided and instructed by the people. Sustaining us, however, would be a sense of duty, commonly discussed as owed to praiseworthy institutions—praiseworthy apart from the problem of legitimacy, apart from questions of consent and obligation, but never to be taken as praiseworthy to begin with unless some compatibility to consent and hence to legitimacy is present in them. The obvious fact to point to is constitutionalism, the Bill of Rights. There is a duty to preserve constitutionalism, understood, however, not only as a conceptually required accompaniment to the electoral procedure but also as valuable for *nonpolitical* reasons. This is especially true of free speech and expression. The preservation of constitutionalism is tied to the preservation of representative democracy.

To indicate the praiseworthiness of representative democracy yet more largely, we would have to depart from Arendt's perspective, as well as from some of her stated likes and dislikes. We would try to show that the electoral procedure (combined with constitutionalism) fosters in all relations of life several commendable moral phenomena that, together, conduce to the emergence of a certain kind of *culture*. These phenomena include: independence, in the twofold sense of a wish to be autonomous (to lead one's own life, to make one's own soul) and of a disposition to say no, to resist inclusion in collective mindlessness or wrongdoing; a wish to democratize as many sorts of human relations as lend themselves to a greater citizenly equality; a wish to ensure that all relations are characterized by the delicacies of constitutionalism, not only fairness but compunctions, hesitations, and avoidances that figure, for example, in amendments four through eight in the American Constitution; and a sense of moral indeterminacy, a sense that though there are absolute limits, a voluptuous uncertainty as to how to judge and what to think and what, even, to want, both is a sign of life and is life itself.[63]

Thoreau as no-sayer is an emblematic figure, but there are others; some, like Whitman's Myself, are more spontaneous and abundant. In the first instance, the idea of the culture of representative democracy is resistance, yet the encouragement of resistance is paradoxically dependent on the health of its political institutions. They must be regarded better than Arendt regards them. With some strain perhaps, one could also try to demonstrate that resistance is not likely to be a salient trait of a culture unless the whole cluster of commendable phenomena existed. Although they are not merely instrumental to the spirit of resistance, they grow best in the same soil as the spirit of resistance. They all grow together. Therefore, to praise resistance may commit one to a warmer appreciation of other phenomena that belong to the same family as resistance.

And then beyond resistance—and Arendt would be the first to say that life is more than resistance—the other commendable phenomena that representative democracy sponsors, fosters, or shelters are valuable for themselves. At this point, the fact of a theorist's temperament must assert itself. Arendt dislikes two tendencies in modern democratic life that naturally emerge from these itemized dispositions. She has no patience with the effort to democratize human relations outside the public arena; and she shows immense skepticism to individuality, which in its positive expression includes autonomy. On the one hand, she is certain that all activities but politics are governed by standards that disallow the presumptuousness of unequal learners and amateurs claiming equality with masters and practitioners. On the other hand, she loves the solidarity of committed equals too much to have any feeling for individual efforts at unpolitical self-realization through conduct that differentiates and distances each from the rest. She says approvingly, "It is in the nature of a group and its power to turn against independence, the property of individual strength."[64] Yet the culture of representative democracy blesses both individuality and the democratization of all human relations. To turn against them is to be averse to representative democracy, but it is also to be averse to some of the more humane possibilities of life in the modern age.

Notes

1. Hannah Arendt, "What is Freedom?" in *Between Past and Future* (2nd ed., New York: Viking, 1968), 155.
2. Arendt, *On Revolution* (New York: Viking, 1962), 273. Hereafter cited as OR.
3. Ibid., 254-55.
4. Arendt, "Public Rights and Private Interests: In Response to Charles Frankel" in Michael Mooney and Florian Stuber, eds., *Small Comforts for Hard Times* (New York: Columbia University Press, 1977), 108. Hereafter cited as PR.
5. OR, 256.
6. Ibid., 284.
7. Arendt, *The Human Condition* (Chicago: University of Chicago Press, 1958), 55. Hereafter cited as HC. See also PR, 105.
8. HC, 52.
9. In Melvyn A. Hill, ed., *Hannah Arendt: The Recovery of the Public World* (New York: St. Martin's, 1979), 317–18. Hereafter cited as Hill.
10. See Arendt, "Truth and Politics" in *Between Past and Future*, 241, 259–62.
11. PR, 105.

12. Ibid., 106.
13. OR, 219. Yet Arendt believes in the institution of property and insists that the government should never own or control the means of production. See "Thoughts on Politics and Revolution" in *Crises of the Republic* (New York: Harcourt Brace Jovanovich, 1972), 212-14.
14. Hill, 317.
15. Ibid.
16. Ibid.
17. Ibid., 319.
18. "What is Freedom?" 169.
19. OR, 220.
20. Ibid., 170.
21. Ibid., 152. See also "Civil Disobedience" in *Crises of the Republic*, 100. Hereafter cited as CD.
22. Arendt, "The Crisis in Education" in *Between Past and Future*, 191. For the distinction between authority in persons and authority in offices, see Arendt, *On Violence* in *Crises of the Republic*, 144. Hereafter cited as OV.
23. Arendt (and others), "The Impotence of Power" in Alexander Klein, ed., *Dissent, Power, and Confrontation* (New York: McGraw-Hill, 1971), 222-23. But she says on one occasion (OR, 272) that people are ruled in a representative democracy.
24. OV, 139-40; Arendt, "Personal Responsibility Under Dictatorship," *The Listener* 72 (August 6, 1964), 185-87, 205.
25. OV, 140.
26. OR, 240.
27. Ibid.
28. OR, 280.
29. Ibid., 281. See also 168, 170.
30. Ibid., 179.
31. Ibid., 167.
32. Ibid., 169.
33. Ibid., 170.
34. Ibid.
35. CD, 85.
36. Arendt, "What is Authority?" in *Between Past and Future*, 133.
37. CD, 78-80.
38. Ibid., 87.
39. Ibid., 86.
40. Ibid., 87.
41. Ibid., 86.
42. OV, 140.
43. Two books are especially relevant to this discussion: Joseph Tussman, *Obligation and the Body Politic* (New York: Oxford, 1960), and Jeffrey H. Reiman, *In Defense of Political Philosophy* (New York: Harper and Row, 1972).
44. OR, 163.
45. CD, 92.
46. Ibid., 88.
47. Ibid., 85.
48. Ibid., 96.
49. Ibid., 97.
50. Ibid., 92.
51. OV, 140.
52. Ibid., n. xi, 193.
53. OR, 200-201.
54. OV, n. 11, 193-94.
55. CD, 88-89.
56. Ibid., 74-75. See also Arendt, "Lying in Politics" in *Crises of the Republic*; and "Home to Roost" in Sam Bass Warner, Jr., ed., *The American Experiment: Perspectives on 200 Years* (Boston: Houghton, Mifflin, 1976), 61-88.
57. CD, 74-75.
58. Ibid., 99.

59. Ibid., 89.
60. Ibid., 93-94.
61. Ibid., 88-89; OR, 280.
62. The need to distinguish between obligation and duty is discussed in John Rawls, *A Theory of Justice* (Cambridge: Harvard University Press, 1971), 111-17, 333-50.
63. I discuss these matters in "The Moral Distinctiveness of Representative Democracy," *Ethics* 9 (April 1981), 357-74.
64. OV, 143

Chapter Five

Modernity

Arendt says that her aim in *The Human Condition* is to reconsider "the human condition from the vantage point of our newest experiences and our most recent fears."[1] In truth, her whole life's work is spent on such reconsideration. Her intellectual passion is devoted to distilling the meaning of modernity, of the new. Even when she tries to penetrate the Greek and the Roman understanding of political action, her ambition is more one of retrieval than it is of historical reconstruction. Aware that a writer may engage in "hidden self-interpretation"[2] when interpreting another (as Broch did in writing on Kafka), she does the same in writing about Walter Benjamin. She says:

> Without realizing it, Benjamin actually had more in common with Heidegger's remarkable sense for living eyes and living bones that had sea-changed into pearls and coral, and as such could be saved and lifted into the present only by doing violence to their context in interpreting them with the "deadly impact" of new thoughts, than he did with the dialectical subtleties of his Marxist friends.[3]

The "break in our tradition"[4] that helps to define modernity ensures that we can neither be unreflectingly intimate with the past nor imitate it faithfully. Nor does Arendt think we can use the past for the sake of furthering a present *practical* purpose. There is no learning useful lessons from the past, certainly not from the remote past. She is as far from nostalgia as it is possible to be and still admire. Her aim is to press the past into the service of establishing the strangeness of the present; the unexperienced strangeness of the past is made to throw its light on the unrecognized strangeness of the present. Not only is modernity discontinuous, it is less and less human. To say what is human, she tears "fragments out of their context."[5] She gives a new life to the ancient world so that our new life—life in the modern world—is seen for the immense anomaly that it is.

Some of "our newest experiences" are the source of, are the equivalent of, "our most recent fears." Nazi and Stalinist totalitarianism in their unprecedented quality are an essential part of the definition of modernity. They are not, in Arendt's rendering, typical of our period; they need not have happened. Rather, they could have happened only in the modern age; they show what only modern Europe was capable of. She does not pretend to know whether anything comparable will happen again. (Arendt did not live to absorb the story of Pol Pot's Cambodia, where mass murder of the innocent was undertaken by non-Europeans infected by a European ideology.) Yet even if totalitarianism did not recur, the meaning of modernity could not be ascertained without a direct intellectual confrontation with it. If we are right in thinking that no contemporary political theory can be adequate unless it shows that it has let the worst evil leave its mark, then we can say that Arendt's work survives one of the tests of adequacy. For all the flaws in her analysis, she has done more than anyone else to present totalitarianism as a phenomenon.

Of course, encompassment of the worst evil is not the sole work of a contemporary political theorist. Let us say that our full expectation is elucidation of modernity, "the modern" (to use Walt Whitman's phrase). The assumption behind this expectation is captured in Arendt's phrase, "break in our tradition." Modern life is, in fundamental ways, new, strange, discontinuous. This is hardly a fresh thought. Hundreds of books and essays attempt to disclose the nature of modernity—some of them great or good. Arendt's work is part of the overall effort. However, because she dares to encompass the worst evil, she is one of the principal theoretical expositors of modernity. But she does more, because more must be done. There is more than one horror and there is more than horror. A rounded sense of modernity will show acquaintance with abysmal depths: but also with heights. It will perhaps suggest whether the same energies that threw humanity into the depths have also made it soar; and whether or not such a fatal connection exists, to suggest, as well, how to consider those heights. Are they only consolation, or could they be positively worthy? Or are they, instead, perversity, disguised evil, depths only a fool could think were heights?

Concerning the depths: Arendt's discussion of totalitarianism reaches beyond itself to other horrors. We can insist on the uniqueness of totalitarianism as methodical and legal genocide and still realize that in the experiences that prepared its way, and in the experiences that its victims suffered, we may find resemblances to other horrors of modern life. Arendt does not insist that the experiences that prepared the way are terrible only because they prepared the way. Nor does she imply that the experiences of dehumanization can happen only in the death camps or in the daily life of a population terrorized by totalitarian dictatorship. Although totalitarianism is a systematic response to a given historical situation, elements of that situation are everywhere around us and can be expected to continue and even worsen. Similarly, elements of the totalitarian response may detach themselves from the system and appear and reappear in various combinations.

Arendt holds that totalitarianism could not have come into being unless large numbers of civilized people felt deeply that they were superfluous, or abandoned and lost, or bereft of meaningfulness. But surely these feelings are never out of sight or out of consciousness for long in the modern world. For example, the mere numbers of people alive may weigh nightmarishly on the consciousness of those not used to such crowding, such "overpopulation." She also offers a grim passage in the midst of wondering whether crimes similar to totalitarianism will be committed in the future. She worries about the practical uses of apocalypse:

The frightening coincidence of the modern population explosion with the discovery of technical devices that, through automation, will make large sections of the population "superfluous" even in terms of labor, and that, through nuclear energy, make it possible to deal with this twofold threat by the use of instruments beside which Hitler's gassing installations look like an evil child's fumbling toys, should be enough to make us tremble.[6]

She says, most generally and chillingly, that "masses of people are continuously rendered superfluous if we continue to think of our world in utilitarian terms."[7]

The sense of being suffocated or the pain and the pathology of feeling superfluous are part of the story of *The Origins of Totalitarianism* and Arendt's other writings on totalitarianism. To read about them there is to be fortified perceptually for their occurrence elsewhere than in the context of pre-Nazi Germany and Europe. In the same way, Arendt's rendering of lostness, or of the craving for meaning in the midst of disorientation, contributes to our general sensitivity to endemic features of modern life. (This is not to say that these features have not existed in the past. The difference between now and then is that there is now a feeling of having become lost, and a self-conscious and deliberate expectation that one should not be lost or have to endure the void of meaninglessness.) In short, Arendt's conception of the conditions exploited by totalitarianism breaks out of its confines productively. It can instruct the imagination of disaster, distress, desolation; it can help the lucky ones avoid numbness in the face of suffering too great for the categories of normal life. As for the importance of Arendt's thought to actual victims and survivors, I cannot say.

Evils and Modernity

Arendt's delineation of the political system of totalitarianism itself enhances our response to political events and arrangements in modern life. On the one hand, the total enclosure within an ideological or mythological frame of mind and emotion can exist without totalitarian consequences. Mystique is almost never avoided in modern life; it grows along with both enlightenment and technical rationality. Her essay on the Pentagon Papers ("Lying in Politics") offers a striking characterization of both the problem-solving mentality and the mentality of ex-Communist anti-Communism as instances of ideological enclosure.[8] These are just two examples taken from Arendt's own work. Obviously, she provides a way of addressing comparable manifestations that she does not take up. On the other hand, the intensely modern impulse to believe that "everything is possible" appears apart from totalitarianism as well as in it. Such overreaching may be a more ambiguous tendency than Arendt characteristically allows. On occasion, she is willing to grant that the modern age "has so strangely intertwined the good with the bad."[9] That sentiment of ambiguity is rare in her work. Yet to follow her in seeing overreaching as intrinsic to totalitarianism is to be prepared at once to see it in other circumstances where it may be only obscurely present and to suspect that its possible unfolding will be demonic. For that reason, we may find some affinity between the suggestiveness radiated by Arendt's theory of totalitarianism and the quite distinct notions of it advanced by Herbert Marcuse in *One-Dimensional Man* and Norman Mailer in *The Presidential Papers* and elsewhere. Arendt's thought encourages hospitality—perhaps partly in spite of her—to metaphoric uses of "totalitarianism," especially where the theorist detects an insidious, illimitable movement of encroachment by "forces" or "the system" or bureaucracies of one kind or another.[10] She may also prepare a reader to receive Foucault's cognate analyses in his books on punishment and sexuality. Her study of totalitarianism has both inherent worth and indefinite suggestiveness.

Besides totalitarianism, Arendt discusses another great evil that helps to define modernity: nuclear weapons. She says that when science "imports cosmic processes into nature,"[11] a decisive breach opens up between the modern age (in its trajectory from Copernicus to the early twentieth century) and the present world ("the world we have to come to live in").[12] Her sense is that the present age is an acute intensification of moral and intellectual passions that first emerge clearly with Galileo and Descartes:

> Without actually standing where Archimedes wished to stand (*dos moi pou sto*), still bound to the earth through the human condition, we have found a way to act on the earth and within terrestrial nature as though we dispose of it from the outside, from the Archimedean point. And even at the risk of endangering the natural life process we expose the earth to universal, cosmic forces alien to nature's household.[13]

The fruit of the modern Archimedean project is nuclear weapons, the existence of which separates us from all the past.

The subject of nuclear weapons is pervasive. No one thinker could possibly have any special relationship to it. It dwarfs even the best as it surpasses all the moral seriousness that may be directed toward it by countless people. It is not a subject, even though another great defining evil—totalitarianism—*can* be transformed, by courageous intelligence, into a subject. Thus no special claims can be made for Arendt's treatment of nuclear weapons in the light of the modern Archimedean project. She doubtless enriches the subject by linking it to something more than its immediate genesis in military ambition; on the nuclear danger, she may influence other writers, as, for example, Jonathan Schell in *The Fate of the Earth*. Yet she shows her more typical power in expressing anxiety over the seemingly beneficent response to the threat of nuclear weapons than in articulating the total nature of that threat. If thought about nuclear weapons is an indispensable part of thought about modernity—indeed, its profoundest part—Arendt once again demonstrates her relevance to philosophizing about "the human condition from the vantage point of our newest experiences and our most recent fears." The relevance is at its most pointed, however, when she allows her long-standing concern for the integrity of the political to guide her.

In an essay prepared for a volume to honor her revered teacher, "Karl Jaspers: Citizen of the World?" (1957), Arendt in effect spells out the significance of the question mark in the title. The very idea of being a citizen of the world strikes her as dangerous to human dignity. She exempts Jaspers's universalism from complicity with it. Yet she is entirely aware of the temptations that prompt people, Jaspers's and herself included, to envisage alternatives to the present world situation. The possibility of human extinction in a nuclear war must be contemplated. The point is not to turn to stone, not to be either hopeless or paralyzed by the sense of future enormity. The more important point is not to succumb to the notion of a unitary world state as a solution to the nuclear danger. She says in a slightly too unmodulated sentence:

> Just as man and woman can be the same, namely human, only by being absolutely different from each other, so the national of every country can enter this world history of humanity only by remaining and clinging stubbornly to what he is. A world citizen, living under the tyranny of a world empire, and speaking and thinking in a kind of glorified Esperanto, would be no less a monster than a hermaphrodite.[14]

Arendt discusses only briefly the question taken up by Jaspers in *The Future of Mankind* (1958); namely, whether a unitary world *totalitarian* state (that is, tyranny) is preferable to human extinction. That is, is Western surrender preferable to mutual extinction? Jaspers does not give an unequivocal answer, but he seems to incline to the view that the risk of the "final destruction of human existence by the atom bomb" may be worth taking if it were necessary to avoid the "final destruction of the human essence by totalitarianism."[15] Before the publication of Jaspers's book, she condemned the view he later inclined to. After its publication, she condemned Jaspers's way of setting up the alternatives as specious, while unreservedly praising his book in a backnote for being free of mental reservation.[16] She said in 1954: "The moment a war can even conceivably threaten the continued existence of man on earth, the alternative between liberty and death has lost its old plausibility."[17] Later on, in considering the slogan "better dead than red" and its reverse, she scorns both sides: "The bad faith of the discussants lies in that both dodge the preposterous alternative they themselves have proposed; they are not serious." Both sides have a "mental reservation." One side does not really think that nuclear losses would ever be so great as to destroy free societies irrecoverably. The other side thinks that slavery "will not be so bad" and will eventually succumb to man's desire for liberation.[18]

Arendt may, in the later discussion, be evading what she really believes. She seems to turn away from the fact that some on both sides are ruthlessly free of mental reservation. She *does* repeat her earlier position that no one can sanely think to risk man's life for the sake of preserving it from universal tyranny, but then she undercuts the position by calling the reverse position equally ridiculous. She hates her real position; so she states it only once without equivocation and then subsequently tries to analyze the dilemma out of existence. Her true feelings also come out when she calls the atomic bombing of Hiroshima and Nagasaki "war crimes."[19]

There are of course harder questions. Suppose that man's life was not at stake, but instead millions of lives in free and in tyrannical societies, as well as in all the middling regimes on earth. Are losses in the millions to be risked—tens or hundreds of millions—for the sake of preventing universal tyranny? Tens of millions died in World War II, after all. How much does it matter analytically that they did not die in one exchange of fire, in one or two presses of a button? that no longlasting ecological trauma accompanied their deaths? that dying from nuclear weapons may often be a lengthy torture? Further, can one even speak of preserving free societies in the midst of nuclear ruins? Is it therefore only a choice between our tyranny and theirs? Would ours be better because it would be built on the memory of freedom and thus tend to undo itself with the gradual restoration of human recuperative powers? One cannot blame Arendt for not answering these questions. It is to a theorist's credit not to try.

Consider Arendt analogous analysis of the adage "Let justice be done though the world may perish." She finds that even Kant could not stomach its real meaning. When, however, truth is put in the place of justice, she says:

> The sacrifice of truth for the survival of the world would be more futile than the sacrifice of any other principle or virtue. For while we may refuse even to ask ourselves whether life would still be worth living in a world deprived of such notions as justice and freedom, the same, curiously, is not possible with respect to the seemingly so much less political idea of truth....No permanence, no perseverance in existence, can even be conceived of without men willing to testify to what is and appears to them because it is.[20]

A world without truthfulness in general is inconceivable. Her point here, however, is not easily imaginable as the basis of a specific future decision where the choice would be between *one lie* and the continuation of all human existence. If that were the choice, she would not hesitate to have the lie spoken. Who would? (Who except Kant would refuse to tell a lie in order to save *just one* innocent person from harm or death?) By remote analogy, it would seem that Arendt would prefer the world red than dead.

In any case, Arendt, like Jaspers, would never try to have us believe that a desperate answer to an inconceivably vast horror could be, in itself and at the same time, a positive good. She is far away from recent "ecological humanism," just as she is explicitly remote from sympathy with the idea of a unitary world state, even if merely technocratic rather than cruelly tyrannical. Both "solutions" threaten a human diminution. If necessary, they would still be awful. We must not let fear of the worst abolish our commitment to preserving what is valuable and humanly distinctive. That is the implicit admonition.

Arendt's emphasis is that any ideal proposal would have to retain fidelity to human plurality. Even a unitary world state that results from peaceful agreement rather than from conquest by a superpower is abhorrent. It corresponds to uniformity of mankind, a universal sameness. Paraphrasing while endorsing Jaspers's argument, she says:

> The unity of mankind and its solidarity cannot consist in a universal agreement upon one religion, or one philosophy, or one form of government, but in the faith the manifold points to a Oneness which diversity conceals and reveals at the same time.[21]

She goes so far as to say that if it were true that there was, as the Enlightenment believed, "a basic human nature underlying the multiplicity of nations, peoples, races, and religions," then human nature would be "a natural phenomenon." If that were so, "to call behavior in accordance with it 'human' would assume that human and natural behavior are one and the same."[22] She rejects the assumption.

Ultimately, hope may lie in a "framework of universal mutual agreements, which would lead into a world-wide federated structure."[23] There would be no more war, and hence the threat of human extinction would disappear, but on terms that do not save humanity while unhumanizing it. Nevertheless, while celebrating Jaspers as a man and thinker by placing him among the small number of those who have risen to the task of reconceiving humanism in a desperate age, Arendt closes the tribute with an expression of distaste even for the political arrangement she has found consonant with such humanism:

> The abolition of war, like the abolishment of a plurality of sovereign states, would harbor its own peculiar dangers; the various armies with their old traditions and more or less respected codes of honor would be replaced by federated police forces, and our experience with modern police states and totalitarian governments, where the old power of the army is eclipsed by the rising omnipotence of the police, are not apt to make us overoptimistic about this prospect.[24]

One might say that it is with relief that Arendt ends the essay in the remark: "All this, however, still lies in a far distant future."[25] She is clearly uncomfortable in the presence of any global project even when attenuated by a genuine humanism and affirmed only when the need seems incontestable. If, then, her work can instruct the imagination of disaster, it by no means seeks to indulge it.

The fact is that Arendt's reluctance, her tentativeness, in discussing any global project reflects one of the basic philosophical convictions inspiring her whole work, which is her rejection of the idea that political action is essentially instrumental, a means to some practically necessary or practically desirable end of a social or economic kind. In the nature of the case, she will be more disposed to face horrors that come from human perversion or human thoughtlessness rather than from human need. If she faces the latter kind at all, she does so only reluctantly. And she is as good at mentioning the price of responding as she is at enhancing our ability to feel the evil. We have already taken up her contention that the passion to relieve economic misery destroyed the sentiments and practices of freedom in revolutionary France and Russia. We have also noticed her view that even when economic troubles are less acute and more amenable to solution, that very solution must be administrative. It cannot be political in the double sense. Political action cannot create wealth, only economic production or theft can; and economic problems must be handled by experts, by having some people tell others what to do. Her political theory is not a theory of the beneficent uses that can be made of executive and administrative powers. It is clear, therefore, that her aversion to a unitary world state is an aversion to a world without true political action.

There is a silent lamentation in her redescription of Kant's utopia of world peace: "But this ideal state would necessarily put an end to politics and political action as we know it today and whose follies and vanities are recorded by history."[26] One wants to say that for her this prospect is as dire as a nuclear holocaust. But one cannot say that: Her own words forbid it. There is simply no way of balancing the great gain of ridding the world of the nuclear peril and the great existential loss sustained by humanity living in an administered world. Freedom is not the conquest of necessity; nor conquered from it. Freedom exists in spite of necessity, or in its absence.

The large implication of this point is that when one considers another actual and future possible horror—starvation because of "overpopulation"—one must admit that Arendt's adequacy as a political theorist of modernity comes under tremendous strain. Clearly it is not that she wants correctable suffering ignored. Rather, she does not want us to think that when governments engage in remedial, purposive activity we are seeing true political action. Remedial activity crowds out the right understanding of political action and, with it, the will to act in a truly political way. The prestige of administration subverts the idea of equal citizenship. In return, Arendt's thought works to withdraw prestige from remedial, purposive activity. In short, her philosophy must lead her to distribute her attention to the horrors of modernity unevenly. Her work demonstrates that in seeking generally to prevent a sense of the worst things from injuring the desire to posit and affirm the best things, and in seeking to deny that a solution for any of the worst things can be good in itself, she may leave some readers feeling that she has deserted them.

Great in her understanding of totalitarianism, she seems to falter or fall silent (say, about possible environmental catastrophes) when other horrors press for consideration. There might be some consolation in remembering that she persistently maintains that acts of spontaneous political audacity can avert what appeared to be a fated horror, or can interrupt and even end an existent one. There may be further consolation in noticing how she turns on her beloved Greeks in her most "Greek" book, *The Human Condition*:

> The miracle that saves the world, the realm of human affairs, from its normal, "natural" ruin is ultimately the fact of natality, in which the faculty of action is ontologically rooted. It is, in other words, the birth of new men and the new beginning....Only the full experience of this capacity can bestow upon human affairs faith and hope, those two essential characteristics of human existence which Greek antiquity ignored altogether.[27]

She goes on to find the *summa* of faith and hope in the words of Isaiah: "A child has been born unto us." To what degree these tendencies in her thought can be used to enlist her in a more desperately purposive and hopeful sense of politics one cannot say. It is probable that the effort should not be made. The limitations of her thought—or the seeming limitations—should instead be taken as a sign of what may be the truth. It may be that no body of thought could possibly possess the resources to contemplate *all* the worst things and still preserve a genuine idealism— in any case, an idealism in which a distinctive sense of political action as the supreme existential opportunity presides. All idealism requires incompleteness.

It is noteworthy in itself that the modern horror about which Arendt philosophizes the most strenuously—totalitarianism— emerged in the very sphere of human activity where she finds what she affirms as the highest existential opportunity open to the generality of mankind. (The life of thinking or of contemplation can be only for a few.) That is, she does not go outside the public sphere to find salvation, even while she is prepared as well as any other philosopher to ponder its malignancy. Furthermore, her praise of political action cannot be reduced to—it can scarcely be related to—the desire to see totalitarianism resisted by the concerted action of its enemies or intended victims. Politics is much more than resistance.

One would expect a writer so determined to persevere in delineating pathology to be overcome by repugnance at the norm: as if to say, if something as bad as this can happen in the public sphere, let us turn away from it altogether. Let us merely endure it, if we can. Let us look to some other sphere. Let us seek consolation, not expecting joy. Let us follow, say, Epictetus, and unaided by revelation or mysticism convert the splendor of nature or the freedom of the will into devices for belittling human society, especially the public sphere; of redefining that realm as trivial and delusive, as nothing in comparison to nature and psyche. Let us manage our impressions and think ourselves into self-sufficiency. Arendt refuses the temptation of Epictetus, the most natural temptation—an achievement that may ease the way to feeling less disappointment concerning Arendt's principled severance of political action from remedial, purposive activity.[28]

The Meaning of Alienation

On the *unmistakable* horrors of modernity, then, Arendt's political theory has much to offer, but some may feel that much is withheld. But, modernity is more than its horrors. Harsh complexity arises when we see that saying what a horror is may cause disagreement. The disagreement may be so acute that a phenomenon perceived as a horror by some may be thought either not so awful as a horror, or, indeed, may be thought a positive good, or at least a mixed good. For Arendt, the spiritual condition of modernity is marked by loss, which she calls, most generally, alienation. She finds in alienation not a specific horror, but a pervasive mentality that is often painful to endure and that is part of the direct or ultimate source of the specific horror of totalitarianism, and the source and also the intensified outcome of smaller wrongs and evils.

By seeing only the horror in alienation, and the horrors that may be connected to it, Arendt fails to deal properly with the heroism and greatness of modernity, which are at the source of alienation. Even more important, she takes little account of the benign effects and intimations of a moderate, everyday alienation, the kind of alienation that helps to define the self nurtured by modern constitutional representative democracy. This benign sort of alienation could not have come into existence unless the acute sort had also. Thus Arendt is at one with all those who lament alienation, even though her analysis contains some novel elements. It may be, however, that lamentation is not the right response, or not the solely right response. Unless alienation inspires more than lamentation in the political theorist, the theory cannot be fully adequate to the work of confronting modernity.

By *alienation* Arendt means two things: first, world alienation, and second, earth alienation. Words like *homelessness* and *decenteredness* catch most of the content, as does the more common synonym, *estrangement*. She is trying to conceptualize the condition in which the rightly expectable is taken away or has always been felt as missing. Quite without elaboration, Arendt assumes this condition is in some of its manifestations painful and will, painful or not, necessarily issue in social and political aberrations, large and small. But aside from the pain and the consequences, alienation is to be lamented as the wrong condition to be in. The largely unargued premise is that the human race exists in order to be at home in the world and on the earth; that our humanity is tied to the absence of alienation—at least, the radical alienation in the modern age. She says in a sympathetic paraphrase of Kant:

> But we saw that purposeless art objects, as well as the seemingly the purposeless variety of nature, have the "purpose" of pleasing men, making them feel at home in the world. This can never be proved; but purposiveness is an idea by which to regulate one's reflections in one's reflective judgments.[29]

These sentiments may be religious in nature; in fact, they may be an important component of religiousness by definition. Arendt rarely spoke of her own religious beliefs, but Alfred Kazin quotes her as saying, "I have never, since a child, doubted that God exists." [30] She also shows a steadfast refusal to use the word *religion* in any extended sense as functionalist social scientists do: She insists on reserving it for the relationship to the nonhuman, the above-human.[31] Let us just say that though she is adamantly untheological, Arendt seems to have a religious commitment to the notion that we exist to be at home in the world and on the earth, and that human identity depends on it. To be sure, the absence of alienation does not automatically mean that people are at home, or at home humanly; only that the opportunity to work on the project of being at home is not hopelessly blocked. She speaks of alienation in connection with mankind or with large masses of people in their commonality when they live fully in modernity. (She does not more precisely locate the bearers of alienation.)

Being at home in the world and on the earth, existentially or religiously right in itself for humanity, is also the precondition for an affiliated achievement: It enables individuals to feel reconciled to their lives. Reconciliation is genuine only when one has lived a life of achieved identity through memorable deeds, deeds fit to be made into stories. Groups of people must be at home in the world first if the frame of memorable deeds, the frame of political action, is to be secured and strengthened. Of course, even without this special kind of reconciliation, not being alienated matters greatly. Yet human capacities have produced world alienation and earth alienation, as well as calamitous or self-deceived efforts to overcome alienation. The hope is that humanity could be at home rightly. The hope is dashed by modernity.

The hope is dashed by the growth of human capacities to master and use nature. In the perspective of *world* alienation, the great series of events that comprise the European "discovery of the globe as a whole,"[32] and the emergence of a global economy spurred by economic ambitions retrospectively called capitalist, are decisive. In the perspective of *earth* alienation, the splitting of the atom and the exploration of space are decisive. These two related sets define modern alienation. Because mankind is just beginning to explore space, and because the full possibilities of splitting the atom are not yet disclosed, we are in a better position to know the meaning of world alienation than of earth alienation. Nevertheless, Arendt says that world alienation is of "minor significance" in comparison to earth alienation.[33]

What is world alienation? Arendt's discussion suggests a dynamic, remorseless process of economic growth, accompanied until fairly recently by immense human suffering:

> Expropriation, the deprivation for certain groups of their place in the world and their naked exposure to the exigencies of life, created both the original accumulation of wealth and the possibility of transforming this wealth into capital through labor. These together constituted the conditions for the rise of a capitalist economy....What distinguishes this development at the beginning of the modern age from similar occurrences in the past is that expropriation and wealth accumulation did not simply result in new property or lead to a new redistribution of wealth, but were fed back into the process to generate further expropriations, greater productivity, and more appropriation.[34]

The essence of the process in its earlier phases was the uprooting of many people from their land and their conversion into "free" laborers. At the same time, the very notion of property as rootedness and as an inviolable private place and shelter was transformed. "Society" replaced the family as "the subject of the new life process," while national solidarity was supposed to make up for the weakening of family solidarity.[35] The ultimate logic of the system is a global society in which cultural singularities fade and the human race experiences the same experiences and is affected by the same happenings.

We have seen that Arendt worried about the unitary world state as a proposed remedy for the problem of nuclear weapons. Abhorrence of a nearly undifferentiated global society in which all people exist, so to speak, in the same time and on the same plane is part of the worry. The fact is that Arendt *defines* the core of world alienation as, precisely, the loss of group differentiation, which is not only the loss of mediation between the individual self and everything else, but the loss of elements that help to compose a self and sanely enlist its energies. She says: "For men cannot become citizens of the world as they are citizens of their countries, and social men cannot own collectively as family and household men own their private property."[36] The unchecked movement to a global society would consummate world alienation. To be in the world one must be in only a part of it, and a part is what it is only because there are distinct other parts. Individual identity depends on group life, which depends on group identity. Every identity, whether individual or collective, requires otherness, not for the sake of developing itself through opposition and awareness of contrast, but because it is real only when perceived and acknowledged by something outside itself and different from itself. The world as a whole is not a world for any person.

"World" here means the common life of a group fixed in a place and extending over the generations. From what we have seen earlier, we can add that the public realm—the realm of political action—is the world in the narrow but deeper sense. The human condition of modernity is characterized by loss of the world in both the wide and the narrow senses: the loss of cultural rootedness and a proper public realm. In another formulation, Arendt says, "The rise of society brought about the simultaneous decline of the public as well as the private realm."[37] The rise of society is the rise of capitalism as a global political economy. She insists, against Marx, that "world alienation, and not self-alienation....has been the hallmark of the modern age."[38] She accepts Weber's thesis concerning the spiritual origins of capitalist conduct and transforms it into "his demonstration that an enormous, strictly mundane activity is possible without any care for or enjoyment of the world whatever, an activity whose deepest motivation, on the contrary, is worry and care about the self."[39] Exploiters alienated the exploited from their roots in the world: That was and is the worst fact about exploitation. But the early exploiters themselves were also alienated from the world, precisely because their work was heedless of the world. It was done for a totally self-regarding purpose: otherworldly salvation.

What is earth alienation? On the one hand, *world* alienation is, above all, the process whereby the many are ruthlessly made into one, whereby peoples and groups are drawn together in ways that weaken or abolish their identity, which cannot exist except in the world. *Earth* alienation, on the other hand, is, most generally, the ruthless transformation of the indefinite into the enclosed, the transformation of the whole earth into just one more object in the universe. In *The Human Condition* and a later essay, "The Conquest of Space and the Stature of Man," Arendt tries to show that the basic meaning of modern science has been to adopt the universe rather than the earth as its true standing point and frame of reference. We have already referred to her view that the intellectual animation behind the ability to make nuclear weapons was the Archimedean project. But she deploys the notion of the Archimedean project as a metaphor for the whole sustained effort to repeat the processes of aboriginal nature through deliberate human capacity and to define man as no more than an observer of the universe. She refers not only to reproducing "cosmic processes" but also to the will to "create or re-create the miracle of life" by the advance of biological knowledge.[40] Writing in 1958, Arendt mentions the recent fact of artificial satellities: humanity was "creating as it were...new heavenly bodies."[41] This fact she calls "second in importance to no other, not even to the splitting of the atom."

Earth alienation became literal, became earth departure, with the commencement of the exploration of space. Not only could men use and exploit nature, not only could they imitate some of its fundamental processes, they would soon be able to employ their inexhaustibly unsettling science and technology to leave the earth itself. But to be able to do so much, to be able to take leave of the earth, is to signify a disposition to a general abandonment of the earth as sufficient place, as the only home. Arendt says:

> The most radical change in the human condition we can imagine would be an emigration of men from the earth to some other planet. Such an event, no longer

totally impossible, would imply that man would have to live under man-made conditions, radically different from those the earth offers him. Neither labor nor work nor action nor, indeed, thought as we know it would then make sense any longer.[42]

The most surprises in Arendt's reflections on alienation, especially on earth alienation, are found in her essay on the conquest of space. Among them is her finding alienation in a condition that at least formally resembles the one theorized by Hegel and Marx as the *end* of alienation. For Arendt, to be totally immersed in a situation in which everything is man-made and recognizable as the result of human effort successfully achieved is to be cut off from nature, but not to have found oneself or man.[43] It is to be lost in a possibly "self-defeating" enterprise.[44] The short life span of any human being sets strict limits on his ability to be an agent of space exploration. Beyond that, the exploration of space seems in Arendt's understanding to substantiate with ever greater force the uncertainty principle of Heisenberg. Although this principle has often been made to lend itself too nicely to literary uses, we must grant Arendt her moment. She is persuaded that the loss of "the very objectivity of the natural world"[45] that Heisenberg himself inferred from the idea that observation is dependent on theory, and that incompatible theories may be used on the same events—that this loss is incurred ever more steeply as modern technology proceeds indefatigably. Space exploration is one of the great instances of technological genius, and as such, it makes an unsurpassed contribution to spreading an overall sense of the loss of objective reality. At the same time, it epitomizes earth alienation.

On the loss of objective reality Arendt says:

> All of this [technolog]y makes it more unlikely every day that man will encounter anything in the world around him that is not man-made and hence is not, in the last analysis, he himself in a different disguise. The astronaut, shot into outer space and imprisoned in his instrument-ridden capsule where each actual physical encounter with his surroundings would spell immediate death, might well be taken as the symbolic incarnation of Heisenberg's man—the man who will be the less likely ever to meet anything but himself and man-made things the more ardently he wishes to eliminate all anthropocentric considerations from his encounter with the non-human world around him.[46]

The extreme of the human is thus unnatural; the abolition of otherness in its otherness, in its strangeness, is the *triumph* of alienation. The further prospect is that once arrived at the Archimedean point with respect to the earth, once having acquired manipulative control over the whole earth, man would "need a new Archimedean point, and so *ad infinitum*. In other words, man can get lost in the immensity of the universe, for the only true Archimedean point would be the absolute void behind the universe."[47]

There is worse yet, by Arendt's account. She uses a formulation of Kafka's for her purpose. Kafka wrote that man "found the Archimedean point, but he used it against himself; it seems that he was permitted to find it only under this condition."[48] She turns this grim irony into a futurist conjecture towards the end of the essay. We find an uncharacteristic rhetorical unsteadiness in what is offered as the culminating expression of pessimism concerning earth alienation. The figurative and the literal mix confusingly. She says:

> Without as yet actually occupying the point where Archimedes had wished to stand, we have found a way to act on the earth as though we disposed of terrestrial nature from outside, from the point of Einstein's "observer freely poised in space." If we look down from this point upon what is going on on earth and upon the various activities of man, that is if we apply the Archimedean point to ourselves, then these activities will indeed appear to ourselves as no more than "overt behavior," which we can study with the same methods we use to study the behavior of rats.[49]

"Seen from a sufficient distance," man appears to undergo a mutation: to become one with his methods of movement and communication, indistinguishable from his technological creations, and rid of "speech and everyday language."[50] Thus would the "conquest of space and the science that made it possible" have approached destroying the stature of man.[51] Arendt thus hazards an answer to the question of what man is, a question she suggests in *The Human Condition* that only a nonhuman entity, only God, could answer.[52] She has the confidence to say here what man is not.

But what does "seen from a sufficient distance" mean? The literal seeing of the earth from space yielded different emotions from those Arendt mentions. The metaphorical seeing—the imagining—is already present in a good deal of social science even when the laboratory study of human beings and the study of animals with human behavior in mind are not pursued. Behaviorism and the statistical handling of human data already imply the wish for an Archimedean point, even if the point has not been reached or can never be reached. It could also be argued that the metaphorical seeing is merely illusion. Close up—that is, understood properly—the human being remains intact and survives all theoretical reduction.

Yet if Arendt stirs up more matters than she manages to shape coherently, her reflections help to give some freshness to the subject of modern alienation. She weakens, perhaps breaks, the Marxist connection between the achievement of human mastery and the overcoming of alienation. Nevertheless, because she specifically repudiates the Nietzschean concept of will to power as the secret of human aspiration,[53] because she rejects the notion of power-drive, "the passion to rule or govern," as the secret of politics,[54] and insists that totalitarian genocide was not explainable by reference to the lust for power or the rational accumulation of power, we cannot say that she performs a simple reversal. She does not suggest that the *search for mastery* is the great cause of alienation (rather than being the key to its overcoming). Nearer to her meaning is the supposition that mastery is a main consequence of some other drive, although certainly present itself in particular instances as a drive itself. The passion for mastery, with its irrespressibility that resembles or counterfeits joy, gives way in Arendt's analysis to something darker: resentment against the human condition. Although she does not use this word regularly, it best captures her theme.

Resentment as a Source of Alienation

Arendt really does not give much attention to the ultimate psychological source of the activities that create alienation. We may be mistaken in trying to find one in her analysis. She may never have thought that such opaque and interconnected matters, stretching over several centuries, could properly be traced to one source, least of all, to a shadowy psychological source. Yet she intimates one, and her analysis of modernity is enhanced by the intimation. Early in *The Human Condition* she speaks of the now manifest "desire to escape from imprisonment to the earth" and of "the wish to escape the human condition" as accounting for the exploration of space, the development of biological engineering, and the effort to extend man's life span.[55] Some future man as imagined now by scientists "seems to be possessed by a rebellion against human existence as it has been given."[56] But her implication is that humanity—most crucially, the scientifically advanced portion of it—is *now* engaged in such a rebellion. We should extend this concept to the events that issued in world alienation as well: exploration of the globe and capitalist exploitation and accumulation.

From Arendt's words, we cannot assume that this resentment is primarily that of the child seeking independence or, even more, to be self-caused, as, say, Norman O. Brown proposes in *Life Against Death*. The resentment would not be appeased by a new relation to the father, the creator. However, Arendt does speak of the modern will to "exchange as it were" human existence with its given limitations for "something he has made himself."[57] And she does attribute to Hegel, Marx, and Sartre a common "rebellion against the very factuality of the human condition" because they espouse versions of "the idea of man creating himself."[58] Nevertheless, the resentment she theorizes is broader.

It is directed at the several "conditions of human existence" (as Arendt proceeds to itemize them). These conditions comprise the human condition, or at least its givens. They are "a free gift from nowhere (secularly speaking)."[59] Arendt lists "life itself, natality and mortality, worldliness, plurality, and the earth."[60] She does not systematically tie any human endeavor to resentment of any particular one of the conditions as she ties political action to joy in natality. Nor does she give primacy to any—say, resentment of mortality. The net sense is that humanity (or at least Western humanity) resents limitation as such. (Perhaps Camus's "metaphysical rebellion" is a similar conceptualization.) Its resentment induces extremist, excessive, unsatisfiable aspiration, exertion, accomplishment. The result is world alienation and earth alienation as a general condition.

If we can say that Arendt's thought contains a dialectic of alienation, it moves from resentment to extremism to alienation. Then the pains of alienation may issue in pathology or help cause it. (It is not the sufficient cause of totalitarianism, but totalitarianism takes advantage of it, intensifying it by the very methods that promise to alleviate it.) But it would seem that the experience of alienation and of its consequences does not press humanity to give up the extremist project (of which the Archimedean project is perhaps the most dramatic form). Sickness is perhaps driven to seek its cure in more sickness. Resentment dominates; and modern science and technology give it ever greater instrumentalities, thus strengthening their own source and inspiration. At one point, Arendt describes alienation as the basic *cause* rather than the basic *result*. She says that it is "a basic condition of our whole life because out of it, and partly at least out of its despair, did arise the tremendous structure of the human artifice we inhabit today, in whose framework we have even discovered the means of destroying it together with all non-made things on earth."[61] Still, her most consistent meaning is that the root of alienation is human extremist exertion, and the root of that, in turn, is resentment of the human condition.[62]

The question arises as to whether Arendt theorizes complete acceptance of the facts of the human condition as she itemizes them. If she did, we would find a quite remarkable combination of elements in her thought: an uninhibited celebration of political action and a deep suspicion of all other human activities insofar as they show resentment of limitation. She would seem to bless only the political uses of human energies (to the point of not always showing theoretical care for their moral cost) and desire restraint and self-restraint everywhere else. Restraint and self-restraint would come from *acceptance* of the human condition and would lead to less alienation. She sometimes speaks as a humanist, and as one who hopes to see humanism revived by being made adequate to modernity in its capacity to engender horrors.[63] Quite clearly, her humanism would not consist in the affirmation of human powers displayed and employed indefinitely and in diverse modes. Her humanism is a humanism of limitation, of confinement—except for political action. In truth, Arendt's tendency is to counsel acceptance of the facts of the human condition. She does not do so as a theologian. She does so as a philosopher, even though she is prepared to endorse the Platonist view that "the true philosopher does not accept the conditions under which life has been given to man."[64] She seems to prefer that resentment lead to extremist exertion than to the characteristic philosophical distillation of resentment: the judgment that until you die "withdrawal into a sect is the second-best cure for being alive at all and having to live among men.[65]" In any case, there is no paradox involved in granting political action all favor while theorizing the desirability of accepting the facts of the human condition and submitting human activities, in general, to the discipline of such acceptance.

Earlier, we noticed Arendt's absolutely serious engagement with Silenian wisdom. That is, she has her doubts, her despair, her temptation to resent—feelings to which we could apply the word "impious" in her behalf, even though she does not do so for herself. She overcomes these feelings: That is what her theory exists to do. The basic proposition is that in the absence of concerted and efficacious resentment of the human condition, in a culture's acceptance of the facts of the human condition, there emerges the chance for an *individual's* reconciliation with other facts: the events and experiences, the suffering, in his or her life in the world. Where resentment of the human condition is not a cultural drive, all those activities that grow out of it and work to alienate humanity from the world and the earth would perhaps abate. If they abated, the possibilities for a positive commitment to the world, both in the broad cultural and social sense and in the specific political sense, would increase. The way is prepared for political action to establish itself as the focus of human energies. One measure of the greatness of politics is that it is, far more than any other human activity, implicated in the hope that each person can be reconciled to his own life. That is why Arendt can release politics while reining in everything else. Everything else tends to alienation and thus to, among other undesirable things, the foreclosure of reconciliation. Modernity makes reconciliation ever more difficult. It strengthens Silenus.

A third concept is even more religious in quality than the concepts of generalized acceptance and individual reconciliation, but it is intimately related to them. That is the concept of wonder at and gratitude for Being. Its presence is most dramatic in *The Life of the Mind*, but its pressure is constant throughout Arendt's work. In *The Human Condition* she refers to "the shocked wonder at the miracle of Being" and finds it expressed in Plato's *Theaetetus.*[66] It is "an essentially speechless" wonder, and it instigates philosophy. She says that Plato and Aristotle, despite all substantive disagreements, agree that speechlessness also characterizes the *end-state* of philosophy, which is "the speechless state of contemplation....the philosophically purified speechless wonder."[67]

In a preliminary way, we may distinguish between wonder or amazement at the fact that there is something rather than nothing, and wonder or awe at the beauty, regularity, or immensity of the universe, of the world in some natural sense. Most famously in recent times, Wittgenstein states the difference, and subordinates one response to another. "Not how the world is, is the mystical (*das Mystische*), but *that* it is."[68] Yet he goes on to say what at least seems dissonant: "The feeling of the world as a limited whole is the mystical feeling."[69] We appear to be back to "how it is" in some sense, not to its "mere" thereness. Probably the same rapid movement from one feeling to the other can be attributed to Arendt. Surely she is responsive to the idea of the world as a limited whole.

The substratum of Arendt's thought on the human and individual is a composite feeling: *wonder* at the fact that there is something rather than nothing, and *gratitude* for the beauty of the world (in a special sense of beauty). The reason for making the distinction between wonder and gratitude when Arendt herself does not is to suggest that each feeling may set up a different field of response. In fact, wonder can set up two, if it forsakes speechlessness. Arendt accepts neither. Wonder at mere thereness can lead to thoughts of a maker and hence to worship and to a search for some system of worship that accommodates wonder. Nothing in Arendt's thought moves toward a *system* of worship. Much less does it look favorably on the question, Why is there something rather than nothing? This question desires the answer that there is a purpose to all that is. "This purpose, like every purpose, must be more than nature, life, or the universe, which immediately, by this question, are degraded into means for something higher than themselves."[70] Or, wonder at mere thereness may lead to a sense of arbitrariness, of accident, of meaninglessness, of Sartre's nausea, and then perhaps to confusion or absurdist disappointment. However, Arendt is not interested in a theodicy to cure confusion or disappointment: Wonder should annul the will to justify existence by reference to some entity or purpose outside itself, or to a hidden harmony. Wonder should not be appeased, but dwelt in. Let human beings deal with meaninglessness by creating their own meaning in thinking and acting.

In short, Arendt does not want wonder to forsake its speechlessness. It too easily does and becomes frozen into a doctrine. Wonder should be present invisibly. In any case, that is how it is present in Arendt's work. It also turns out that she is not philosophically content with wonder, with amazement at the thought that there is something rather than nothing. Wonder may be too closely allied to shocked passivity. The components of her feeling are not equal: The major one is gratitude for the beauty of the world. Gratitude for beauty is more compatible with action. But her understanding of beauty is not confined to those shining appearances she praises, and praises the Greeks for praising, in *The Life of the Mind*. Not in a treatise, but in a public letter to a friend made angry by *Eichmann in Jerusalem* she enunciates a doctrine of thereness as beauty. It is a nonesthetic sense of beauty, and it has profound existential consequences. Writing to Gershom Scholem (July 24, 1963), she says:

> I have always regarded my Jewishness as one of the indisputable factual data of my life, and I have never had the wish to change or disclaim facts of this kind. There is such a thing as a basic gratitude for everything that is as it is; for what has been given and was not, could not be, *made*, for things that are *physei* and not *nomo*.[71]

What is involved here is more than the belief (mentioned above) that we exist to be at home in the world and on earth, and that we can be so only if we do not resent the facts of the human condition. Beyond the facts of the *human* condition is the way things are; this way must be regarded as worthy of acceptance and as fit for gratitude; as beautiful in the sense of being worthy of acceptance and fit for gratitude. The desire "to change or disclaim" what cannot be changed is stilled. Also stilled is any inclination to find all that exists condemnable by the standard of morality.[72]

It is legitimate to transfer Arendt's view concerning the apprehension of works of art to the apprehension of the way things are. In effect, she would have us see the way things are, as beautiful even if we cannot think they were made, or made to be beautiful. In regard to actual works of art and things of beauty, she says, adapting Kant, that taste is needed. Taste is purely disinterested; it is free of life interests and moral interests, and any care for use.[73] Its exercise requires distance, and distance is established when we do not seize what we admire, but "let it be as it is, in its appearance."[74] What is expected of us is Kant's "disinterested joy." Taste is an emanation of judgment; judgment, in this context, is "being prepared to meet the phenomena."[75] In order to be so prepared, thinking (in Arendt's sense) must cleanse the mind of rigid preconceptions and the mechanical habit of subsuming disparate phenomena under the same rule or generalization. Above all, there must be a self-emptying, a self-forgetting, if beauty is to be seen and felt. Similarly, if what there is, as it is, is to be seen and felt, not as beautiful but as worthy of the emotions aroused by beauty, and not merely used or changed or despised because unusable or unchangeable, then the person must begin and end in gratitude. Things as they are do not need to be beautiful to be beautiful.

Of course, there is much beauty, in the esthetic sense, radiated by nature and the human world.[76] This beauty helps to create receptivity, which then can teach itself to take in all things on their own terms, even the least digestible esthetically. Receptivity, however, passes beyond the discriminations of estheticism, beyond the range of taste, no matter how wise and tolerant taste may learn to become. Estheticism is *aufgehoben*. In her tribute to Heidegger, Arendt makes a certain distinction in speaking of wonder at Being that better fits the notion of gratitude for things as they are, for the way they are. She distinguishes between "the mere surprise or astonishment that arises in us when we encounter something strange" and (in Heidegger's words) "the faculty of wondering at the simple."[77] The former inspires the sciences, but the wonder that inspires thinking "applies to the everyday, the matter-of-course, what we are thoroughly acquainted and familiar with."

Arendt questions Heidegger for his quiescent openness to Being, for his will-not-to-will, for his *Gelassenheit*.[78] Yet she comes close to *Gelassenheit* in a passage in "The Concept of History":

> When Sophocles (in the famous chorus of *Antigone*) says that there is nothing more awe-inspiring than man, he goes on to exemplify this by evoking purposeful human activities which do violence to nature because they disturb what, in the absence of mortals, would be the quiet of being-forever that rests or swings within itself.[79]

Nevertheless, it is not passivity she deduces from gratitude. She escapes too literal an *amor fati*. What is changeable certainly should be changed, only without rancor or envy. By willed definition, however, political action, more than any other human activity (except thinking), is traceable to gratitude, in spite of the fact that changing the course of things defines its greatness. In its unequaled commitment to the world, it truly manifests what it means not to resent the human condition. It also best prepares for reconciliation with one's life in the world. It could play neither role unless those who engaged in it had some sort of prior acceptance of Being.

There is another accompaniment to grateful acceptance. In the letter to Scholem, Arendt says of philosphical gratitude:

> Such an attitude is pre-political, but in exceptional circumstances—such as the circumstances of Jewish politics—it is bound to have also political consequences though, as it were, in a negative way. This attitude makes certain types of behavior impossible.[80]

She means, in this passage, behavior stemming from shame or self-rejection, from resentment, to use that word again. Her point can be made general for her theory and applied to other than "exceptional circumstances." The ultimate guarantor against atrocities is gratitude for "everything that is as it is." She explicitly links totalitarianism to "contempt" for the given.[81] When such contempt turns into the feeling that any change is better than none, totalitarian leaders have found a mass sentiment to organize and articulate. Arendt does not distinguish between the facts of the human condition and specific social conditions when she speaks of such contempt. We may assume that the contempt extends to both and can work so awfully because, to begin with, there is no gratitude for Being, and also, inevitably, no wonder at it. She indissolubly ties the avoidance of political horror to an unreluctant willingness to accept what cannot be changed—perhaps even to accept many things that can be changed. She says:

> This whole sphere [of political action], its greatness notwithstanding, is limited....It does not encompass the whole of man's and the world's existence. It is limited by those things which men cannot change at will. And it is only by respecting its own borders that this realm, where we are free to act and to change, can remain intact.[82]

In sum, gratitude helps both to inspire the will to act politically and to diminish the possibility that action will be unjust or atrocious.

Yet so restless is Arendt's thought concerning thinking itself and the experiences of wonder and gratitude that adhere to it, she can say—and, appropriately, in an unpublished paper—that "the speechless horror at what men may do in political life and what the world may become is in many ways related to the speechless wonder or gratitude from which the questions of philosophy spring."[83] The presence of the evil double of political action is here acknowledged and linked to the speechlessness that may issue in suicidal world-rejection. This acknowledgment is not allowed, however, to have any place in Arendt's formal discourse.

Altogether, wonder at and gratitude for Being may help to diminish resentment of the human condition, just as inflamed resentment may close off susceptibility to wonder and gratitude. Where resentment proceeds—and its successes intensify its course—alienation ensues and works to block widespread commitment to the world (as culture) and to the life of political action. Alienation consequently prevents reconciliation to one's own experiences and sufferings, because reconciliation is founded on the stories that can be told about what one has done in action and therefore about who one is. One's reconciliation depends on the prior existence of a common home with others. The culminating formulations reach beyond Arendt's interpretation of the choral ode from Oedipus at Colonus wherein the exhilaration intrinsic to action done in cooperation and competition with one's peers gives it redemptive value. Arendt at times transfers the value of action from the actual doing and experiencing to the words later said about it. "No philosophy, no analysis, no aphorism, be it ever so profound, can compare in intensity and richness of meaning with a properly narrated story."[84] The words create a story which by its power achieves the supreme result: acceptance of all that one has done and endured.

Experience exists for the sake of language. "We can no more master the past than we can undo it. But we can reconcile ourselves to it." Reconciliation consists in acceptance. There is nothing to regret or excuse: there is, instead, "consent."[85] Quoting Isak Dinesen's words; "My life, I will not let you go except you bless me, but then I will let you go" she adds: "The reward of storytelling is to be able to let go."[86] In "Truth and Politics," Arendt expands the point:

> It is perfectly true that "all sorrows can be borne if you put them into a story or tell a story about them," in the words of Isak Dinesen.... She could have added that joy and bliss, too, become bearable and meaningful for men only when they can talk about them and tell them as a story.... The political function of the storyteller—historian or novelist—is to teach acceptance of things as they are... this acceptance... can also be called truthfulness.[87]

The notion of acceptance unites Arendt's thought on Being, the human condition, one's existence. Even the freest and most creative activity—political action—is finally consecrated because it is the truest road to acceptance.

Resentment and Acceptance

Unless alienation inspires more than lamentation, modernity's greatness cannot be seen clearly or given its due. All the more so, when alienation is conceptualized by reference to acceptance and hence to the connected themes of resentment (which is the source of alienation) and reconciliation (which is the greatest prize for individuals when humanity is not alienated). Arendt's philosophy is inhospitable to modernity through and through. She converts almost all its leading phenomena into horrors or sees them from the perspective of their contribution to horrors. She comes close to doing what Jaspers warned against doing: letting fear of the worst preclude taking risks for the best. This is not to suggest that she actually succumbs. After all, her sense of the best is not essentially modern, even when it takes a peculiarly modern form. If political action is the greatest existential opportunity, modernity must be seen as deficient, despite the fact that council governments and civil disobedience are the practical inventions of modernity.

At one point, Arendt is willing to suggest that her praise of the council system that arose in the Hungarian Revolution of 1956 is "hard to reconcile with [her earlier] assumption that the *only* clear expression of the present age's problems up to date has been the horror of totalitarianism."[88] In this instance, the peculiarly modern is not perverse but partakes of the best. And it would be a mistake to think that Arendt's praise of modern political action is only a compensatory device to allay her loathing of totalitarianism or a vicarious method for vanquishing it or a way of imagining a world in which it could never have arisen. Her commitment to political action, whether Greek or modern, is not solely traceable to such an origin. But this overriding commitment must necessarily set her at war with modernity, despite the presence of distinctive political action in it. Yet it cannot be denied that totalitarianism makes a difference in her thought even when it is not the subject. Ingratitude, resentment, and the compensatory use of ideology and myth to make masses feel at home are all involved in totalitarianism, reflected and magnified. It came in part from, exploited, and increased, alienation. Knowledge of it must tend to blight any sensitive person's effort to achieve reconciliation and acceptance. Given her love of political action and her dread of totalitarianism and and whatever shows any affinity to it, Arendt could never praise alienation or its source, resentment. She therefore could not praise modernity. She does not. Are we wrong to try? This question has no answer. One is once again in the realm of the unarguable. Let it be merely an act of faith to say that the existential opportunities as well as some of the achievements of modernity deserve praise. We can say that and still believe that no amount of greatness can weigh as much , or outweigh, the horrors. There is no commensurability, no wish to strike a balance. The horror of totalitarianism is unforgivable: incommensurate with other evils and with all greatness. Other evils are also horrors and also incommensurate with all greatness. Still, there is a life, a life in modernity. Political theory must try to take it in, in its vast indefiniteness. All we can do is to raise certain questions of Arendt's work—questions that she inspires and enables. Resentment and alienation may be commendable, and reconciliation may not be. Thus acceptance as the unifying idea must be indicted in behalf of modernity.

Is resentment of the human condition as significant for modern extremist aspiration, endeavor, and achievement as Arendt says? Athough she deplores resentment, she never makes it a small passion or sees it at the service of envy, or of the will to undermine or tarnish. It is not Nietzsche's *ressentiment*. To the contrary, it drives those who feel it to overreach. Arendt sees its largeness of spirit, but she is offended and dismayed by it. At the same time, she beautifully imputes to the scientists who worked on the space program, for instance, an utterly unself-interested submission to the task of understanding nature[89] This submission is not totally dissimilar from the disposition to be a spectator, free of all interests, whom Arendt follows Cicero in calling "the most noble group of the free-born men, for what they were doing: to look for the sake of seeing only was the freest, *liberalissimum*, of all pursuits."[90] She is also fully aware of the heroism of space feats. Yet for all these contrary motions against herself, the force of her theory is to see resentment of the human condition behind the dynamism of modern life.

Arendt does not give a sufficient place for motives other than resentment. Disinterestedness added to resentment still does not make a complete enough picture. The effects, of course, are what they are, whatever the motives may be. Nevertheless, such matters as the exploration of space, the development of biological knowledge (on the one hand) and the pursuit of wealth on a global scale (on the other hand) show delight, virtuosity, perfectionism, restlessness, a sense of craft, and a fearlessness that are humanly admirable, even though streaked with cruelty and rapacity. They show that disdain for the merely utilitarian that Arendt herself expresses when discussing art or political action.

Yet even if resentment were the major animating energy, perhaps that is the way it should be. Arendt says in *On Violence*: "rage and violence that sometimes—not always—goes with it belong among the 'natural' *human* emotions, and to cure man of them would mean nothing less than to dehumanize or emasculate him."[91] One could say, analogously, that without resentment of the human condition humanity would become dehumanized or emasculated. To give acceptance of the human condition the last word is to court cowardice or sterility. The celebration of political action is not adequate to rid Arendt's theory of this danger. Not all heroism is political heroism. Political action cannot exhaust the best human energies and capacities. It leaves too much out of the spectrum of human nature for it to be considered the definitively human activity—even if it were not as morally problematic as it in fact is. That it may be the best road each person may have of honestly reconciling himself to his life's events and pattern may call the notion of individual reconciliation into doubt.

The projects of modernity are caught best by Emerson in "Circles." At the beginning of the essay, he writes:

> Our life is an apprenticeship to the truth that around every circle another can be drawn....Every end is a beginning....
> This fact, as far as it symbolizes the moral fact of the Unattainable, the flying Perfect, around which the hands of man can never meet, at once the inspirer and the condemner of every success, may conveniently serve to connect many illustrations of human power in every department.[92]

Thus the energy to try to complete a project is in itself a warning that every completion is only temporary. The will to perfection guarantees that in spite of every effort, no achievement will ever permanently satisfy as perfect. Following Emerson, we could say that perhaps the deepest resentment is not of the human condition, but of human imperfection. Operative is not the will to be superhuman, but to be human. The will is unappeasable. The dignity is in the self-rejection by the species. If that quasi-Emersonian thought is plausible, we can say either that resentment is philosophically defensible or that resentment, refracted through an Emersonian prism, is not rancor, but mobility. Correspondingly, the hope for reconciliation with one's own life may be less exalted than a certain kind of individual self-rejection. "Don't you see," Arendt says, "if you want something better, and better, and better, you lose the good."[93] No thought could be more foreign to modernity than this one.

By no means does the Emersonian perception require loyalty to a current of thought in Heidegger, which Arendt knew and detested—the eager fatalism that consists in wanting to see every extreme tendency go its length with the philosopher's blessing, so that in its full expression it will do what it must, and by so doing, help prepare for its supersession.[94] In a letter to J. Glenn Gray, Arendt speaks of Heidegger's "grotesque idea" that National Socialism was "an encounter between global technology and modern man."[95] Heidegger's idea is worse than grotesque; but Emerson's idea, Emerson's blessing of extremist aspiration, is not Heidegger's. Emerson could say in "Circles" that " 'Blessed be nothing' and 'The worse things are the better they are' are proverbs which express the transcendentalism of common life."[96] But this attitude is an expression of defiant will, not of metaphysical resignation to the excesses of others. At the furthest edges of his view of "compensation," Emerson could not have lent himself to seeing the highest good as the "saving power"[97] in relation to the greatest evil. At most, he is urging that a seeming evil may not be a real evil, but a blessing. The highest good must be a good defined apart from evil, even if the energies of good are intertwined with those of evil. The evil cannot be willed or wanted or philosophically tolerated, whatever good it may lead to unintentionally. Emersonian innocence consists in its entire lack of that historicism that sometimes tainted Heidegger.

On the question of resentment of the human condition, one last thing can be said. If it is possible that resentment is not wrong in itself, even when it is what Arendt says it is, and that many phenomena that seem to stem from it (if only partly) are not to be condemned but praised, it may also be the case that it is compatible with wonder at and gratitude for Being. Only, wonder and gratitude would have to be somewhat different from those proposed by Arendt. They would have to have room for the Weberian sentiment, "In spite of all."[98] This sentiment is caught by Emerson's carefully phrased answer, in "Compensation," to Hamlet's question: "It is worse not to be than to be." To have that sentiment is not to preach Silenian wisdom on a cosmic scale; to wish that there had never been anything. It is only to work very hard to keep feeling gratitude. The wonder would survive the strain; actually, it is severable from gratitude. Despite its risks of passivity, wonder may be the superior passion.

When the young Marx tried to imagine a life in which social conditions were so right for man that the human condition was no longer resented, he foresaw the evaporation of God. He said, "the question about an *alien* being, about a being above nature and man—a question which implies the admission of the inessentiality of nature and of man—has become impossible in practice."[99] These words suggest that a perfect acceptance of the human condition, facilitated by social conditions that allow people to feel at home in the world, seems to be quite capable of strangling wonder at and gratitude for Being. What is at stake is not rescuing belief in God, but, to the contrary, adhering to "the inessentiality of nature and of man." As a matter of course, unbelief goes better with the sense of inessentiality than belief. Wonder and gratitude are keenest when one is smitten by that sense. Arendt has no wish to overcome inessentiality. To say that man (to leave aside nature) is essential is to assume the propriety of the *degrading* question, Why is it necessary for man to exist at all?[100] and then to answer it theologically, or as Marx does, humanistically. Both answers are as degrading as the question. Both presume to be able to say, finally, what man is, and thus to cure him of his indefiniteness. Arendt does not think, however, that some kind or degree of resentment may help to keep that sense of inessentiality alive. Yet if it does, we may conclude that the ideal of acceptance of the human condition is an obstacle to the wonder and gratitude that Arendt cherishes. And if resentment of the human condition is understood with Emerson's help, then one might say that it is the very expression of gratitude, because it radiates a greater trust in the way things are.

Alienation and Exclusion

Modern resentment of the human condition engenders attempts and achievements that alienate humanity from the world and the earth. The feeling of being at home is weakened. Masses of people feel disoriented, lost, cut off from coherence and meaningfulness, which require stability and boundedness. For the time being, world alienation is the more actual and widespread experience. (We are only at the beginnings of earth alienation.) The question arises as to whether the condition of world alienation is in itself as clearly lamentable as Arendt says. Not only may resentment and the achievements spurred by resentment be praiseworthy, but so also may resentment's ultimate consequence, alienation .

As always with Arendt, there are contrary moments. Most impressively, the essay on Lessing contains a noteworthy contention (present elsewhere, but not as vividly). She there speaks of the fraternity of persecuted or enslaved peoples, instancing European Jews before their emancipation in the nineteenth century. She says that the persecuted may manifest their humanity in "dark times," in the darkness of their exclusion and maltreatment, by bonding together, huddling, treating each other compassionately. Indeed, these "pariahs" can develop "a kindliness and sheer goodness of which human beings are otherwise scarcely capable."[101] In describing their response to life, Arendt even employs a formulation she normally reserves for the ecstatic thinker's relation to reality. She says that pariahdom can be "the source of a vitality, a joy in the simple fact of being alive, rather suggesting that life comes fully into its own only among those who are, in worldly terms, the insulted and injured."[102] But she insists that this state shows loss of the world; it is not another way of being at home in it. Pariahdom, in its intense humanity, signifies a radical absence of those qualities that are created only by having a world to be at home in and take care of. The persecuted and enslaved suffer an "atrophy of all the organs" that people use to engage with the world: common sense as well as "the sense of beauty, or taste, with which we love the world."[103] The humanity of the pariahs is thus dearly bought. The "great privilege of being unburdened by care for the world" sponsors their humanity.[104]

Thus Arendt makes it clear that the world (understood as a culture that has a politics) is not meant to be a warm place, any more than it is meant to be a place of oppression. It is cool and hard; a place of struggle. It must be made a home, and it can be kept a home only precariously. A home is what necessitates sacrifice. Likewise, it is not a place of intellectual uniformity or certainties: Politics works on opinions; its food is disagreement growing out of human diversity. Yet all these characterizations do not suffice. To be at home in the world is for a people to be free, to be responsible politically for the cultural totality. To be alienated from the world may not always mean oppression or even physical or mental hardship. Pariahs can be comfortable, although usually they are not. What matters finally, however, is to have a world: the place of the highest existential opportunities as well as the greatest dangers. It gives individuals identity and the chance for reconciliation, but also it may ask that not only comforts but also life itself be given up.

When therefore we say that Arendt dreads alienation from the world, we do not mean to suggest that she falls for one of the worst modern temptations, that of pining for an intimate community, for some anthropologically induced tribalism. Her antimodernism is free of this excessively modernist antimodernism. She theorizes the need for distance between peers, not only their need for mutual presence and common undertakings. Yet is there something to be said in behalf of world alienation—something other than what she has said about the vitality and warm humanity of certain excluded or exploited groups of people?

We may begin negatively. We say something in alienation's behalf when we try to tally the cost of being at home in the world. Obviously Arendt's strong sense is that by arming resentment scientifically and technologically, modernity fosters alienation. The conclusion must be that all the achievements that are thus tied to alienation should, ideally, have never come to be. In fact, whatever the role of resentment in their making, humanity would be better off without them. It may be impossible to talk sensibly about undoing, but it is clear that many would prefer a world without the human ability to create nuclear weapons. For a moment, ignore that ability. Consider all the achievements since the time we now call the dawn of modernity—the time of European global exploration, the Reformation, the Renaissance, the start of the system of capitalism. We cannot wish all this undone. Not even the most feudal Catholic could, except in an insubstantial mood. To undo the productions of later capitalism? We do not have to be Marxists to repel the thought.

It is not that we seek here to transfer the sentiment of acceptance to precisely the one area from which Arendt withholds it. Rather, it is to say that humanity is no longer imaginable without these and related happenings. Who would we be without them?[105] Their costs have been and will continue to be stupendous: costs of the sort that Arendt keenly theorizes, and other costs as well. But we cannot undo, except in fantasy, but not in imagination, five centuries. Then, too, it is hard to resist the feeling that the fruit of the science and technology of these centuries has been such an enhancement of human experience that perhaps the true response is, after all, the sentiment of acceptance. We are not at home; we have too much at our disposal merely to construct a home. There must be some other metaphor than home for the desired condition, even when home is as richly difficult a place as Arendt conceives it. The metaphor cannot be architectural. The modern world is not solid, but misty or particulate.

The Costs of Being at Home in the World

The costs of alienation are great; so would be the costs of trying to ensure its absence. It must be emphasized that Arendt's idea of being at home in the world involves hostility toward other things besides those that pertain to capitalism and to modern science and technology. First, Arendt expresses a continuous guardedness toward modern subjectivity. Second, she speaks approvingly of Greek friendship and Roman *humanitas*, both of which she says rested on the deliberate exclusion of various human endeavors, especially the search for knowledge. Third, in her last intended book, she brings philosophical thinking itself under extensive indictment as a force for alienation. In effect, the world is always threatened. So much of what human beings try to do conflicts with the health of the world. Modernity is not alone in threatening it. Nor does Arendt say that resentment is the source of everything that alienates. By the time we survey all the things that must be suspected because they contribute to alienation from the world, we might be dismayed by the variety. Not only are the great achievements of modern science and technology regarded with a cold eye, but so is much of the long-standing human effort to gain ever more truth and experience. The critique of this effort goes hand in hand with Arendt's disparagement of the nonpolitical, especially the biological, the domestic, and the social, which we discussed in Chapter 1. The world is the stake.

Leaving aside the complex case of thinking (see the Appendix), consider Arendt's view of modern subjectivity. In Chapter 1, we dealt with her verdict on romantic inwardness: a hopeless entanglement with unreality. We may notice in passing here that her pages on the Cartesian *cogito* in *The Human Condition* try to trace subjectivism to a distrust of the senses and hence to a distrust of everything outside one's mind. Although she realizes with an exemplary acuteness that the great early astronomers had given sufficient reason to distrust the senses as invariable sources of truth concerning the natural world and the universe, Arendt meditates on the Cartesian project with remorse.[106]

There is another possible source of Arendt's antagonism to modern subjectivity. When she says that the heart is a dark place and means that it is not fit to be explored or lived in, she may be saying that intensive self-analysis will always discover filth. Modern psychology in its relentless truth-seeking excels at discovering filth. The cultivation of subjectivity thus flows into the ungovernable search for knowledge.

Arendt seemed to fear the disclosure of too much psychological truth because it enfeebles commitment to the world, by catching the individual in a trap of loneliness. In a chapter added to the second edition of *The Origins of Totalitarianism*, she says that the loneliness of modern masses makes them receptive to totalitarian domination because loneliness disposes a person to seek relief in the rigidity of an ideological system. But her discussion includes the comment that there is some underlying complicity between the dominated and those who dominate. She says, following Luther, that a lonely man "always deduces one thing from the other and thinks everything to the worst."[107] One could infer here that the worst means the worst about oneself: Loneliness facilitates self-discovery, which nourishes self-loathing. She says also that the "extremism" of totalitarian regimes consists in "this deducing process which always arrives at the worst possible conclusions."[108] She had already remarked on how totalitarianism prepares each individual equally well to be executioner or victim.[109]

In short, from this perspective, the secret resource of totalitarianism—and perhaps of all forms of political cruelty—is guilt induced by self-analysis of the sort that modern loneliness promotes. The distance between self-analysis and the institutionalization of analysis by psychological experts is not great. The latter heightens the danger. (Freud's affirmation of our innocence at the end of *The Interpretation of Dreams* may be too qualified.) D. M. Thomas's novel, *The White Hotel* (1981) appears to say what Arendt would have accepted completely. Self-analysis combined with psychoanalysis can always either find or plausibly confect reasons for self-accusation of the most searing kind. The premonition of destruction is a yearning for punishment. But the person, for all the filth inside, is still innocent, even if self-convicted. Arendt could have said that unless the darkness within remained unapproached, a ruinous loneliness would grow, the world would be lost, and the acceptance of victimization prepared. These are the bitter results of cultivated subjectivity. Self-knowledge, not just self-absorption, is self-alienation. The courage of self-knowledge is perhaps the one kind of courage she refuses to insist on.

Even without this uncertain example in which increased knowledge and the cultivation of subjectivity are in each other's baleful service, Arendt unmistakably links the search for cognitive truth, for knowledge of every kind, to world alienation. It is not just a matter of knowledge that can be converted into world-alienating and earth-alienating technology. She never says that she wishes such a search and such knowledge had never existed. Rather, she persists in admiring what she thinks they have made altogether less likely, if not impossible. She certainly does not locate human dignity in the endless accumulation of knowledge.[110] The level of abstraction (or degrees of vagueness) of the question as to where to locate human dignity is so great that one can scarcely say a relevant word.

Still, we had better see that a determined philosophy of the world as home and of political action as the exemplary relationship to the world is continuously at odds with the project of indefinite knowing. This tension is not the immemorial one between the alleged requirements of order and stability and the corrosive effects of inquiry; nor is it the other immemorial one between the commitment to action and the commitment to reflection. The latter certainly figures in Arendt's thought; the former concern would not have suited her natural rebelliousness. The issue is related to the immemorial ones but nevertheless distinct. Knowledge, in the period of modernity, makes the world more and more strange and thus cultivates estrangement from the world. The effect of the accumulation of knowledge may paradoxically increase uncertainty about the ability of humanity to know; or contrastingly, by establishing certainties it may freeze the play of opinion.[111] In either case, her implication is that there may be such a thing as knowing too much for the good of the world.

Arendt finds antecedents for her attitude. She tries to recover Greek, but especially Roman, notions of humanness, all of which demand limitations on the pursuit of knowledge (and beauty). She deploys several considerations. First, she proposes that the very political notion of friendship present in Greek thought—personal friendship as linked to public citizenship; citizenship as a kind of friendship; and friendship as in itself political because, like citizenship, it is made from the discourse of equals—provides a starting point for thought about what matters are fit for utterance. She says that there can be no "humane" world unless it is "the object of discourse." Talk with others is what creates the world, which "remains 'inhuman' in a very literal sense unless it is constantly talked about by human beings."[112] Similarly, we learn to be human in the course of speaking. Yet if the world is to be humane and its inhabitants are to be human, the very idea of the human must be delimited. She extends the Greek idea:

Whatever cannot become the object of discourse—the truly sublime, the truly horrible or the uncanny—may find a human voice through which to sound into the world, but it is not exactly human.[113]

With the phrase "not exactly human," rather strict limits are placed on the publicly expressible. The public realm undergoes a purfication. But the powers of human expression thus confined may in turn undergo atrophy.

In the same essay, Arendt praises Lessing not only for seeing that "single absolute truth" would mean the end of human discourse, but for taking pleasure in this insight. She joins him in exulting in the fact that "the truth, as soon as it is uttered, is immediately transformed into one opinion among many, is contested, reformulated, reduced to one subject of discourse among others."[114] She also exults in the "distress" this vicissitude caused Plato and Parmenides. But this point is preliminary to a more radical one that she finds unhesitatingly present in Lessing's work. *Nathan the Wise* is her text; and the point she makes her own is that "Nathan's wisdom consists solely in his readiness to sacrifice truth to friendship."[115] Once again, the political notion of friendship works to discredit truth. Truth here is not knowledge, but moral or metaphysical truth. The trouble is that Arendt does not distinguish between the fallacy of thinking that in every particular case submitted to disinterested judgment there is one and only one right answer instead of a range of equally or almost equally eligible answers; and thinking rightly that a basic principle can be accepted by all participants. The latter condition is usually the necessary precondition for meaningful and robust dispute of the sort she idealizes as the talk of the world. Thus the search for the principle,[116] or for greater clarity about it, is surely as compatible with the well-being of the world as it is indispensable to the health of a friendship. Only a rigidly Kantian notion of moral truth, extending from the principle to all cases that arise under it, works with the devastating effect on the world that Arendt feared.

Other antecedents for her desire to limit the pursuit of knowledge or truth she finds in a formulation from Pericles' funeral oration, and in Cicero's views on truth in relation to culture. The Periclean formulation in Alfred Zimmern's English is: "We are lovers of beauty without extravagance, and lovers of wisdom without unmanliness."[117] Arendt calls the formulation untranslatable and offers a paraphrase: "We love beauty within the limits of political judgment, and we philosophize without the barbarian vice of effeminacy."[118] She interprets this text to mean that "it is the polis, the realm of politics, which sets limits to the love of wisdom and of beauty." The gist is that "a kind of overrefinement, an indiscriminate sensitivity" is barbarian; while "the lack of virility, the vice of effeminacy, which we would associate with too great a love of beauty or aestheticism, is mentioned here as the specific danger of philosophy."[119] She suggests that the danger of philosophy is that it may lead to contemplative inactivity, since it begins in wonder and ends in "the speechless beholding of some unveiled truth."[120] She seems to endorse the description of inactivity as effeminacy. There is the slightest hint in Arendt's discussion that Socrates was not a citizen, as if there were only one way of being citizen.

The cause of truth is also assaulted in Arendt's discussion of Cicero. She once again takes hold of a formulation and expands its sense. She quotes Cicero from the first book of the *Tusculan Disputations*: "I prefer before heaven to go astray with Plato rather than hold true views with his opponents."[121] She thinks this remark is "an outrageously bold statement," but she interprets it with entire sympathy. Her thesis is that Roman humanism, as incarnated in Cicero, gave ascendancy to the faculty of *taste*. Taste is "the political capacity that truly humanizes the beautiful and create s a culture."[122] It is a political capacity because its principle is "to take care and preserve and admire the things of the world."[123] Of course, taste does not operate brutally as censorship. The method of exclusion is subtle. It insists on one's freedom as a man of the world (and hence as a citizen). She says:

> This Roman *humanitas* applied to men who were free in every respect, for whom the question of freedom, of not being coerced, was the decisive one—even in philosophy, even in science, even in the arts.[124]

Worldliness is a rejection of the absolute claims of any art or discipline in behalf of the preservation of the world as home. There is no home, only unsettledness, when human creativity strains toward autonomy.

The costs, in sum, of the lamentation of alienation and the affirmation of being at home in the world are immense. Every human struggle against limitation, or every aspiration to perfection except the political one (rightly understood), comes under scrutiny or indictment. As Arendt's political theory unfolds, the full cost of avoiding alienation so that groups of people may aspire to be at home in a culture with a politics is demonstrated. The cost appears as immense in the cultures that may be said to have lived for politics—the Greek and the Roman. The costs are nearly total for modernity. The cost would not be worth paying, even if it were possible to pay it.

Now we do not praise alienation in itself when we point out that its abolition has a prohibitive cost. At its worst, it is a condition that must be endured for the sake of our humanity, even though it is sometimes implicated in appalling events. However, there is a good form, a *moderate* alienation, that can be praised. An idea of a culture of good alienation exists. The events and achievements that cause alienation in its gross forms help to prepare but do not define moderate alienation. There is a way for a people to be at home by not being at home. There is, consequently, a way of achieving individual reconciliation that does not depend on living a life that lends itself to a "properly narrated story."

The Defense of Alienation and of Modernity

The true beneficiary of all the dislocations and uncertainties of modernity is the democratic individual living in a culture of moderate alienation and himself sharing in that alienation. Arendt (and others) are probably right to see individualism in general as a symptom and expression of alienation. The theory of democratic individuality, however, is the conversion of this distress and loss (whether or not felt as such) into a great good. Each individual becomes individual because the general condition of moderate alienation provides the opening. More than anyone else, Emerson, Thoreau, and Whitman have shown how that may be so. We cannot do anything more than point in the direction of their ever-fresh teaching.

The moral unit in any discourse on the rightness of moderate alienation is the individual, not humanity or masses of people heaped together traumatically. The individual is the democratic individual, not some unconditioned and unsituated ghost. The key to his stature is self-consciousness carried to the point of what Emerson calls, with mixed feelings, the "double consciousness" in "The Transcendentalist" and "Fate," and what Thoreau calls "doubleness" in *Walden*. Its essence is self-objectification: to be ready to treat oneself as another. It is a form of practiced alienation. This doubleness is conceptually related to the Socratic "two-in-one" that Arendt makes paradigmatic for the experience of thinking and fundamental to the avoidance of atrocity; but it is not altogether the same. It is not altogether the same either as the Kantian "enlarged mentality" that allows one to understand how another person looks at the common world; and when alone, to "think in an anticipated communication with others" by thinking in the place of everybody else.[125] It is also far removed from the late Stoic conceptualization as found in Epictetus and Marcus Aurelius (and borrowed by St. Augustine), which counseled a *double life*. The Stoic doubleness consists in following the rules of society outwardly, but inwardly thinking one's own thoughts and managing one's impressions. The double life is like living a lie: You act as if the rules you were following behaviorally were good, or not to be questioned, not at all changed. The world and the self are separated and left untouched. Thoreau explicitly calls such a life a "failure."[126]

The American romantic doubleness is most radically present in Whitman's *Song of Myself* (section 4):

Apart from the pulling and hauling stands what I am,
Stands amused, complacent, compassionating, idle, unitary,
Looks down, is erect, or bends an arm on an impalpable certain rest,
Looking with side-curved head curious what will come next,
Both in and out of the game and watching and wondering at it.

The capacity being invoked in these lines is that by which one becomes all the more active because detached; all the more active because constantly enlarging one's passivity and receptivity; all the more active because one knows of certainties that underlie the futility and imprecisions of action. There is no *social* identity worth holding on to. The self is loose-fitting. There is no chance that bad faith will substitute itself for reconciliation. There is restlessness, contradiction, bursting all confines. There is serious play, without winning and losing. Taste is put down, because everything is allowed in, everything can be poetized. There is no pretense that the classical understanding of excellence or virtue is being reproduced in a democracy; nor is there the lesser pretense of "cultured" personalities issuing from that process of self-improvement that Arendt scorns as philistine, but which is not in any case the aim of democratic individuality.[127] Emerson's and Whitman's "spontaneity" also scorn the deliberate putting together of a beautiful self. The enlargement of human powers is an enlargement of the power of *each* individual to experience and to poetize experience. Modernity stands for such enlargement. Courage and generosity promote and employ alienation in *each*. Modernity, when it is benign, or can be made benign, or can be twisted into benignity, supplies this good alienation. Modern democracy is the unsettled "home" of moderate alienation. The risks are great of course; so are the costs; so are the perversions and failures.

If, however, one does not find in the culture of moderate alienation the best of modernity, where then? In exasperation Arendt says of America:

> And this body politic has at least endured to the present day, in spite of the fact that the specifically modern character of the modern world has nowhere else produced such extreme expressions in all nonpolitical spheres of life as it has in the United States.[128]

She also complains that modern (especially American) society "introduces between the private and the public a social sphere in which the private is made public and vice versa."[129] In both cases, she has decried tendencies that actually are signs of the vitality of the democracy: the will to extend its spirit throughout the society and not restrict it to the public realm. American democracy is expressed in and thrives on "extreme expressions in all nonpolitical spheres of life" and on the mutual moral permeability of public and private. (And so, to a degree, did Athenian democracy.)

To wrest something fine from modernity requires sympathy to the ideal of democratic individuality. We have seen that Arendt finds individuality, serious or not, unserious and even repugnant. Naturally, she will not be able to do for the best of modernity what she is able to do for the worst: present its innermost meaning. For her,

> The true forerunner of modern mass man is this individual, who was defined and indeed discovered by those who, like Rousseau in the eighteenth century or John Stuart Mill in the nineteenth century, found themselves in open rebellion against society.[130]

With such a coarse reduction, her political theory of modernity exposes its shortcomings.

The curious thing is that when Arendt writes about "men in dark times"—the men and women who are courageous and generous in the gloom—she articulates the ideal of individuality with an exceptional clarity and, what is more, sympathy. The trouble is that she confines its possibility to a few; and these few are writers (and include one pope and one revolutionary). She cannot contemplate an idealism, like that of the American romantics, that aspires to the encouragement of a poetical or a philosophical relation to reality on the part of all to some untrivial degree. Democratic individuality is the doctrine of every person as poet or philosopher, not as writer, but as one who sees beauty everywhere, even in the commonplace or ugly; as one who spends himself in the service of the desire to understand otherness, even when it is supposed to be hateful or despicable; as one who, emptied of self-interest, is liberated all the more for strenuous exertion. Modern democracy finds its highest justification in the sponsorship and protection of this ideal. It rests on the belief that more than a few can see, imagine, and act like the best few; and that the extension of the ideal enhances it rather than cheapening it. One may say that the romantic poetical or philosophical relation to reality is the democratically refined sense of wonder at and gratitude for Being.

We should notice some of Arendt's formulations because they are serviceable for a doctrine that she does not want us to embrace. It is not accidental that they all come from *Men in Dark Times*, which turns out to be a book of reflections on defiant individuals.

She refers to Jaspers's "high-spirited independence" that does not so much make him rebel against conventions as keep his distance from them: "the conventions are always recognized as such, never taken seriously as standards of conduct." He was always capable of resisting enlistment; he was "inviolable, untemptable, unswayable." This independence was sustained by confidence: "the secret trust in man, in the *humanitas* of the human race."[131] She also praises Waldemar Gurian for his lifelong decision "never to conform and never to escape, which is only another way of saying that it was built on courage."[132] With all these words we are suddenly in the world of Emerson's "Self-Reliance." He makes us see that democracy robs convention of its majesty by reinforcing its citizens in the idea that political authority is constructed and artificial, and so must be most of the laws that come from it. What is true of laws must also be true of social conventions. To see such truth is the beginning of emancipation into democratic individuality. But Arendt writes as if only someone of Jaspers's genius could possibly live a life with such a tenuous connection to convention.

In summarizing Jaspers's theory of the "axial" period between 800 and 200 B.C., she says words about a few "great personalities" that Emerson and Thoreau endeavor to make commonly available:

> Great personalities appear everywhere who will no longer accept or be accepted as mere members of their respective communities but think of themselves as individuals and design individual ways of life.[133]

When Thoreau says that "we should be men first, and subjects afterward"[134]—"afterward" can only mean not at all—he is speaking to his neighbors in the democracy. The scorn in Arendt's phrase "mere members" could have come from Thoreau. Arendt praises Lessing for the reason that he "never felt at home in the world as it then existed and probably never wanted to, and still after his own fashion he always remained committed to it."[135] She insists that "special and unique circumstances governed this relationship."[136] But why must they? Why cannot Lessing's relationship to the world be envisaged as the norm, as the aspiration, as approachable by democratic individuals who redefine the notion of world and of being at home in it?

Arendt speaks of Rosa Luxemburg as one of those persons "whose genius forced them to keep the world at a certain distance and whose significance lies chiefly in their works, the artifacts they added to the world, not in the role they played in it."[137] But why restrict the choices to two: works or role? The *vita activa* is not exhausted by labor, work, and political action; the sole alternative to the *vita activa* is not the *vita contemplativa*. There is the unstructured immensity in which people idle, observe, ruminate, imagine, move about, encounter, travel down the open road; in which, in short, they experience. For them, too, the world in its commitments must be kept "at a certain distance" if the unstructured immensity of possible experience is to be entered. The modern technologies of communication and travel, the modern technological media of art and entertainment, and the modern methods of reproducing and disseminating art and the works of culture all transform the very nature of experience as well as its content. The achievements of modernity have made individuals more able to see, have given them more to see, have devised new ways of seeing. They have created utopia as vision. The key to the modern transformation of experience is to be found in the emancipation of sight more than in the emanicipation of all the other senses (to use Marx's early formulation).[138] This is an unmeasurable advance.

In her great essay on Brecht, Arendt pictures him as a young man wandering through Germany after the horrors of World War I:

> As it appeared to Brecht, four years of destruction had wiped the world clean, the storms having swept along with them all human traces, everything one could hold on to, including cultural objects and moral values....It was as though, fleetingly, the world had become as innocent and fresh as it was on the day of creation....Hence it was life that the young poet fell in love with—everything that the earth, in its sheer thereness, had to offer.[139]

She abandons, for Brecht's sake, the view that being at home is necessary if one is to love the world. The very feeling of strangeness—a kind of *Verfremdungseffekt* for the theater that life in society is—tightens the tie to the world and one's life in it. This is not the same as moderate alienation, which does not presuppose a literal calamity. Rather, the condition of democratic individuality is the regularization of a culturally encouraged and self-perfected *Verfremdungseffekt*, both as a continuous and domesticated perspective (Whitman's "in and out of the game"), and as an exceptional possibility now and then made actual and ecstatic, as Emerson, for one, describes it in the famous passage about crossing the town common in *Nature*.[140]

For Brecht, Arendt even lets go of her religiousness. She thinks that no one has excelled him in conveying "the clear understanding that what Nietzsche called 'the death of God' does not necessarily lead into despair but, on the contrary, since it eliminates the fear of Hell, can end in sheer jubilation, in a new 'yes' to life."[141] The doctrine of democratic individuality, on the other hand, goes beyond this jubilation, great as it is. It is Emerson who best sounds the note. In the Divinity School Address of 1838, he says, "men have come to speak of the revelation as somewhat long ago given and done, as if God were dead."[142] The assassin of the old God is democracy as the culture of human self-positing of values and projects; as the culture where everything becomes "thematized," a subject for discussion. He knew that the traditional God was dead, but such knowledge is preliminary:

> Heartily know,
> When half-gods go,
> The gods arrive.[143]

Religiousness is restored, but altered, and understood as the spiritualization of democratic individuality. This is the "new 'yes' to life," and it bespeaks a cultivated alienation, which builds a saving doubt into the "yes."

Finally, in an exuberant passage in her memoir of Waldemar Gurian, Arendt seems to break away from the disposition to confine individuality to a few. In doing so, she comes to the center of the doctrine of democratic individuality:

> It remains the greatest prerogative of every man to be essentially and forever more than anything he can produce or achieve, not only to remain, after each work and achievement, the not yet exhausted, sheer inexhaustible source of further achievements, but to be in his very essence beyond all of them, untouchable and unlimited by them.[144]

Oddly, these words were written more than ten years before the contrasting words quoted above from the essay on Rosa Luxemburg. There is an untypicality in them, not because they are charged with hope, but because they do not go well with a concentration on the world as home, as the object of devotion and sacrifice. Neither do they merely repeat Arendt's idea of freedom as unpredictable action. These are words, instead, of individual transcendence. Their expression is full of unintended echoes of Emerson, Thoreau, and Whitman. These words comprise the faith of modernity. How startling is their appearance in the work of this great antimodernist!

Notes

1. Hannah Arendt, *The Human Condition* (Chicago: University of Chicago Press, 1958), 5. Hereafter cited as HC.
2. Arendt, "Hermann Broch: 1886–1951" in *Men in Dark Times* (New York: Harcourt, Brace & World, 1968), 117. Hereafter cited as Broch.
3. Arendt, "Walter Benjamin: 1892–1940" in *Men in Dark Times*, 201.
4. Arendt, "Tradition and the Modern Age" in *Between Past and Future* (2nd ed., New York: Viking, 1968), 26; also 25-27. The whole essay is relevant for the subject of modernity's difference from all the past. See also her Preface to this book, 13-15.
5. "Walter Benjamin: 1892–1940," 202.
6. Arendt, *Eichmann in Jerusalem* (2nd ed., New York: Viking, 1964), 273. Hereafter cited as *Eichmann*.
7. Arendt, *The Origins of Totalitarianism* (rev. ed., Cleveland: Meridan, 1958), 459. Hereafter cited as OT.
8. Arendt, "Lying in Politics" in *Crises of the Republic* (New York: Harcourt Brace Jovanovich, 1972).
9. OT, viii. Also in the Preface, vii, to *Men in Dark Times*, she joins as if symbiotically "the political catastrophes" and "moral disasters" of the first half of the twentieth century to its "astonishing development of the arts and sciences."
10. See Arendt's denunciation of bureaucracy as the unaccountable "rule by nobody" and hence as tyranny in *On Violence* in *Crises of the Republic*, 137-38. Hereafter cited as OV.
11. HC, 268.
12. Ibid.
13. Ibid., 262.
14. Arendt, "Karl Jaspers: Citizen of the World?" in *Men in Dark Times*, 89.
15. Karl Jaspers, *The Future of Mankind*, trans. E. B. Ashton (Chicago: University of Chicago Press, 1961), 168.
16. Arendt, *On Revolution* (New York: Viking, 1963), 287. Hereafter cited as OR.
17. Arendt, "Europe and the Atom Bomb," *Commonweal* 60 (September 17, 1954), 578-80.
18. OR, 4.

19. *Eichmann*, 256.
20. Arendt,"Truth and Politics" in *Between Past and Future*, 229.
21. "Karl Jaspers: Citizen of the World?" 90.
22. Arendt, "On Humanity in Dark Times: Thoughts about Lessing" in *Men in Dark Times*, 12. Hereafter cited as "Lessing."
23. "Karl Jaspers: Citizen of the World?" 93.
24. Ibid., 93-94.
25. Ibid., 94.
26. Ibid., 91. Arendt goes so far as to say, "Kant knew quite well that a world government would be the worst tyranny imaginable." Arendt, *Lectures on Kant's Political Philosophy*, Ronald Beiner ed. (Chicago: University of Chicago Press, 1982), 44. Hereafter cited as *Lectures*.
27. HC, 247.
28. Arendt discusses Epictetus in *The Life of the Mind* (2 vols., New York: Harcourt Brace Jovanovich, 1978), vol. 2, *Willing*, 73-84. Hereafter cited as *Willing*.
29. *Lectures*, 76. Arendt also says that "I do not believe in a world, be it a past world or a future world, in which man's mind, equipped for withdrawing from the world of appearances, could or should ever be comfortably at home" (*Willing*, 158). She derides nostalgia and utopia as false homes. Is she also deriding the very concept of being at home in the world? If so, she is departing from her usual position. The words are ambiguous.
30. Alfred Kazin, *New York Jew* (New York: Vintage, 1979), 306.
31. Arendt, "Religion and Politics," *Confluence* 1-2 (September 1953), 105-26. She also claims that however much man may understand or "can discover and handle without true comprehension," the "unknown that is the region of faith" remains intact. HC, 270-71.
32. HC, 264.
33. Ibid.
34. Ibid., 254-55.
35. Ibid., 256.
36. Ibid., 257.
37. Ibid.
38. Ibid., 254.
39. Ibid.
40. Ibid., 269.
41. Ibid., also 1.
42. Ibid., 10.
43. Arendt, "The Concept of History: Ancient and Modern" in *Between Past and Future*, 88-90. Hereafter cited as "History."
44. Arendt, "The Conquest of Space and the Stature of Man" in *Between Past and Future*, 276. Hereafter cited as "Space."
45. "Space," 277.
46. Ibid. Compare Martin Heidegger, "The Question Concerning Technology" in *The Question Concerning Technology and Other Essays*, trans. William Lovitt (New York: Harper, 1977), 27.
47. "Space," 278.
48. Ibid.; also HC, 284-85.
49. "Space," 279.
50. Ibid.
51. Ibid., 280.
52. HC, 10-11.
53. Ibid., 245.
54. OR, 280.
55. HC, 2
56. Ibid
57. Ibid., 3
58. OV, 114–15.
59. HC, 2.
60. Ibid., 11.
61. "History," 53-54. Compare another analogous deviation from her usual position: "the more at home men feel within the human artifice—the more they will resent everything they have not produced, everything that is merely and mysteriously given them. "OT, 301. Instead of

saying that resentment issues in achievements that prevent people from being at home, she says that being at home *creates* resentment toward the given. The whole passage is remarkable but inconsistent with what she says elsewhere.

62. Compare Martin Heidegger, *What is Called Thinking?* trans. F.G. Wieck and J.G. Gray, (New York: Harper, 1968), 85-110. He discusses the theme of revenge in Nietzsche.

63. See Elisabeth Young-Bruehl, *Hannah Arendt: For Love of the World* (New Haven: Yale, 1982), 222. Hereafter cited as Young-Bruehl.

64. *Lectures*, 22.

65. Ibid., 23.

66. HC, 302. See also *The Life of the Mind*, vol. 1, *Thinking*, 179-93, hereafter cited as *Thinking*; and Arendt, "Thinking and Moral Considerations", *Social Research* 38 (Autumn 1971), 417-46.

67. HC, 302; also Arendt, "The Crisis in Culture: Its Social and Its Political Significance" in *Between Past and Future*, 214. Hereafter cited as *Culture*.

68. Ludwig Wittgenstein, *Tractatus Logico-Philosophicus*, trans. C. K. Ogden (London: Routledge & Kegan Paul, 1922), 6.44:187. Consult also the translation by D. F. Pears and B. F. McGuinness (London: Routledge and Kegan Paul, 1961), 149. See Wittgenstein's earlier formulations in *Notebooks, 1914-1916*, G. H. von Wright and G. E. M. Anscombe, eds., trans. G. E. M. Anscombe (New York: Harper, 1961) 86e.

69. Ibid., 6.45:187.

70. *Lectures*, 12; also 13, 58.

71. Arendt, *The Jew as Pariah*, Ron H. Feldman, ed. (New York: Grove, 1978), 246. Hereafter cited as *Pariah*.

72. Arendt could never have traversed the trajectory of her contemporary, Marcuse. He started in defiant hope: "In the process of civilization, Nature ceases to be mere Nature....Civilization produces the means for freeing Nature from its own brutality, its own insufficiency, its own blindness, by virtue of the cognitive and transforming power of Reason," *One-Dimensional Man* (Boston: Beacon, 1964), 236, 238. Yet there is the sound of defeat in almost his last words: "The world was not made for the sake of the human being and it has not become more human," *The Aesthetic Dimension* (Boston: Beacon, 1978), 69. Her thought is averse to such defiance and such despair: the poles of rejection. Marcuse's humanism is anthropocentric; Arendt's goes beyond man, but not to any theology.

73. "Culture," 222. See also the extended discussion of beauty and taste in Kant's philosophy in *Lectures*, 13-15, 51-77.

74. *Culture*, 210.

75. Quoted in Young-Bruehl, 452-53.

76. Arendt approvingly quotes Kant: "The fact that man is affected by the sheer beauty of nature proves that he is made for and fits into this world" (Lectures, 30).

77. Arendt, "Heidegger at Eighty," *The New York Review of Books*, October 21, 1971, 50-54. Compare Emerson in "New England Reformers": "that is ever the difference between the wise and the unwise: the latter wonders at what is unusual, the wise wonders at the usual." *The Complete Essays and Other Writings of Ralph Waldo Emerson* (New York: Modern Library, 1940), 468. Hereafter cited as *Emerson*.

78. *Willing*, 158, 188-89. This volume contains an extended discussion on Heidegger and his thought on will, 172-94.

79. "History," 42.

80. *Pariah*, 246. Arendt examines how Kant tried to separate the moral-practical from the sense of beauty, so that the spectator's viewpoint not become the principle of action. She finds that Kant eventually united the actor and spectator: He wanted action to create the conditions for "the greatest possible enlargement of the enlarged mentality" (*Lectures*, 52-58, 74-77). In Arendt's thought, a special sense of beauty may have great consequences for action.

81. Roger Errera, "Hannah Arendt: From an Interview," *The New York Review of Books*, October 26, 1978, 18. Hereafter cited as Errera.

82. "Truth and Politics," 263-64.

83. Quoted in Young-Bruehl, 519.

84. "Lessing," 21.

85. Arendt, "Isak Dinesen: 1885-1963" in *Men in Dark Times*, 105.

86. Ibid., 97.

87. "Truth and Politics," 262.

88. Quoted in Young-Bruehl, 201-2.
89. "Space," 272, 275-76.
90. "Culture," 219.
91. OV, 161.
92. *Emerson*, 279.
93. Errera, 18.
94. Martin Heidegger, "The Question Concerning Technology," 28-35; "The Turning," 42; and "The Age of the World Picture," 137, 153; all in Lovitt.
95. Quoted in Young-Bruehl, 443. For Heidegger's formulation see *An Introduction to Metaphysics*, trans. Ralph Manheim (New York: Anchor, 1961), 166; see also *What is Called Thinking?* 57-75.
96. *Emerson*, 287.
97. "The Question Concerning Technology," 28, 34-35.
98. Max Weber, "Politics as a Vocation" in H. H. Gerth and C. Wright Mills, *From Max Weber: Essays in Sociology* (New York: Oxford, 1958), 128.
99. Karl Marx, "Private Property and Communism" (*Economic and Philosophic Manuscripts of 1844*) in *The Marx-Engels Reader*, Robert C. Tucker, ed. (2nd ed., New York: Norton, 1978), 92.
100. *Lectures*, 12-13, 58.
101. "Lessing," 13.
102. Ibid.
103. Ibid.
104. Ibid., 14.
105. Compare *Willing*, 31.
106. HC, 273-89.
107. OT, 477.
108. Ibid.
109. Ibid., 468.
110. Compare Isaiah Berlin, "'From Hope and Fear Set Free'" in *Concepts and Categories*, Henry Hardy, ed. (New York: Viking, 1979), 173-98.
111. Lessing, 10, 26-31.
112. Ibid., 24.
113. Ibid., 25.
114. Ibid., 27.
115. Ibid., 26.
116. See Arendt's sympathetic account of Broch's effort to arrive at an absolute principle, Broch, 121-30, 140-51.
117. Thucydides, II, 40. Zimmern's translation of the entire oration is in *The Greek Commonwealth* (1911) (New York: Modern Library, 1956), 202-11.
118. "Culture," 214.
119. Ibid.
120. Ibid.
121. Ibid., 224.
122. Ibid.
123. Ibid., 225.
124. Ibid.
125. These formulations are from "History," 51, and "Culture," 220. See also, *Lectures*, 42-44; "Truth and Politics," 241-42.
126. Quoted in Joel Porte, *Emerson and Thoreau: Transcendentalists in Conflict* (Middletown, Conn.: Wesleyan University Press, 1966), 207.
127. "Culture," 198-205.
128. Hannah Arendt, "What is Authority?" in *Between Past and Future*, 140.
129. Arendt, "The Crisis in Education" in *Between Past and Future*, 188.
130. "Culture," 199.
131. Arendt, "Karl Jaspers: A Laudatio" in *Men in Dark Times*, 76-77.
132. Arendt, "Waldemar Gurian: 1903–1954" in *Men in Dark Times*, 261-62.
133. "Karl Jaspers: Citizen of the World?" 89.
134. Henry David Thoreau, "Civil Disobedience" in *The Variorum Walden and the Variorum Civil*

Disobedience, Walter Harding, ed. (New York: Washington Square Press, 1968), 344.
135. "Lessing," 5.
136. Ibid.
137. Arendt, "Rosa Luxemburg: 1871-1919" in *Men in Dark Times*, 33.
138. "Private Property and Communism," 87.
139. Arendt, "Bertolt Brecht: 1898–1956" in *Men in Dark Times*, 229.
140. *Emerson*, 6-7.
141. "Bertolt Brecht: 1898–1956," 233. But Arendt warns that "God is dead" "certainly" does not mean that God has died. If "anything is dead, it can only be the traditional *thought* of God" (*Thinking*, 10).
142. *Emerson*, 75.
143. "Give All to Love."
144. "Waldemar Gurian: 1903–1954," 257. .

Appendix

The Life of the Mind

One of Hannah Arendt's great powers is the ability to refresh perception. She tries to get us to look again at subjects on which there already exists perhaps too much writing and therefore too much confident understanding. By her further reflection, she tries to save these subjects for our further reflection. Her re-discovery is actually discovery. The reader experiences a shock not of recognition, but of revelation. Certainly in her analysis of antisemitism, or Nazism, or the American Revolution, or Greek thought about action, or "the banality of evil," she may be said to achieve originality, to compel us to open ourselves up to new thoughts that are often harsh or strange. In her last work, *The Life of the Mind*, this power is fully present. The voyage of rediscovery is, if anything, more arduously undertaken than ever before; the results may be, as the book is slowly absorbed over the years, as unsettling as any she had earlier induced.

Coming to terms with a book by Arendt should never be easy. Each is so richly unexpected that it resists one's natural tendency to see it as part of a larger tradition or tendency of thought, or to enlist it in some ideological cause. Her work just does not cooperate with the techniques we all have for arranging the contents of our mental universe. *The Life of the Mind* offers this kind of resistance to a degree that is unusual even for Arendt. In responding to the book, however, one must know that not only did she always write to shake us out of settled habits, but also that when she died in December of 1975 her last book "was not in final shape,"[1] as Mary McCarthy, the book's editor, tells us in a remarkable Postface. It seems to me that the book is sometimes digressive, uneven in its proportions, or lacking in explicit connections and emphases. Even more important, Arendt did not live to finish the work, to write the third part, *Judging*. So we must be somewhat tentative in what we say. Yet I think the book is extraordinary; I do not feel the need to be tentative in saying that.

At the start of the first volume, *Thinking*, Arendt says that she is leaving "the relatively safe fields of political science and theory" to take up questions that are more strictly philosophical.[2] After all, to try to disclose the nature of thinking and willing is to be engaged in a kind of epistemological inquiry rather remote from political philosophy and reminiscent, say, of William James's *The Principles of Psychology*. Arendt does mention that one of the sources of her concern was her belief that a person like Eichmann could help to administer a system of atrocity without feeling any hatred, or indeed any passion, toward those he put to death. Eichmann could do what he did because he was incapable of thinking: that was Arendt's hunch. The hunch played a part in *Eichmann in Jerusalem* and was worked out in a preliminary way in an essay published almost ten years later, "Thinking and Moral Considerations." So, Arendt's theoretical absorption with politics is not suppressed. But the book is deeply political through and through. The fact that it is politically instigated is only one indication of the book's direct and indirect involvement with political things.

The two volumes have one aim: to *accuse* thinking. No sooner is that said than a knowledge of Arendt's inevitable complexity presses back the simple assertion. I should say instead that the two volumes are a *qualified* accusation of *philosophical* thinking; an accusation qualified by love of the accused; a love constantly shown and expressed as the book's arguments unfold. Still, it would be too safe to say that all that Arendt is doing is having a lover's quarrel with thinking. There is an indictment in the book, an indictment of thinking in a book provoked by the dread hunch that much of the worst evil done in the world is done by those who are not capable of thinking.

To put it crudely, Arendt calls thinking as an activity to account because it is a withdrawal from the life of the senses, and because it is characteristically hostile to willing and hence to free spontaneous action. Her philosophical commitment is to the world—the world as our cultural home and the world as the realm of political action. This commitment seems to confer, despite great difficulties, coherence on the book. What Arendt did in her last book, then, was to cope with an expanded range of considerations that were adversary to her commitment.

What is thinking? It is the silent speech that takes place inside oneself, "the soundless dialogue between me and myself,"[3] when one is disengaged from either the activities of life or even the mere observation of them. As Arendt defines it, its content may be any past experience, any event or situation in one's life or the lives of others. All thinking is animated by the search for meaning. Yet Arendt is mostly occupied with a particular sort of search, the effort to search out the meaning of existence as such. This is *philosophical* thinking. It starts, like all thinking, with experience, but it does not confine itself to the meaning of the particular, as more ordinary thinking does. Philosophical thinking must be seen as the attempt to answer unanswerable questions, like the great traditional ones concerning God, freedom, and immortality.

The actual world is not enough for the thinking mind when it works with a greater intensity than the ordinary mind, that is, when it is philosophical. Philosophical thinking is alienation from the world; and "world alienation" has always figured in Arendt's writings as one of the crucial aspects of the modern human condition. But where she had described this condition in previous work she referred to great masses in Europe, especially victims, whether of capitalist exploitation, or the traumas of two world wars, or the general condition of modern life. Millions were uprooted and battered. Millions came to feel a terrifying loneliness and lostness, a feeling of being superfluous, which totalitarian movements and regimes exploited, apparently assuaged, but actually furthered systematically. Now this very concept of world alienation is turned on philosophers all through the ages. Of course, Arendt traces it to a source that is not sociologically related to the condition of the European masses in the modern age. Philosophers deliberately and continuously, like the rest of us now and then, *cultivate* their alienation. They seek it out: To think is to leave the world. (One wants to say, to take leave of one's senses.)

Arendt is eloquent on the capacity of the "thinking ego" to be driven restlessly, or to drive itself restlessly, to find or impute meaning and then to dissolve that meaning and look for another one. There is no doubt that she finds philosophical thinking heroic. It is a heroism built into the very nature of humanity. Although some never think philosophically, and most only now and then, there will always be some who will think because they cannot help it. In casting about for a metaphor to represent the activity of thinking, she finally settles on "the sensation of being alive."[4] At the other extreme, men like Eichmann, who are not only unphilosophical but altogether unthinking, are "sleepwalkers."[5] Truly, Arendt loves philosophical thinking, loves it so much as to consider a hypothetical world without it as nonhuman.

Nevertheless, it is as if thinkers had to be reminded that there is a world, the world. "The sensation of being alive" is too close to being dead to the world and is purchased at the cost of "de-sensing,"[6] dematerializing the things in it. The senses may not ultimately rebel and derange the thinker, but Arendt in the magnificent first part of *Thinking* speaks for them. When she dwells especially on seeing and being , she celebrates the glory of the physical world. There is the glory radiated by the being of creatures who are endowed with sensory capacities of varying kinds and all of whom seek innately to explore and inhabit their world by means of those capacities. There is the greater glory created by the disposition that Arendt thinks all creatures have to self-display, to individuate themselves. She says:

> *whatever can see wants to be seen, whatever can hear calls out to be heard, whatever can touch presents itself to be touched.* It is indeed as though everything that is alive....has an *urge to appear*, to fit itself into the world of appearances by displaying and showing, not its 'inner self' but itself as an individual.[7]

To read these pages is to have as striking an instance of Arendt's power of rediscovery as any in the body of her work. She enables us to look freshly; the look of things is made fresh. Paradoxically, she uses ideas to save the world of appearances. She claims that "nothing we see or hear or touch can be expressed in words that equal what is given to the senses."[8] That may be, but she educates the sense of beauty, especially that of persons who often philosophically express contempt for "mere appearances." The affinity with early Greek thinking is strong, but there is a philosophical desperation in Arendt that makes her own expression work more intimately on us.

Thinking is withdrawal from appearances, a self-blinding to the shining of beautiful appearances. However, some sources of thinking retain a connection to appearances. Such a connection, intentionally or not, implies praise for the glory of the sensory world. Arendt devotes the third part of *Thinking* to the question, What makes us think? She takes up a number of Greek, Roman, and modern texts in order to detect an answer. She says that she must use inference because there is so little directly said by the thinking ego about its own necessities. She finds, as she was wont to find, the initial clue in Greek reflection before Plato. Then the presiding view was Pindaric: "Both the world and men stand in need of praise lest their beauty go unrecognized."[9] Appearances shone, but they did not manifest meaning. To see the meaning of human and natural phenomena there had to be a withdrawal into thinking. Meaning had to be distilled only by the kind of blindness that accompanies thinking. The greatest of all the poets who saw the meaning of past action and who made it into an immortal story was literally blind, and that blindness became emblematic for all seers, prophets, and bards. Blindness in the service of sight, thinking in the service of praising life—Arendt's sympathies are here, although she will explore other answers to the question, What makes us think?

Arendt takes up the answer Plato gave once in passing: Thinking in the form of philosophy begins in wonder, admiring wonder.[10] The wonder comes from the hidden harmony of the whole rather than from the splendor of any particular. Appearances intimate an order: They have the dignity of leading us on to something better than themselves. The world seems to sustain a loss when the metaphysical is posited as superior to the physical. Yet, in one of those turnings back on the self that Arendt excelled in, she suggests that there is an unexpected guarantee of reality to the physical when it is made to depend on the metaphysical. The loss of the "suprasensory" is the loss of the sensory, at least in a world totally lacking in all credible religious doctrine.[11] In any case, Greek philosophy stays in touch with the world of appearances, even when Platonic wonder turns into Aristotelian perplexity.

Since the Greeks, Arendt finds no answer to her question that honors the world and life in it, unless it be Nietzsche's. The unappeasable quest for meaning that drives all thinking did not and does not find sponsorship in "admiration, confirmation, and affirmation."[12] The sense of the world's hostility is what impelled the Roman Stoics to thinking and to find an inner refuge or a kind of medicine in it. Although this escapism is as old as wonder, Arendt maintains that no one acknowledged it before Cicero and Lucretius. Thinking for the Romans became a substitute world, a world elsewhere. In later thinking there is something like wonder at its source—shock that the world exists, that there is something rather than nothing. Even here, however, faith in God is presupposed, and demand for such a presupposition suggests the loss of the Greek ability to admire and affirm. The work of Hegel, directed as it is by the desire to find the basis for reconciling mind with existence, shows the same Roman terror of existence, and the same Roman impulse to overcome terror by "transforming occurrences outside yourself into your own thoughts."[13] When philosophers cannot praise life, they turn to theodicies. Nietzsche wants to bless life; Heidegger wants to see the origins of thinking in thanking, in being thankful that there is something rather than nothing, that Being calls to be heard. Yet in both there is finally an attitude toward Being that approaches abnegation or *Gelassenheit*, and this, for Arendt, seems to place human life in great jeopardy.

The history of the sources of thinking since the Greeks is a mostly uninterrupted though richly various avoidance of ravished wonder at the beauty of the world of appearances and the wish to shape that wonder into an imputation of meaning. Because of that, *Thinking* is a work of regret, if not of mourning. There is a contrary moment. Arendt says too hurriedly that the trouble with wonder as the source of thinking and with thinking as thanking is the amount of evil in the world.[14] Her hurriedness is all the more surprising, yet it is forgivable because it comes from a writer who is unsurpassed in delineating evil's modern forms. Still, she insists that to see only or mostly evil is to want there to be nothing rather than something. This is humanly intolerable, and in its coldness it engenders no sustained thinking.

Who could speak of thinking and not consider Socrates? Arendt certainly could not. He was the hero of her first essay on thinking, "Thinking and Moral Considerations," the essay that grew out of her controversial assertion that Eichmann was unable to think. After discriminating among the sources of thinking that she finds in the history of the thinking ego's self-analysis, and feeling that her presentation is inconclusive and that her own general notion of the search for meaning as the source of thinking is too vague, she turns to Socrates. She presents him as the model thinker. He was possessed by the love of wisdom, an erotic need to apprehend the true nature of things. This need drove his mind in circles, never satisfied with a conclusion, constantly perplexed and wishing to have others share his perplexity. His effect was to intensify their sensation of being alive though perhaps inhibiting their public life. But, oddly, after praising Socrates for having a democratic soul, Arendt asserts that the Socratic location of the source of thought in eros must necessarily turn into an elitist separation of the few from the many.[15]

What *initially* makes Socrates the model thinker for Arendt's purposes, however, is not so much that he was driven erotically to know and hence to question, doubt, and refute, as that he discovered the reason why the activity of thinking may tend to make the person forbear from terrible evil. Her discussion (already present in earlier writings) is based on the two related contentions that Socrates makes in the *Gorgias*. First, "It is better to be wronged than to do wrong." Second, "It would be better for me that my lyre or a chorus I directed should be out of tune and loud with discord, and that multitudes of men should disagree with me rather than that I, being one, should be out of harmony with myself and contradict me." The first follows from the second. If one is disposed to think, one will be reproached by an inner voice if one does wrong. Thinking is precisely this two-in-one, this doubleness of mind, this talking to and talking back to oneself. The thinking person cannot bear reproach, self-reproach: It is worse harm than the harm another can inflict. There is no worse harm than inner division.[16]

Arendt thus elaborates on the notion that those not able to think may cause much of the evil in the world. Here is the completion of the work on Eichmann and the banality of evil. Yet such a result is incidental to the work as a whole. Not only does she seem almost too determined to distinguish the Socratic thinking ego from the common conception of conscience[17]—as if to exonerate Socrates from the charge of moralizing the virility out of Athens—she herself is not interested in yolking thinking to goodness or even to decency. Doing so would cast a shadow on the passion for "admiration, confirmation, and affirmation." It may be that the amount of evil in the world creates "trouble" for this passion, as Arendt says. Despite that concession, Arendt wants to free thinking from any strict moral association, to liberate it for that admiring wonder that transcends moral categories. If Socrates is *finally* the model thinker, that is not because the attempt to be like him would help make one incapable of atrocity, but rather because he is the eroticist of thinking. He is so energetic in his thinking and yet so ruthlessly without conclusions. Arendt's wish to explore the connections between the banality of evil and the absence of *ordinary* thinking or thoughtfulness is thus displaced by the project of determining the impulses behind *philosophical* thinking.[18] This displacement is not sufficiently prepared for, and it requires the reader to adjust his expectations.

Philosophical thinking is least under accusation when it begins in wonder. How pitifully small the number of philosophers who have begun there. Arendt's attack on those who begin instead with the need to escape from or justify the world takes not only the form of redescribing the physical world as a world suited to wonder and gratitude, but also the form of explaining reductively the famous doctrincal conclusions, the finished products of thinking, which comprise the history of Western metaphysics. The real object of her critique is here: the tendency to produce doctrines and systems, which consummate as they betray philosophical thinking. Throughout *Thinking* she refers to the most frequently studied philosophical systems as "fallacies." She means this term to cover such achievements as the Platonic doctrine of Forms, the Kantian concept of the thing in itself, and the Hegelian phenomenology. She is their close student, full of respect; she is scornful of those "Oxford" philosophers who with a literal mind, see mistakes in the metaphysical books. At the same time, she says toward the end of *Thinking* that her work is part of the *dismantling* of philosophy.[19]

The dismantling consists in the novel interpretation Arendt offers of the great systems. Knowingly or not, their great makers have in almost all cases produced metaphors of the activity of thinking itself. In seeming to speak the truth about reality and the mind's relation to it, they have actually been throwing off hints about the process of thinking itself, the very process that inevitably engenders formal doctrines about reality and mind (except in the case of a pure thinker like Socrates, who was pure because he espoused no doctrine). Arendt means to free us of the criterion of truth when we approach metaphysical systems. She insists that truth is the proper criterion only of the labor of the *intellect*: trains of thought that issue in everyday or scientific "cognition" or knowledge. Meaning, on the other hand, is the criterion of the work of *reason*: trains of thought that issue from thinking.[20] But it seems that some of the time Arendt concentrates the meaningfulness of metaphysical systems into one property, that of throwing some indirect illumination on thinking. To be freed of the criterion of truth is troubling enough to anyone who looks to philosophy for help in understanding the way things are. More troubling still is the claim that thinking is mostly about itself; or that, for philosophers, the world exists so that the incredible difficulties connected with the phenomena of self-consciousness could be projected on to it and thus made perhaps a little less difficult. It is not merely the case that we all must use physical metaphors taken from the world of appearances to talk about the phenomena of consciousness.

Arendt does not say that the doctrine a philosopher propounds about reality is totally shaped by the understanding of mind that a philosopher has. But she thinks there is a strong connection. What is it that permits such variety of philosophical doctrines? I suppose that Arendt's answer is twofold. The mind is elusive. *Metaphysical* knowledge of objective reality is beyond human powers. (Or is it that the very notion of metaphysical knowledge is theological, overtly or not?) The mind is so elusive that it will yield many patterns that can be projected onto objective reality. And because objective reality is unknowable, because it will never allow certain questions about it to be answered, it will accommodate a great variety of such patterns.

At times, Arendt seems to concede that philosophers, in fact, think about something other than thinking; that they have an independent interest in objective reality. Do they know, however, that metaphysical knowledge concerning objective reality is impossible? The answer is not clear. She says that "men have an inclination, perhaps a need, to think beyond the limitations of knowledge."[21] In any case, philosophers persist. They want to know in a special way what is outside their minds, what is really there. They continue to desire what they cannot have. Her concession—if she makes it—nevertheless does not contribute to the honor of philosophy. Philosophers persist by pretending to know what cannot be known, and they cover up their pretense by deliberately or helplessly converting reality into patterns that repeat those of mental activities. Arendt therefore leaves us with the double sense that the scarcely knowable (mind) is employed as a model in the vain effort to promote knowledge of the unknowable (reality from a metaphysical, a more-than-human point of view); and that the real though hidden subject of self-confident doctrines about the unknowable is the scarcely knowable, the mind.

I believe that Arendt's deep wish is that thinkers had turned away from their absorption in mind and in metaphysics—if only they could have. But they could not; she knows it. Her deep wish is not her deepest: if men were to "cease to ask unanswerable questions, [they] would lose not only the ability to produce those thought-things that we call works of art but also the capacity to ask all the answerable questions upon which every civilization is founded."[22] But the burden of her book is not to praise philosophical thinking.

Surely what Arendt says is profoundly suggestive; but it seems that something has been needlessly lost when metaphysical doctrines are no longer studied as truth-obsessed responses to the mysteries of objective reality. They all are curious, willful, slanted, and confusing. But are not their aims and modes of expression determined other than by the experience of thinking? At least, somewhat? Arendt is right to attack the positivists who belittle metaphysicians for taking so many seemingly unrewarding pains. I wonder, however, if metaphysicians would want to be understood as Arendt proposes. They may find they lose less dignity from positivist derision. The largest point is that the metaphysical investigation of the physical world of appearances does not have to imply ingratitude toward its beauty, or plain indifference to it, or outright loathing of existence because of pain and evil. The necessities of rational inquiry—not the needs of the thinking ego—may lead the metaphysician on, just as they do the scientist. Some unanswerable questions are rational. I can do no more than suggest that Arendt's war on philosophical thinking, carried on alternatively by the praise of appearances and by the reductive interpretation of metaphysical doctrines, is driven by the desperate sense that thinking strengthens a pervasive suicidal tendency in the culture as a whole. World alienation, deriving from contempt for appearances, turns into self-destruction. (The theme of suicide is quietly but persistently present in both volumes, as indeed it is in much of her work.)

We can schematically say the following. The incapacity for *ordinary* thinking that Eichmann and other "desk murderers" show works direct evil. The capacity for *philosophical* thinking may indicate an abandonment of the world of appearances. The doctrines of philosophers often condemn existence, despite the radiance of appearances. The story Arendt tells about thinking in its two forms is in effect a story about how desperately needed is ordinary thinking for decent life, but how threatening to a commitment to life in the world, especially to political life as the most worldly life, is the beautiful intensification of ordinary thinking: philosophy. Thoughtlessness and philosophy form a strange alliance. This is the political theory of *Thinking*.

Two reasons account for the indictment of thinking. The first has to do with thinking's tense relation with the world of appearances. The second is the hostility of most thinkers to the will, which is the source of free action. *Willing* is marked by the effort to show that with rare exceptions, philosophers have been unaware of the will or have tried to destroy it by force of argument. What is willing? Arendt gives no definition. It seems that willing is the silent speech that takes place inside oneself concerning future action or projects. It thus bears some resemblance to thinking, but thinking is mostly about the past, and its living experience resembles the *nunc stans*, the standing now, the present as eternity.[23] Willing looks to the future as undetermined and hence as awaiting the will's determination.[24]

Arendt insists that willing is not reducible to thinking, just as no aspect of the life of the mind is reducible to any other. Acts of willing typically take the form of making resolves, deliberating, forming intentions, giving thought to what is to be done. Willing is not to be confused with desire, passion, or appetite. It is purely a verbal phenomenon; it has no biology. Arendt says that willing is truly known when the inner observer notices that willing is often divided against itself: No sooner do I make a resolve than I immediately discover resistance in myself to that resolve. A "counter-will" accompanies will.[25] Or, I will to do one thing and find myself doing the contrary. The two-in-one are enemies rather than friends. Christian thinkers—St. Paul and St. Augustine—are the great founding theoreticians of the will. The Christian experience is the precondition of this enlarged subjectivity. Later philosophers bear the brunt of Arendt's anger. She says that every theory of the will is a product of the thinking ego. The thinking ego prizes order and regularity; it hates contingency.[26] Only with a principled belief in contingency does the will emerge as a sign of human honor, and it does so as the exploiter of contingency, as the initiator of spontaneous, unpredictable, causally inexplicable action; as a power capable of even more than making a free (rational) choice between alternatives or realizing a given potentiality.[27]

Arendt praises Duns Scotus as one of the few who may be said to have reveled in contingency. The Greeks knew the splendid reality of action, but they did not recognize the faculty of willing. Once that faculty is recognized, almost all conspire to obliterate it as a disturbance to the philosophical peace. For Arendt the stakes are huge. Her life's work is in defense of freedom. She insists that after the will has been "discovered" it must be preserved conceptually. The philosophers for the most part must be fought. She knows that the very notion of spontaneous action, of freedom as free will, is exceptionally problematic. But unless it is true, freedom is a lie. Freedom is not a lie. Although she continues to insist that the individual's free will is not the same as political freedom, that the "I-will" is not the same as the "we-can," there is no doubt that the philosophical defense of free will is implicated in the defense of politics as freedom. Common to both is the human capacity to do something new, unpredicted, unpredictable, creative—perhaps even great and heroic. Common to both is a mysterious beneficence. Arendt uses the same formulations about one kind of freedom that she uses about the other. In *The Origins of Totalitarianism* she already says "Freedom as an inner capacity is identical with the capacity to begin."[28] The concept of willing has no direct political application in Arendt's system; but if it is ignored or disparaged by philosophers, politics as freedom is threatened.

At the end Arendt takes us back to those beloved men of revolutionary action whom she vivified in *On Revolution*. They demonstrated in their very deeds that freedom is no lie. They, not the philosophers, are the guarantors of human possibility. Yet she gives the very last word to a philosopher, St. Augustine, the subject of her doctoral dissertation and first book, published more than fifty years ago.[29] She finds in him the saving idea of *natality*. We are free because we are first babies and then children before we are adults. Natality may unperplex the idea of freedom. The freedom is in the freshness of beginning, and in that freshness the world renews itself with every human individual. She had earlier spoken of "the free development of characteristic qualities and talents....the uniqueness that distinguishes every human being from every other, the quality by virtue of which he is not only a stranger in the world but something that has never been here before."[30] It is right that her last written work serve "admiration, confirmation, and affirmation," and that they point to the simplest of facts and refresh our perception of them.

Notes

1. Hannah Arendt, *The Life of the Mind* (2 vols., New York: Harcourt Brace Jovanovich, 1978), vol. 1, *Thinking*, 226. Hereafter cited as *Thinking*. Vol.2, *Willing*, is hereafter cited as *Willing*.
2. *Thinking*, 3.
3. Ibid., 31, 185, and *passim*.
4. Ibid., 123, 178, 197.

5. Ibid., 191.
6. Ibid., 87.
7. Ibid., 29.
8. Ibid., 8.
9. Ibid., 132.
10. Ibid., 144 ff.
11. Ibid., 10.
12. Ibid., 151.
13. Ibid., 166.
14. Ibid., 150.
15. Ibid., 179–80.
16. Ibid., 180–93.
17. Ibid., 190–91.
18. Arendt refers to the "two rather different origins" for her "preoccupation with mental activities" (Ibid., 3).
19. Ibid., 212. The influence of Heidegger is great here; indeed, the whole work owes much to him.
20. Ibid., 15, 77-78, and *passim*.
21. Ibid., 11–12.
22. Ibid., 62.
23. Ibid., 86.
24. *Willing*, 13, 18, and *passim*.
25. Ibid., 69.
26. Ibid., 23-34.
27. Ibid., 20, 29-31, 62.
28. Arendt, *The Origins of Totalitarianism* (rev. ed., Cleveland: Meridan, 1958), 473.
29. Arendt, *Der Liebesbegriff bei Augustin* (Berlin: Springer, 1929).
30. Arendt, "The Crisis in Education" in *Between Past and Future* (2nd ed., New York: Viking, 1968), 189.

List of Selected Writings on Hannah Arendt

Auden, W. H. "Thinking What We Are Doing." *Encounter* 12 (June 1954), 72-76.

Bernstein, Richard J. "Hannah Arendt: The Ambiguities of Theory and Practice." In Terence Ball, ed., *Political Theory and Praxis:New Perspectives*. Minne apolis: University of Minnesota Press, 1977.

Botstein, Leon. "Hannah Arendt: The Jewish Question." *The New Republic*, October 21, 1978, 32-37.

Canovan, Margaret. *The Political Thought of Hannah Arendt*. New York: Harcourt Brace Jovanovich, 1974.

—. "The Contradictions of Hannah Arendt's Political Thought." *Political Theory* 6 (February 1978), 5–26.

Cooper, Leroy A. "Hannah Arendt's Political Philosophy: An Interpretation." *Review of Politics* 38 (April 1976), 145–76.

Crick, Bernard. *In Defence of Politics*. Baltimore: Penguin, 1964.

Donoghue, Denis. "After Reading Hannah Arendt." *Poetry* 100 (May 1962), 127–30.

Dossa, Shiraz. "Human Status and Politics: Hannah Arendt on the Holocaust." *Canadian Journal of Political Science* 13 (June 1980), 309–23.

Germino, Dante. *Beyond Ideology: The Revival of Political Theory*. New York: Harper and Row, 1967.

Gunnell, John. *Political Theory: Tradition and Interpretation*. Cambridge: Winthrop, 1979.

Heather, Gerald P., and Matthew Stolz. "Hannah Arendt and the Problem of Critical Theory." *The Journal of Politics* 41 (February 1979), 2–22.

Hill, Melvyn A., ed. *Hannah Arendt: The Recovery of the Public World*. New York: St. Martin's, 1979. This collection contains essays by Elisabeth Young-Bruehl, Bernard Crick, Mildred Bakan, Bikhu Parekh, Kenneth Frampton, Robert W. Major, Peter Fuss, James Miller, Stan Spyros Draenos, J. Glenn Gray, Michael Denneny, and Melvyn A. Hill.

Hughes, H. Stuart. *The Sea Change: The Migration of Social Thought, 1930–1965*. New York: Harper and Row, 1975.

Jay, Martin, and Leon Botstein. "Hannah Arendt: Opposing Views." *Partisan Review*, 45, no. 3, 348–80.

Kariel, Henry S. *In Search of Authority: Twentieth-Century Political Thought*. Glencoe: Free Press, 1964.

Kateb, George. "Hannah Arendt." In David L. Sills, ed., *International Encyclopedia of the Social Sciences: Biographical Supplement*. New York: Free Press, 1979.

Knauer, James T. "Motives and Goal in Hannah Arendt's Concept of Political Action." *The American Political Science Review* 74 (September 1980), 721–33.

Lowell, Robert. "On Hannah Arendt." *The New York Review of Books,* May 13, 1976, 6.

McCarthy, Mary "Saying Good-by to Hannah." *The New York Review of Books,* January 22, 1976, 8–11.

Macdonald, Dwight. "A New Theory of Totalitarianism." *The New Leader* 34 (May 14, 1951), 17-19.

Mack, Arien, ed. *Social Research* 44 (Spring 1977). The issue consists of essays on Hannah Arendt by Jurgen Habermas, Hans Jonas, J. Glenn Gray, Robert Nisbet, Judith N. Shklar, Sheldon S. Wolin, Bernard Crick, Hans Morgenthau, Dolf Sternberger, Erich Heller, Ernst Vollrath, and Elisabeth Young-Bruehl.

McKenna, George. "On Hannah Arendt; Politics: As It Is, Was, Might Be." *Salmagundi,* no. 10–11 (Fall 1969–Winter 1970), 104–22.

Moors, Kent F. "Modernity and Human Initiative: The Structure of Hannah Arendt's *Life of the Mind.*" *Political Science Reviewer* 10 (1980), 189–230.

Nelson, John S. "Politics and Truth: Arendt's Problematics." *American Journal of Political Science* 22 (1978), 270–301.

Oakeshott, Michael. Review of Hannah Arendt, *Between Past and Future. Political Science Quarterly* 77 (March 1962), 88–90.

O'Sullivan, N. K. "Politics, Totalitarianism and Freedom: The Political Thought of Hannah Arendt." *Political Studies* 21 (June 1973), 183–98.

—. "Hannah Arendt: Hellenic Nostalgia and Industrial Society." In Anthony de Crespigny and Kenneth Minogue, eds., *Contemporary Political Philosophers.* New York: Dodd, Mead, 1975.

Parekh, Bhikhu. *Hannah Arendt and the Search for a New Political Philosophy.* Atlantic Highlands: Humanities Press, 1981.

—. *Contemporary Political Thinkers.* Baltimore: Johns Hopkins University Press, 1982.

Pitkin, Hanna Fenichel. "Justice: On Relating Private and Public." *Political Theory* 9 (August 1981), 327–52.

Shklar, Judith N. Review Essay on Hannah Arendt, *Between Past and Future. History and Theory* 2, no. 3 (1963), 286–92.

Spitz, David. "The Politics of Segregation." In *The Liberal Idea of Freedom.* Tucson: University of Arizona Press, 1964.

Stern, Peter, and Jean Yarbrough. "Hannah Arendt." *American Scholar* 47 (Summer 1978), 371-86.

Voegelin, Eric. Review of Hannah Arendt, *The Origins of Totalitarianism. Review of Politics* 15 (January 1953), 68–76, 85.

Whitfield, Stephen J. *Into the Dark: Hannah Arendt and Totalitarianism.* Philadelphia: Temple University Press, 1980.

Wolin, Sheldon. "Stopping to Think." *The New York Review of Books,* October 26, 1978, 16–18.

Young-Bruehl, Elisabeth. *Hannah Arendt: For Love of the World.* New Haven: Yale University Press, 1982.

—. "Reflections on Hannah Arendt's *The Life of the Mind.*" *Political Theory* 10 (May 1982), 277–305.

Index

Absolutism. *See* Christian absolutism; Socratic absolutism
Achilles, 9
Action: deficiency of, 2; to be hidden, 3–4; nonpolitical modes of, 22–25. *See also* Political action
Administration, 120–21
Alienation: defense of, 178–83; meaning of, 157–62: and resentment, 163–74. *See also* Earth alienation; Reconciliation; World alienation
Ambition, 25–26
American Constitution, 19, 43, 135. *See also* Constitution
Antisemitism, 56, 57; reasons for, 58–61
Apocalypse, 151
Apology (Socrates), 100–101
Arendt, Hannah: novelty of, 3; theory's moral nature, 28–42. Writings: "Civil Disobedience," 98, 124; "The Conquest of Space and the Stature of Man," 160; *Eichmann in Jerusalem*, 35, 73, 95; *The Human Condition*, 3, 4, 35, 42, 62, 89, 116, 124, 149, 160, 163; "Karl Jaspers: Citizen of the World?," 152; *The Life of the Mind*, 85, 108, 188–96; *On Revolution*, 1, 3, 19, 92, 98, 116, 124, 125, 127, 128, 130, 134, 140; *On Violence*, 109, 170; *The Origins of Totalitarianism*, 20, 52–58, 116, 175; *Rahel Varnhagen*, 6
Aristotle, 31
Authority, 126, 130–31
Autonomy, 137

Being, 1
Benjamin, Walter, 149
Billy Budd (Melville), 27, 91
Boers, 63
Bourgeoisie: attack on, 63–64; and imperialism, 62; and totalitarianism, 66–68
Brecht, Bertolt, 182

Burden of Our Times, The. *See Origins of Totalitarianism, The*
Capitalism, 120, 122
Christian absolutism, 89–96. *See also* Morality
Citizen participation, 7, 21
Citizenship: abdication of, 126; active, 125; bourgeoisie effect on, 67; and common good, 66; nonpublic, 40, 41; types of, 42
Civil disobedience, 20–21, 27, 97–98, 123, 127; and conscience, 104–12; defense of, 98; justification for, 141–44; and nonviolence, 105; and political authority, 131; as pressure politics, 107–8; and Socrates, 103–4
"Civil Disobedience" (Arendt), 98, 124
Compassion, 27, 94; and pity, 93; as self-interest, 95
"Conquest of Space and the Stature of Man, The" (Arendt), 160
Conscience, 27; Christian, 98; and civil disobedience, 104–12; political, 105; politics of, 96–97; as self-interest, 102
Conscientious obeyers, 106
Conscientious objector, 104
Consent, 134–35; and dissent, 138; to be governed, 124–32; individual, 136; meanings of, 133; and obligation, 139–41; politics of, 138
Constitution, 43, 119, 136–38; deliberation about, 18–19. *See also* American Constitution
Contract: and lawbreaking, 142; social, 128–29, 139; theories of, 127–30; types of, 134
Corruption, 118
Council democracy, 43–44
Council government, 19–20

Democracy. *See* Council democracy; Representative democracy

Dinesen, Isak, 169
Disraeli, Benjamin, 60
Dissent, and consent, 138

Earth alienation, 159–61, 173
Economic interests, 66, 116–17
Economic policy, 21
Economics, 117, 121–22
Eichmann, Adolf, 73–74, 78, 80; and thinking, 195
Eichmann in Jerusalem (Arendt), 35, 73, 95
Election, and consent, 130–31, 136
Electoral system, and political authority, 129
Elite: gullibility of, 80; and totalitarianism, 64–65
Emerson, Ralph Waldo, 132, 171
Emotion, 25
Empathy, 53, 58, 63
Entitlements, 121
Equality, 14, 23
Erikson, Erik, _Young Man Luther,_ 104
Evil: lesser, 86–88; and modernity, 151–57; political, 28. _See also_ Totalitarianism

Forgiveness, 35
Freedom: abdication of, 6; and natality, 196; and nature, 4; and politics, 7; and worldliness, 2
French Revolution, 91, 92
Future of Mankind, The (Jaspers), 153

Generosity, of understanding, 52, 57, 61–62, 63, 65
Genocide, 77–78, 80, 83 n.50; cause of, 81. _See also_ Totalitarianism
Gillette v. United States, 106
God, 172
Goodness, 26, 89–91
Gorgias (Socrates), 99, 100
Governing, and ruling, 126–27, 129
Government. _See_ Council government; Representative government
Gratitude, 165–69, 172
Great War, 68, 71
Gurian, Waldemar, 181

Happiness, 124–25
Hegel, Georg Wilhelm Friedrich, 161; _Phenomenology of Mind,_ 92
Heidegger, Martin, 167, 171–72
Heisenberg, Werner, 161
Himmler, Heinrich, 78
Hitler, Adolf, 30, 75–76, 81; and genocide, 77; racism of, 78; teachers of, 56–57
Hobbes, Thomas, 18, 88, 128–29; and vertical contract, 134
Human behavior, versus political action, 32
Human condition. _See_ Resentment

Human Condition, The (Arendt), 3, 4, 35, 42, 62, 89, 116, 124, 149, 160, 163
Human existence, 163
Humanness, 176–77
Hungarian Revolution, 19, 169

Identity, 9
Immortal soul, doctrine of, 4
Imperialism, 56, 62
Inner life. _See_ Mental life
Interests, play of, 116–24

Jaspers, Karl, 154–55, 181; _The Future of Mankind,_ 153
Jefferson, Thomas, 19–20, 118
Jesus, 26, 89–90, 96
Jews, 59–61
Judging, 38
Jury, 119, 120–21

Kafka, Franz, 161–62
Kant, Immanuel, 38, 166
"Karl Jaspers: Citizen of the World?" (Arendt), 152
Knowledge, 176

Law, 137, 140
Lawbreaking, 133, 141–42
Lawfulness, 20–21
Lazare, Bernard, 60
Legitimacy, imperfect, 144–46
Lessing, Gotthold Ephraim, _Nathan the Wise,_ 177
Life, primacy of, 5
Life of the Mind, The (Arendt), 85, 108, 188–96
Locke, John, 129–30; and horizontal contract, 134; on representative government, 128–29
Loneliness, and totalitarianism, 175
Love, 26
Luxemburg, Rosa, 181

Machiavelli, 13
Maoism, 83 n.52
Marcuse, Herbert, _One-Dimensional Man,_ 116–17
Marshall, Thurgood, 106
Marx, Karl, 160, 161, 172
Masses, 4–5, 70–72, 74; creation of, 67
Mayflower Compact, 128
Meaning, criterion of,, 193
Melville, Herman, _Billy Budd,_ 27, 91
Mental life, 5
Mob, 64; creation of, 67; defined, 68–69
Modernity: defense of, 178–83; and evil, 151–57; and nuclear weapons, 152–54; and totalitarianism, 149–52. _See also_ Alienation

Modern subjectivity, 174-75
Morality: absolute, 85, 88-89; and politics, 85-86. *See also* Christian absolutism; Oridinary morality; Political morality
Moral judgment, disallowance of, 30-33

Nathan the Wise (Lessing), 177
Nature, 4
Nazism: and earlier movements, 56; leaders of, 72-73; and lesser evil, 87; and modernity, 149; motives of, 29; as punishment, 81
Nietzsche, Friedrich, 3
Nixon, Richard M., 21
No Exit (Sartre), 14

Obedience, and obligation, 133-34
Obligation: and consent, 139-41; and obedience, 133-34; theory of, 124-25
One-Dimensional Man (Marcuse), 116
On Revolution (Arendt), 1, 3, 19, 92, 98, 116, 124, 125, 127, 128, 130, 134, 140
On Violence (Arendt), 109, 170
Ordinary morality: and proportionality, 104-5; versus political morality, 34-35
Origins of Totalitarianism, The (Arendt), 20, 52-58, 116, 175, 196

Paine, Thomas, 131-32
Phantasm, 3
Phenomenology of Mind (Hegel), 92
Pity: and compassion, 93; effects of, 93; as self-interest, 94
Plato: *Theaetetus,* 165; on thinking, 191
Plurality, 14
Polis, 1, 7
Political action: analysis of, 6-8; content of, 15-22; denaturing of, 25-28; and economic interests, 66, 116-17; and economic policy, 21; equality criterion, 22; existential achievement of, 8-14; existential supremacy of, 6-28; as game, 16-17; versus human behavior, 32; ideal, 29; modes of, 14-15, 25; moral limitations on, 30-33; moral nature of, 43-44; and philosophy, 2; as political speech, 15-16; primacy of, 3; as relation of equals, 23; relocation of, 40, 41; revelatory capacity of, 8-10; revision of, 39; and vindication, 1, 3
Political actor: first analysis, 10; ideal characteristics of, 34-35; second analysis, 10-11; third analysis, 11-13
Political creation. *See* Constitution
Political morality, versus ordinary morality, 34-35
Politics: and disadvantaged, 120; and economic interests, 66, 116-17; and freedom, 7-8; liberal, 28; power, 18; reformist, 121

Principle, and action, 12-13
Private life, 4
Promise-keeping, 35
Protestant Ethic, The (Weber), 76-77
Public, 119
Public life, 3-4

Racism, 58-59; in Africa, 61-63; and genocide, 78-83
Rahel Varnhagen (Arendt), 6
Reality, 193-94
Reconciliation, 165, 168-70
Representative democracy: and atrocity, 132; and civil disobedience, 108-10; as consent of governed, 144-45; as culture, 145; dissent in, 123; and economic interests, 116-18; legitimacy of, 115-16; and passivity, 124-25; politics of, 121-23
Representative government: and freedom, 23-24; nature of, 126-28
Resentment, and alienation, 163-74. *See also* Gratitude; Wonder
Revolutionaries, 91-92
Robespierre, 30, 90-93
Roles, 11
Rousseau, Jean Jacques, 24, 92
Ruling, and governing, 126, 129

Sartre, Jean-Paul, *No Exit,* 14
Self-absorption, 5-6
Self-defense, 86
Self-interest: and absolute morality, 91; socratic, 101-2
Selfishness, 119
Self-regardingness, 119
Slavery, 97
Socrates: *Apology,* 100-101; and conscience, 99-100; *Gorgias,* 99, 100; and thinking, 36-37, 192-93
Socratic absolutism, 88-89, 96-104; and self-interest, 99-100
Solidarity, 93, 96
Song of Myself (Whitman), 179
Speech, 39, 122; modes of, 16; and relations of inequality, 22-23; and totalitarianism, 30; as true political action, 15; and truth, 10-11; and willing, 195
Stain, Joseph, 75-76, 77; and genocide, 77; teachers of, 56-57
Stalinism, and modernity, 149
Stories, 14

Talk. *See* Speech
Tennyson, Alfred Lord, "Ulysses," 14
Theaetetus (Plato), 165
Thinking, 5; accusation of, 189-90; implications of, 36-38
Thoreau, Henry David, 97; *Walden,* 110-12

"Thoughts on Politics and Revolution" (Arendt), 109
Thucydides, 17–18
Totalitarianism, 157; as black miracle, 55; coming of, 56–57; elements of, 69–70; and elite, 63–65; essence of, 74–82; as exorcism, 81; functionaries of, 74–82; and ideal political action, 29–30; justification for, 31–32; leaders of, 74–82; and loneliness, 175; and modernity, 149–52; and psychological analysis, 53–55. *See also* Genocide
Truth, criterion of, 193–94
Tyranny, 83 n.53; defined, 75

"Ulysses" (Tennyson), 14
United States Constitution. *See* American Constitution
United States Supreme Court, 140
Universal suffrage, 108

Utilitarianism, 86

Violence, 39–40
Voting, 118

Walden (Thoreau), 110–12
Weber, Max, 160; *The Protestant Ethic*, 76–77
Whitman, Walt, *Song of Myself*, 179
Willing, as silent speech, 195
Will to act, 34–35
Wisdom of Silenus, 1, 13, 41–42, 165; rebuttal of, 6–8
Wonder, 165–66, 172
World: as home, 174–78; meaning of, 2; and morality of love, 89
World alienation, 158–60, 190
Worldliness: and freedom, 2; and nature, 4
Worldly self, as real self, 9
World War II. *See* Great War

Young Man Luther (Erikson), 104